Norman. Frederick William
McPherson.

1945.

LIFE OF IAN MACLAREN

Noreen Kirby, Liverpool, photo. Emery Walker Ph. sc.

John Watson.

'Ian Maclaren'

LIFE OF THE

REV. JOHN WATSON

D.D.

BY W. ROBERTSON NICOLL

HODDER AND STOUGHTON

LONDON MCMVIII

First and Second Editions printed October 1908.

Third Edition printed November 1908.

TO

MRS. JOHN WATSON

'I'm apt to think the man
That could surround the sum of things, and spy
The heart of God and secrets of His empire,
Would speak but love—with him the bright result
Would change the hue of intermediate scenes
And make one thing of all theology.'

PREFACE

Of Dr. Watson it is most true that 'no man is able to show to those who knew him not what he was; no man could show this to those who knew him in a way that they would feel satisfying.' His sympathy, his tenderness, his kindly humour were to those who knew him inseparable from his presence, and all attempts to describe or report him must be sadly inadequate. But for the friendship with which he honoured me and for the love I bore him, I have done my best. There is nothing in this book which is not based on indisputable authority. I have thought it my duty to set him forth as he was, and to give his own views as nearly as possible in his own words. It will be seen that on important points he differed seriously from the majority in his own Church, and it was thought by many that he sometimes fell into indiscretions. I do not agree with this view. His 'indiscretions' were generally the frank statement of his differences. He would never allow himself to be misconceived, and while he had the greatest patience with the opinions of others he firmly maintained the right to assert his own.

I have had throughout the most valuable co-operation of his son Mr. Frederick W. Watson, B.A., who has helped me largely in almost every part of the book. If these pages do not reveal John Watson as a man of many gifts, of large and generous nature, of unwearied fidelity in service, and above all as a devoted minister of the Christian Church, I have completely failed.

Cordial thanks are due to many friends who have given their aid. My obligations to Lady Grainger Stewart; Mrs. Stephen Williamson; Principal Oswald Dykes; Vice-Chancellor Dale; the Rev. Dr. C. F. Aked; the Rev. R. C. Gillie; Mr. John Lea; Sir Oliver Lodge; Mrs. De Horne Vaizey; Mr. G. A. Mackenzie; Dr. D. M. Ross; Mrs. Thom; Mr. Harold Peirce, and many others, are very great.

HAMPSTEAD, *September* 1908.

CONTENTS

CHAPTER VIII

CHAPTER IX

CHAPTER X

CHAPTER XI

CHAPTER XII

CHAPTER XIII

CHAPTER XIV

CHAPTER XV

CHAPTER XVI

CHAPTER I

EARLY DAYS

THE personality of John Watson was complex and many-sided. I am convinced that the best helps to the understanding of it are the facts that he was a Celt, that his ancestry on the mother's side was Roman Catholic, his grand-uncle being a well-known and influential priest in the Highlands, and in particular that more than most he was acutely sensitive and responsive to the environment in which he found himself.

Without unduly anticipating what is to follow, the Celtic character of Ian Maclaren's nature may be briefly indicated. He possessed all the leading characteristics of the Highlander, for he was a Jacobite, he was fiercely patriotic, and he was superstitious. A few words may be added in illustration of these points. He was a Jacobite through and through, and like his Roman Catholic blood, so this Jacobite strain came to him through his Highland mother. He could bring all the weight of his logical mind to bear on the question. He could tear the claims of the

Stuarts in shreds, but his heart always prevailed, and it was his love of that sweet Scots song, 'There grows a bonnie brier bush in oor kail-yaird,' which furnished the name to his most popular book. The Jacobites wore this flower as an emblem of their cause. 'I chose this title,' he said, 'because the suggestion of the book is that in every garden, however small and humble, you may have a flower. . . . This is the whole idea of my writing, to show the rose in places where many people look only for cabbages.' He had a great love for the old Scots songs. He would be strangely affected by such as 'The Earl of Moray,' a special favourite of his, and 'Wae's me for Prince Charlie,' and one with the lines

> 'He turn'd him right an' round about,
> Upon the Irish shore,
> An' gae his bridle reins a shake,
> With Adieu for ever more, my dear,
> With Adieu for ever more.'

He considered this the saddest and most beautiful of tunes. In this he showed the strong vein of romance and melancholy of the Highlander, who is moved to tears by the tales of long ago. It was difficult for him in his books to avoid some reference to the '45. We hear of it in *Kate Carnegie*, and even in that unromantic study of *The Scot of the Eighteenth Century* he cannot help mentioning the Rebellion when he says: 'In my possession I have a Theophrastus printed in Greek and Latin in the seventeenth century, which came down to me through the eighteenth century, when it was carried to the Rebellion in the pocket of a Highland Chief, so that on his march to restore Prince Charlie he might read the chapter "De Desperatione," and I am bound to say there has also come down to me with the Theophrastus a silver Quaich or drinking-cup, with which the worthy Chief would refresh himself when weary, without stopping to drink at the brook.' He sometimes spoke of writing a novel on the '45 period, and his collection of Stuart books was of a very beautiful and costly nature.

He was extremely patriotic, and always had a great affection for the Army. He used to tell how he played truant at Stirling School to watch the Highland regiments drilling in the fields below the Castle, for his ancestors were either soldiers or farmers. Among his early recollections was one of pictures in the *Illustrated London News* giving some of the scenes in the Mutiny. All Scotland rang with the exploits of the 78th Ross-shire Highlanders, who had followed Sir Colin Campbell to the relief of Lucknow. When that regiment returned home, it was ordered to Edinburgh, and was publicly reviewed in the Queen's Park. Watson's father thought that the boy ought to be taught patriotism, and that his memory should be stored with a recollection of mighty deeds. For weeks before this review he told his son the history of the Highland regiments, from the days after the rebellion of 1745 on to the Crimean war, and especially he aroused his enthusiasm with the description of the long marches and gallant deeds of the 78th as they went to save the women and children from death. He was taken to Edinburgh and never forgot the scene. After the 78th had left the ground they marched before the hotel in Princes Street where the Empress of the French was then staying, and she, who had seen many soldiers, declared that she had never looked upon a stronger or more martial body of men. As they passed that day in company, and as soon as the General had returned their salute, the people up and down the line burst into cheers, crying, 'Well done, 78th!' 'You saved the women and children!' 'The Highlanders for ever!' Then it was that the boy's heart—he was only eight—gave way and he wept. Even the processions in which he took part gave, I imagine, quite a pleasurable sensation to his dramatic and poetic mind. It was largely through his influence that the Liverpool Scottish Volunteers were incorporated, and as Chaplain he was one of the keenest members. One only had to see him marching behind the battalion mopping his brow, but full of delight in everything, to realise that the divine, the novelist, the public speaker were for the time gladly put in abeyance. In the period of the South

African War he was full of enthusiasm. He preached sermons on Patriotism which made a very great impression in Liverpool, and influenced many young men to volunteer for active service. I believe he was more proud of his son going to the front than of any achievement of his own. His address to the Volunteers was not the calm exhortation of a modern divine: it was more the harangue of a Celt in whose mind Scotland and the deeds of ancestry were supreme. And then, as their fortune ebbed and flowed, but for the most part ebbed, he became greatly depressed, and on opening the paper one morning, and seeing the terrible disaster to the Highland Brigade at Magersfontein, he flung the paper down. 'Oh, dear!' was all he said, but he scarcely spoke that day, so near to his heart lay the fortunes of his race. Patriotism with Watson was not a braggart jingoism. He steadfastly taught with Regnault, that a true patriotism means a serious, pure, and honourable life.

He was superstitious, as his mother was before him. She would turn the carriage home again if a hare crossed the road. There can be no doubt that there was a distinct strain of superstition among his connections. When he was living in Logiealmond Free Manse, he had a housekeeper who worked for him during the day and returned in the evening to the village, leaving him alone. One night, he said, he heard footsteps in the room above. They came downstairs very slowly, halted before his door a moment, then continued down to the kitchen. Although feeling somewhat nervous, he opened the door and called 'Martha,' wondering why his housekeeper had stayed so late. He received no answer, and went downstairs. No one there. He searched the whole house. Every window and every door was locked, and yet he says he was working, and in no way sleepy.

On another occasion he heard a tremendous crash in the kitchen like the falling of a great number of dishes. He hurried down, but everything was in its place, and the room was cold and empty. He believed thoroughly in the supernatural nature of these strange occurrences, and had a fervent conviction of the reality of spiritual communications. Though he did not tell his stories to every one, he would relate to some that one day he felt an uncontrollable desire and anxiety to see a friend in Glasgow. Believing thoroughly in the mysterious impulse, he journeyed north without delay, and was in time to speak to his friend before he died. While visiting one afternoon, he suddenly had a strong desire to see a certain member of his congregation. It seemed absurd, however, to yield to this vague feeling, because it meant a long and perhaps useless walk in the opposite direction. He resisted it for some time, but at last surrendered his will, and turned and reached the house. 'O Dr. Watson, how extraordinary, and how fortunate!' the lady of the house said. 'My daughter is taken suddenly very seriously ill, and she has been terribly anxious to see you, but of course we knew that you would not be at home.' He had some curious compact with his mother which was made on her deathbed, and he firmly believed that he was in touch with her all his life. He called it his mother's Tryst, and said that this influence had been a great bulwark against temptation. The inquiries of his friend, Sir Oliver Lodge, and the Psychical Research Society, of which he was a member, moved him to the profoundest interest. He considered the veil between the two worlds to be very thin. Along with his friend, Henry Drummond, he studied the subject of hypnotism at Edinburgh, and within two years of his death he was making a close investigation of patients under hypnotism in the consulting rooms of a scientific doctor. Spiritualism interested him, I think, not so much from a scientific, as from a religious standpoint. Though Watson did not trouble sceptics with his spiritualistic views, he was unusually intolerant on the subject, and did not hesitate to describe the people who sneered at Spiritualism as ignorant fools. I may add that the shadow of early death brooded over his most intimate talk and letters, and that amidst the crowding engagements of his prime he seemed to be very conscious that all these wanderings were drawing towards the inevitable rest.

John Watson's Roman Catholic ancestry made a factor not to be ignored in his life. He never, so far as I know, had any sympathy with the sacerdotal theory of the Latin Church, indeed in almost the only public controversy he ever undertook he set himself to the demolition of that theory. All the same, as we shall see, the asceticism of the Roman Church had a strong fascination for him. He thoroughly believed in the sincere Christianity of Roman Catholic priests and people. Sometimes in moments of doubt and perplexity his heart went back to the Churches where the faithful were peacefully singing the Hallelujah of the Resurrection, as to a last inviolate sanctuary. He was once in a Roman Catholic church in Italy. Before the altar of the Virgin there was a woman, her lips moving devoutly in prayer. As she was making her way to the door after ending her devotions, Watson asked her in Italian some question about the points of interest in the building. By and by the conversation turned upon the differences between the Roman Catholic and Protestant religions, especially in regard to the fact that Protestants do not address prayers to the Virgin. 'Don't you ever pray to the Mother of God?' 'No,' said Watson, 'for it seems to me that all you find which is holy and helpful and adorable in the character of that most revered and beautiful of women, all that and infinitely more I find in her Divine Son.' 'Yes, sir,' she said wistfully, 'I understand that, but you are a man, and you do not know how a woman needs a woman to pray to.' 'My dear, good soul,' said Watson very gently, 'yes, yes, I understand. I think I know something of a woman's heart, of a woman's needs. I take back all I said. Forgive it, forget it. Do not let any word of mine stand between you and your prayers to the Mother of our Lord.' On Sunday evenings in Liverpool, when he had completed his hard and honourable labour, he delighted in the company of Roman Catholic priests, and some of them, like Father Day and Father Castle, were among his warmest, most appreciative, and most beloved friends. Catholic mysticism always possessed for him a great and holding charm.

Never was a man more susceptible to the atmosphere around him. He simply could not live in a hostile air. He could be overborne by views of religion which in fact were not really his. Though he had plenty of courage, and could stand by a losing cause, his thoughts did not flourish in inhospitable soils or chilling winds. For his work he needed the warm and sunny consciousness of sympathy. He could face contradiction and opposition, but not the steady environment of antagonism. It followed that when he was played upon by crossing influences his real power was to a considerable extent paralysed.

Though John Watson prided himself on his Scottish ancestry, it was his fortune to be born at Manningtree, a little old-world village in Essex, on November 3rd, 1850. In this he was the victim of circumstances. His father was a Receiver of Taxes, and became in the end Receiver-General of Taxes in Scotland. When his son and only child was born he was stationed at Manningtree, pleasantly situated on the banks of the Stour at a point where it broadens into the estuary which has Harwich at its mouth. Manningtree has a population of only a few hundreds, a large percentage of whom derive their livelihood from seafaring occupations. But the child remained only a very short time in the place, and was never influenced by it. The preacher whom he most admired, Robertson of Brighton, had as father and mother Scots of very old family, but Robertson was mainly affected by his English environment. Watson, on the other hand, though his great work was done in England, considered himself a Scot of the Scots. 'I am a pure Highlander,' he once confessed to an admirer. 'My mother was a Maclaren and came from Loch Tay, and spoke the Gaelic tongue. My father was born at Braemar, and Gaelic was the language of my paternal grandfather.'

At about four years of age Watson was taken back to Scotland and lived with his parents at Perth, where later he attended the Grammar School. His father, so far as is remembered, was a somewhat stern, methodical Scotsman, a devout Free Kirk elder, not without some sense of humour, but of too grave and businesslike a nature to be attracted very greatly by the ludicrous. A servant of the Government, he was most particular that no word disparaging either to his Queen or employers should be permitted in his presence, and every Sunday the toast 'The Queen' was drunk with much grave loyalty. John Watson followed his father in adhering to the Conservative side in politics, though he took little part in the political controversies of his day. Watson's mother possessed an extraordinary gift of mimicry, and a keen sense of humour. It was from her that he inherited his power of story-telling and repartee. Many a time his father endeavoured to check appreciation at the successful mimicking of some pompous personage whose peculiarities and mannerisms had formed the subject of her sport immediately after his departure. A splendid and fearless horsewoman, she accustomed her son to ride from infancy, and in spite of the expostulations of her husband, and sometimes, though more timidly, of her child, she mounted him on the wildest of farm colts.

Of Watson's boyhood in Perth, Mr. G. A. Mackenzie, his schoolfellow and oldest friend, has most kindly written to Mr. Frederick Watson:—

I fancy we got to know one another from the fact of our

families being near neighbours and of his father and mine being fellow office-bearers in St. Leonard's Free Church. We lived then in No. 10 Marshall Place, Perth, and Mr. Watson first at No. 19 and afterwards at No. 4 Marshall Place. I find that Mr. Watson was ordained a Deacon in St. Leonard's in 1855, so that your father and I must have known one another from the time we were about five years old at least. I was about six months his senior. We were together when we were very small at a Ladies' Boarding School where young gentlemen of tender years received the elements of education. I have no very definite recollections of what we learned, but I remember one class of 'Useful Knowledge' which we thought very amusing, and he used to 'chaff' me for getting as a prize, *The Little Child's Book of Divinity*. The good ladies—some of whom still survive — have been lifelong friends. Whenever your father visited Perth, he made a point of calling at the old School, and I know he was warmly welcomed and pointed to as an example of all the virtues. From the Misses M——'s establishment we passed to Perth Academy, and he has chronicled our experiences there in *Young Barbarians*.

We usually spent our Saturdays together, and I was always particularly keen to make out that it was my turn to come to his house. I suppose this is the way of children, but I think it also indicates that Mr. and Mrs. Watson were very kind to young folks. Of course, we played all sorts of children's games together, and I remember especially the attraction of some splendid 'bricks'—wooden blocks for building houses, and all sorts of wonderful erections. The special charm was to build a castle which, if our architecture was successful, was topped by a pinnacle carrying a red silk flag. There was also a magic lantern which was exhibited on very special occasions, and I think John was usually the exhibitor, assisted by his father. It was the first magic lantern I had seen and left a very vivid impression, although I think now, with all the modern improvements, it would be considered a very poor affair. John had a canary which was kept in a brass cage, and sometimes as a great treat we were allowed to see the canary having a bath. We moved in 1858 to No. 1 Athole Place, and the principal amusement when he came to my house was playing 'keerie' in the back green when my brother and sister joined us, and sometimes having an encampment under big trees at the far end of the back garden. In wet weather we had 'hide-and-seek' indoors, and one of the last times I saw him he recalled how once we were certain that somebody had hid in a particular closet because the door, when pushed open, always quietly swung back, giving the impression that there was some one behind it. Sometimes we had evening parties at one another's house, and there is a tradition in our family that John, who was rather a delicate child, used to be carried along by his nurse rolled up in a warm plaid. On arrival he was deposited in the hall, and carefully unwound.

I have been trying to remember what our story-books were, but I can recollect nothing except *The Swiss Family Robinson*, *Peter Parley*, and *Men that have risen*. *The Swiss Family* must have made a deep impression, because I remember among our favourite haunts a place at the top of the South Inch which we dubbed 'Falcon's Nest,' where we attempted to reproduce the most vivid incidents from that story. I can point out the place to this day. When the weather was good, we used to have frequent excursions to 'Craigie Knowes' and the 'Woody Island.' The latter figures largely in *Young Barbarians*. I should like to say here, however, that in that book, as in all his tales, it is impossible to identify real characters. He had too much good feeling to paint actual portraits, although those familiar with the scenes in which he moved, and the people he met, knew that his characters were drawn from life. For instance, Dr. Davidson, the minister of Drumtochty, is in no sense the portrait of the parish minister whom he knew at Logiealmond, or of any parish minister who was ever there, although he told me he had in view a parish minister whom he met in his boyhood and for whom he had a great esteem. In the same way, while the scene of *Young Barbarians* is laid at Perth Academy, many of the characters, both masters and boys, are, I fancy, taken from his life at Stirling.

I must not omit to mention a great expedition which I made with him to Kinross and Loch Leven. Your grandfather, as you know, held the post of Collector of Customs at Perth, and in the discharge of his duties had to pay a yearly or half-yearly visit to Kinross. On the occasion referred to, John and I were to accompany him. I remember well the excitement of my having to go the night before from Athole Place to Marshall Place to sleep in order to be ready for an early start in the morning. We drove in a waggonette by the Great North Road through Bridge of Earn and Damhead to Kinross. The 'Collector' held his collection in the Inn on the main street in the town. We boys supposed we were very helpful in counting the cash paid by the various small merchants and old wives who took out licences to deal in tea and tobacco, and after the business of the day was over and the books closed, we all sallied forth to the shore of Loch Leven where we spent the afternoon. That was my first visit to that historic scene, and made a very deep impression on my mind.

Watson, who had a humorous way of depreciating himself, used to describe himself as averse from study, retiring, and slow-witted in his childhood. His father once threw a book at his head, and remarked with much frankness that 'of all the stupid blockheads he stood alone.' While at Perth he paid frequent visits to his maternal uncles, the Maclarens, who farmed their own land near Blairgowrie. In fact till the end of his college days he was accustomed to return during holidays and vacations to the farms, and in this manner acquired not only a knowledge of the country, but a great love for farming, and a desire to follow that profession. His friend, the Rev. Dr. D. M. Ross of Glasgow, writes:—

In the summer of 1871, it was my good fortune to have many a talk with Watson. My father was a near neighbour of his uncles Archibald and William, who were successively tenants of the farm of Grange of Aberbothrick. There was a good deal of coming and going between the two farms, especially when the two students were at home for the summer holidays. Watson had by this time 'discovered' Dr. Barty, the parish minister of Bendochy, who supplied him with many a touch in his subsequent portraits of the Scottish parish minister. He had also 'discovered' Dr. Baxter of Blairgowrie, whose evangelical earnestness struck deeper chords in his nature; what with his characterisation of the sayings and idiosyncrasies of ministers in the neighbourhood, of farmers at market or at roups, and of ploughmen in the fields or in the bothies, and with his never-ending sallies, he made the tea-table at Grange or Leitfie a lively centre of wit and merriment. Now and again, his father, courtliest of men, would intervene with an 'O John!'

Much of the colouring of the sketches of Drumtochty was borrowed from the Grange, and from the farms of his other uncles a few miles off in the neighbourhood of Blairgowrie. For example, within a short distance of the Grange, is, or rather was, for a bridge has now been built, the Barmondy ford in the river Isla. In my boyhood, a horse and cart with the driver were swept into the deep water below it and were lost. Watson told me in later years that this incident had coloured his description of the crossing of the Drumtochty ford.

He had a minute knowledge of the details of farm work and farm life, long before he became minister of Logiealmond. It was on the large farms of Strathmore he got his insight into the seamy side of the life of farm-servants and the extra hands employed in harvest time, and in potato lifting I believe that he several times acted as paymaster for the casual labourers on behalf of his uncles, and was thus brought into close contact with them. His experience of their moral laxity was, I believe, exceptional. With reference to this experience, he said to me in later years, that if he were to depict some phases of rural life, as he had known it, *The House with the Green Shutters* would have been considered, in comparison, a flattering portrait. The occasions for the abuses he deplored were absent on the smaller farms in the Logiealmond district. But if in his literary sketches he idealised life on a Scottish farm, this was due not to ignorance of the grim realities but to his high conception of the moral functions of literature.

My mother and he were greatly drawn to each other. In later years when he had become famous, he never missed a chance of calling upon her, and it was a joy to him to get a clap on the shoulder from one who had known and liked him as a young lad. With that tender thoughtfulness which was characteristic of him, he sent her a beautiful little letter of congratulation on her 87th birthday.

It happened occasionally that he and I rode together or drove about the country in a gig. One drive I recall. He was at the time under call to St. Matthew's, Glasgow. We started from my home to drive to Glenisla and climb Mount Blair—a distance of fifteen miles. We had to put up our horse at the farm of Abrick (on the lower slope of the Mount), owned and tenanted by a well-known godly man, Mr. John Mackenzie, an esteemed friend of Dr. Alexander Whyte. We had to introduce ourselves, the one as a minister of the Free Church, the other as a divinity student. (This was in 1877, when the Robertson Smith controversy was just beginning.) Before the good man would have anything to do with us, he put two searching questions; 'Had ye ony whisky at the inn as ye came by?' 'D'ye belong ti thae infidel young men o' oor kirk?' Our reception was discouraging. But when I let it out that my friend was under call to be colleague to Dr. Samuel Miller, frigidity gave way to effusiveness. Straightway, Watson was deep in talk upon theological problems with the good man, and so prolonged was their talk that I feared we should never see the top of the hill. We did the ascent, and on our return to Abrick there was a bountiful 'spread' for Dr. Miller's future colleague.

One letter only survives from his earliest years, and I quote it:—

Drumlochy, May 3rd, 1862.

My dear Papa and Mama,—Uncle and I have been twice seeing Uncle Duncan, and found him pretty well. The first time that we went we took the lamp with us and it arrived quite safe: The second time the gingerbread cake, and we got some very fine sweet butter home with us, as aunt has none.

I was down at Church last Thursday being Aunt's fast day. We had the Revd. G. Stewart of the Free Middle Church, Perth, in the forenoon, and Mr. Crichton of Arbroath in the afternoon, and from both we heard very good sermons. Uncle William has had a very bad cold and cough, but it's getting better. I have nothing but porridge and milk for breakfast, and I like them very much. Aunt and Uncle say that I am improving every day. We are all pretty well and all join in warmest love to you all. —I am, Your ever affectionate son, JOHN WATSON.

PS.—You need not alarm yourself about Uncle, as he is almost well.

It will be observed that Watson was brought up under the ministry of the Rev. John Milne, of St. Leonard's, Perth. Mr. Milne belonged to what was known in Scotland as the M'Cheyne school. This was made up of men who were noted for their sanctity and their evangelistic zeal. Milne left his ministry in Perth to become a missionary in Calcutta, and after an interval returned to his old church. His life was written by Dr. Horatius Bonar, and he has been most felicitously described by the Rev. Dr. John Hunt, Vicar of Otford, Kent, and author of many important books on the history of theology. Dr. Hunt, who in his early years attended Mr. Milne's church, says:—

We have said that Mr. Milne's ministry was successful. He had no great gifts of intellect; he had no eloquence;

his learning was not extensive; in fact, his reading seems to have been unusually limited. What, then, was the secret of his power? We might say at once it was that he preached religion rather than theology; and he lived what he preached. If he did not know the difficulties that beset men who think, he yet knew the wants of men in general. He knew the power of sympathy, and he knew that the story of the life and the death of Jesus will reach men's hearts to the end of time. And then he had mastered the evil that was in himself. No one ever knew him to be angry. Even his wife could only once remember any approach to hastiness, and it was when the servant had omitted to tell him of a case of sickness to be visited. He could bear opposition; he could suffer to see himself despised or thrust aside if any good came of it. He used to buy things at a shop in Perth where the shopkeeper was not civil to him. He was asked why he continued to go where his custom was not wanted; and he answered that he was trying to soften that man by kindness. He could not enter into the thoughts of men who are perplexed with the ways of Providence, or have doubts about revelation, or who do not understand revelation in the same way as he understood it; but he did not rail against them as atheists, infidels, neologians, or sceptics. He knew that men were not to be won by hard names. Nor did he speak evil of Christians who did not belong to his own party. Writing to a servant in England who had been a member of his congregation, he said, 'You must not despise the Church of England. If I know the Lord at all, it was in her that He was first revealed to me.' In India he sometimes preached in the chapels belonging to the Church of England, getting a civilian or an officer to read the liturgy. His religion was not made up of certain opinions; it was a *life.*

It appears that in his youth Mr. Milne had a fall which

affected his head. How far this served as a thorn in the flesh to crucify him to the world we do not know: his zeal often seemed to surpass the bounds of reason. He refused to go into society where he could not make religion the sole subject of conversation. He was out of sympathy with what is secular or 'worldly.' In some company, when a favourite Scotch song was sung, beginning 'There's nae luck aboot the house,' Mr. Milne said it was only true of King Jesus, to whom also all the Jacobite songs were applicable. To little boys in the street he would speak of a little boy in Germany who wrote a letter to the 'dear Lord Jesus.' Walking in a friend's garden, he found the gardener lamenting that the frost was destroying the strawberries; he took the gardener into the summer-house and prayed for a good season. He lived in daily expectation of the second advent. Mr. Milne was one of those happy souls over whose head heaven is still open, and the angels of God ascending and descending. The Bible was to him a book of which every letter is divine, and all its figures realities. His faith was that of a child—as simple, as sincere, as living, as earnest.

One of Watson's chief recollections of early church-going was of the ordination of a minister. It seemed to the child as if the proceedings would never come to an end, and as one minister after another mounted the pulpit and each began a new sermon, despair seized his heart. His mother, ever weaker than his father, conducted him to the door of the church and set him in the direction of home. The father contented himself next morning with expressing his assurance that, whatever John might be fit for in after life, he had no hope whatever that he would become a minister of the Church.

A more pleasing memory was that of the solemn administration of the Lord's Supper. In the procession of the elders the child was specially interested in an old man with very white hair and a meek, reverent face. Some time after he was walking on the road and passed a man breaking stones. The white hair caught his attention, and he looked back and recognised the elder who had carried the cup. Full of curiosity and wonder, he told his father the strange tale. His father explained to him that the reason why the old man held so high a place in the Church was that although he was one of the poorest men in all the town, he was one of the holiest. 'Remember,' said his father, 'the best man that ever lived upon this earth was the poorest, for our Lord had not where to lay his head'; and he added, 'James breaks stones for his living, but he knows more about God than any person I have ever met.' So he learned that evening, and never departed from the faith, that the greatest thing in all the world is character, and the crown of character is holiness.

It was at one of the Blairgowrie farms that Watson made acquaintance with Spurgeon's sermons, as he has related in one of his happiest sketches. He tells how the farmer was instructed by his good wife to bring home from the market town the tea and sugar, the paraffin oil and other necessities of life. 'And, John, dinna forget Spurgeon. Spurgeon was the weekly number of the Metropolitan Tabernacle Pulpit. As the provident woman had written every requirement—except the oil which was obtained at the ironmonger's, and the Spurgeon which was sold at the draper's—on a sheet of paper, and pinned it on the topmost cabbage leaf which covered the butter, the risk was not great; but that week the discriminating prophecy of the good man's capabilities seemed to be justified, for the oil was there, but Spurgeon could not be found. It was not in the bottom of the dogcart, nor below the cushion, nor attached to a piece of saddlery, nor even in the good man's trousers pocket—all familiar resting-places—and when it was at last extricated from the inner pocket of his top-coat—a garment with which he had no intimate acquaintance—he received no credit, for it was pointed out with force that to have purchased the sermon and then to have mislaid it, was worse than forgetting it altogether. 'The Salvation of Manasseh,' read the good wife; 'it would have been a fine-like business to have missed that; a 'll warrant this 'ill be ane o' his sappiest, but they 're a' gude.' And then Manasseh was put in a prominent and honourable place, behind the basket of wax flowers in the best parlour till

Sabbath. When Sabbath came the lads from the bothie were brought into the kitchen and entertained to tea. Then afterwards the master of the house read a sermon by Spurgeon. On that particular evening the little gathering was held in the loft because it was harvest time, and extra men were working. It was laid on the boy as an honour to read Manasseh.

Whether the sermon is called by this name I do not know, and whether it be one of the greatest of Mr. Spurgeon's I do not know, nor have I a copy of it; but it was mighty unto salvation in that loft, and I make no doubt that good grain was garnered unto eternity. There is a passage in it when, after the mercy of God has rested on this chief sinner, an angel flies through the length and breadth of heaven crying, 'Manasseh is saved, Manasseh is saved.' Up to that point the lad read, and further he did not read. You know, because you have been told, how insensible and careless is a schoolboy, how destitute of all sentiment and emotion . . . and therefore I do not ask you to believe me. You know how dull and stupid is a plowman, because you have been told . . . and therefore I do not ask you to believe me.

It was the light which got into the lad's eyes and the dust which choked his voice, and it must have been for the same reasons that a plowman passed the back of his hand across his eyes.

'Ye 'll be tired noo,' said the good man; 'lat me feenish the sermon,' but the sermon is not yet finished, and never shall be.

It will be seen that Watson was brought up under powerful evangelical influences, and there can be no doubt that they touched him to the core of his heart. But it is right to say that his mother was of a broader school. He wrote himself in 1905: 'My mother, I believe, would have gladly seen me a minister of the Established Church. She was a Moderate in theology, and had a rooted dislike to amateur preachers and all their ways, believing that if you employed a qualified physician rather than a quack for your body, you had better have a qualified clergyman rather than a layman for your soul. From her I received the main principles of my religious thinking. She taught me that all doctrine must be tried by human experience, and that if it was not proved by our reason and conscience, it was not true; and especially I learned from her to believe in the Fatherhood of God and to argue from the human home to the divine family. She always insisted that as we were all the children of one Father, He would make the best of us, both in this world and that which is to come. This, however, was the theology of the Moderate school, and not of the Free Church.' He also draws the contrast between the two Churches as they appeared to him in early days. 'The Free Church of that day was more intense, dogmatic, self-righteous, and evangelistic; the spirit of the Established Church was more liberal and humane, and possibly some would add less spiritual. While I greatly honoured the leading Free Church minister of my country days, both as a religious man and a friend of the family, I felt much more at home with the parish minister, who in his courtesy of manner, his practical interest in the parish, his reasonable preaching and avoidance of all extravagance, seemed to me the ideal representative of the Galilean faith. Besides, I believed in an Established Church, and even then, although I had not given my mind much to such questions, was convinced that the alliance of the Church with the State was not only a good thing for the State, but also a good thing for the Church, saving her from sectarianism and bigotry. I used to resent the denunciation from Free Church pulpits of sport, walking on Sundays, amusements, and the reading of fiction, and I remember being very disgusted with an evangelist who was much petted, and who asked impertinent questions, and who suddenly disappeared.' It is evident that the two strains of religious feeling in the father and in the mother were silently in conflict, and the current of the lad's existence was twisted hither and thither.

One of his early heroes was a 'Moderate' minister, the Rev. Dr. Barty of Bendochy, who was Moderator of the Church of Scotland. Dr. Barty was the original of Watson's favourite character, Dr. Davidson, and he referred to him in a speech made at Blairgowrie:—

He wanted to pay tribute to one who seemed to him to

be the very ideal of a country minister—their neighbour, the late respected Dr. Barty of Bendochy. He was the father of the parish. His very appearance carried authority and kindliness with it. He saw him standing in the pulpit on the Sacrament day, moving about the parish speaking with the farmers, and wherever he went always a Christian gentleman, bringing to bear the principles of our religion on daily life in a kindly and wise fashion. Long might Scotland have ministers in their parishes like Dr. Barty, and long might the country districts rear men such as Strathmore had reared! for upon the country districts, on the intelligence and ability, on the physical health and high purpose and godly fear of the country districts depends the welfare of the commonwealth.

I attribute the comparative lateness with which he attained his full intellectual stature to the fact that his mind was disquieted in his youth.

All this may be premature, but I do not think it is. When Watson was twelve his father was promoted to Stirling, and his association with the town is of peculiar interest. It was at Stirling High School that he became the friend of Henry Drummond. No influence in his life was stronger. Watson was one of the warmest of friends, but he was discriminating, and he very rarely spoke of any one with extravagant praise, though of all with kindness. But he would admit no flaw in Henry Drummond. After Drummond's death he wrote his memory of their first meeting:—

The sun was going down behind Ben Lomond, in the

happy summer-time, touching with gold the gray old castle, deepening the green upon the belt of trees which fringed the eastern side of the park, and filling the park itself with soft, mellow light. A cricket match between two schools had been going on all day, and was coming to an end, and I had gone out to see the result—being a new arrival in Stirling, and full of curiosity. The two lads at the wickets were in striking contrast—one heavy, stockish, and determined, who slogged powerfully and had scored well for his side; the other nimble, alert, graceful, who had a pretty but uncertain play. The slogger was forcing the running in order to make up a heavy leeway, and compelled his partner to run once too often. 'It's all right, and you fellows are not to cry shame'—this was what he said as he joined his friends—'Buchanan is playing A1, and that hit ought to have been a four; I messed the running.' It was good form, of course, and what any decent lad would want to say, but there was an accent of gaiety and a certain air which was very taking. Against that group of clumsy, unformed, awkward Scots lads, this bright, straight, living figure stood in relief, and as he moved about the field my eyes followed him, and in my boyish and dull mind I had a sense that he was a type by himself, a visitor of finer breed than those among whom he moved. By and by he mounted a friend's pony and galloped along the racecourse in the park till one only saw a speck of white in the sunlight, and still I watched in wonder and fascination—only a boy of thirteen or so, and dull—till he came back, in time to cheer the slogger who had pulled off the match—with three runs to spare—and carried his bat.

'Well played, old chap!' the pure, clear, joyous note rang out on the evening air; 'finest thing you've ever done,' while the strong-armed, heavy-faced slogger stood still and looked at him in admiration, and made amends.

'I say, Drummond, it was my blame you were run out. . . .' Drummond was his name, and some one said 'Henry.' So I first saw my friend.

What impressed me that pleasant evening in the days of long ago I can now identify. It was the lad's distinction, an inherent quality of appearance and manner of character and soul which marked him and made him solitary. What happened with one strange lad that evening befell all kinds of people who met Drummond in later years. They were at once arrested, interested, fascinated by the very sight of the man, and could not take their eyes off him. Like a picture of the first order among ordinary portraits he unconsciously put his neighbours at a disadvantage. One did not realise how commonplace and colourless other men were till they stood side by side with Drummond. Upon a platform of evangelists, or sitting among divinity students in a dingy classroom, or cabined in the wooden respectability of an ecclesiastical court, or standing in a crowd of passengers at a railway station, he suggested golden embroidery upon hodden gray. It was as if the prince of one's imagination had dropped in among common folk. He reduced us all to peasantry.

Watson in later life used to say that Drummond was the most vital man he had ever known; that his eyes had a power and hold which were little else than irresistible, and almost supernatural; that when he preached, his words fell one by one with an indescribable awe and solemnity in the style of the Gospels, and reached the secret place of the soul. He acknowledged that, in spite of Drummond's sense of humour and sweetness of nature, there was about him a curious aloofness and separateness from human life. He seemed to be master of himself and passionless. Though he would help any one in trouble to his last resource, he neither asked nor wished for aid from others. He received many confidences; he gave none; he refused the accustomed paths and took his own meteoric way. He belonged by nature to the pre-theological age. Christ was his unseen Friend with Whom he walked in life, by Whose fellowship he was changed, to Whom he prayed. The man was greater than all his books, and while competent in science was a master in religion. 'From his youth up he had kept the commandments, and was such a man as the Master would have loved. One takes for granted that each man has his besetting sin, and we could name that of our friends, but Drummond was an exception to this rule. After a lifetime's intimacy I do not remember my friend's failing. Without pride, without envy, without selfishness, without vanity, moved only by goodwill and spiritual ambitions, responsive ever to the touch of God and every noble impulse, faithful, fearless, magnanimous, Henry Drummond was the most perfect Christian I have ever known or expect to see this side the grave.' While Drummond lived constant communication was sustained between the two. Even from Central Africa a letter arrived one day after months of travel by negro couriers, and with many adventures. 'It is very hot here,' wrote Drummond, 'and I am wearing a helmet and five mosquitoes.'

Another friend of these days at the High School of Stirling was William Durham, the 'lad o' pairts.' Speaking at Stirling in 1897, Dr. Watson said :—

One recollection of that school has been to me a great inspiration, and I refer to the life and character and work of my distinguished schoolfellow, William Durham. When I came into that form he was *facile princeps*, and while two of us—the Rev. George MacNaughton of whom I have heard to-night, and myself—fought hard for the second place, none of us had the impudence to try to have the first place. That belonged absolutely, with a wide gulf between, to William Durham, and we were willing to give him the place not only on account of his conspicuous ability, but also on account of his excellent disposition. He was an honour to the High School then, and an honour to the school afterwards in Edinburgh; and more than that, he was a sanctifying and Christian influence upon all who knew him. He was taken away at the age of twenty-one, and was buried in the cemetery at St. Ninians. There is a monument raised to him, but his memory remains with all the pupils as one standing out from our schooldays, one of the noblest and most impressive figures, and I do not deny, but am rather anxious to confess, that he inspired the character of George Howe in *The Bonnie Brier Bush.*

He went on to speak of the beautiful churchyard in Stirling, 'which is one of the most beautiful things in this place, and surely nowhere is there a "God's acre" which stands higher, nearer the sky, and nowhere one on which the sun shines more constantly. . . . There lies the mortal dust of one of my dearest friends, and one of the brightest intellects given to the Church in our time, and one of the holiest lives given to the generation. . . . If I would venture to give any advice to the young men in this excellent institution, it would be to keep before them such lives as those of my schoolfellow, William Durham, known to some who are present here not perhaps quite young any more than myself; and the life of Henry Drummond, known to all of you, a brave soldier of the Cross, a good knight of God, and a pure and saintly man from his first days to the end.'

Of Watson's days in Stirling I am able to give a brief recollection from Mr. J. W. Drummond, Professor Drummond's brother:—

My recollection of John Watson as a schoolboy is that of one of rather slender build, with pale, refined features. In manner he was more sedate than most boys; but he had a hearty laugh, and was always delightful company. Even then he had a keen sense of humour; and sometimes it was difficult to know whether he was talking seriously or in jest. In his case the boy was more the father of the man than in that of most people. To the last he retained an interest in his old schoolfellows; and always inquired for them when opportunity permitted. In his time the organised games connected with the High School of Stirling were limited to cricket, for which two elevens were with difficulty forthcoming; and I do not remember that he often joined in them. He occasionally played golf with his father or another of the half-dozen men who were then the only votaries of the game in the King's Park of Stirling. He was frequently to be seen walking with his father and mother, the former a dignified gentleman with a face which to a boy seemed somewhat sad, but with great kindliness of manner; the latter the essence of good nature; and both closely attached to their only child.

His cousin, who was an inmate of the home, has also sent a recollection:—

I was about five years of age when I remember John Watson first, and I lived with his father and mother at that time in Stirling. I often used to hear my aunt speak of John when he was a little fellow; she was very fond of him, and as a child he was not at all strong, and often lived with her for months at a time at Drumlochy, as the doctors wished John to be in the country as much as possible.

He was rather a precocious child, and one story I remember aunt used to laugh at, and told how she and his mother were crossing a field one day where there were some cattle. Aunt had remarked somewhat strongly to her sister regarding them, and John hearing this ran up to his mother and said: 'Isn't Aunt Jane a naughty girl to use words like that?' His mother answered, 'Yes, John, you are right, she is naughty.' 'Don't you think Satan has gone into Aunt Jane's heart?' 'Well, John, perhaps he has,' at which he answered, 'And don't you think he has gone in and shut the door?'

I fancy he would be five or six years of age at that time.

When I remember him first he was tall and thin, in fact very thin and pale, and not at all strong-looking. At that time and from then onwards Professor Henry Drummond and he were great friends, and the latter used to come to John's house a great deal.

John was always full of humour and tricks. He got me into disgrace with his mother when I was a small child, for asking me to open my mouth and shut my eyes, when he popped an almond sweet into my mouth, which had been previously broken, the interior taken out, the almond filled with mustard, and all put neatly together again. My screams alarmed the house, and there was considerable trouble for John.

My uncle had an estate called the Grange where John and I often spent our holidays together. He used to ride a beautiful cream pony given to him by his father, and uncle used to keep it all winter for him. He had it for seven or eight years, and used to talk to it so much that the pony seemed to understand everything he meant.

John was a great favourite always wherever he went. When in the country with his uncle he used to go and chat with the ploughmen, enjoy their talk, and seemed to study all their ways. Uncle had an old grieve who had been with him for years, and sometimes took a 'drappy' too much. Peter was his name, and John said a chat with Peter after one of those outbreaks was very amusing. He used to come in and relate the story to aunt while he was doubled up with laughter. I feel sure he gathered a great lot of his matter for *The Bonnie Brier Bush* from those people, although I am sure at that time he never dreamt of writing.

In Stirling the Watsons attended the ministry of the Rev. Dr. Alexander Beith, a pre-Disruption minister of vigorous intellect and character, who in later life strongly defended the orthodoxy of Robertson Smith. Watson said :—

I shall always remember here is the church where I worshipped with my people, and the figure of Dr. Beith, moving through this town with a certain dignity which I think we of the younger generation of clergy have not been able always to sustain, and preaching in the pulpit with a note of authority which the pulpit now very seldom has, always fills up a page in my memory. He was a type of the clergyman of the past in all his ways, and left a deep impression on the generation following.

CHAPTER II

THE UNIVERSITY

In 1866 John Watson became a student in the University of Edinburgh. His father, who had been promoted to the highest place in his profession, had removed to Edinburgh, and lived in the Grange. He attached himself to the Grange Free Church, and became an elder there under the ministry of Dr. Horatius Bonar. Dr. Bonar, who is best known as a hymn-writer, had been an intimate friend of M'Cheyne, and was ultimately the biographer of Milne of Perth, the minister of Watson's boyhood. Thus the evangelistic influences of which I have spoken continued to play upon him. But he had very little to say in after life about Dr. Bonar, save that there was a strong element of mysticism in his teaching. Few famous men have owed so little to the University as John Watson. He flowered late, and it is my belief that his force and passion were partly checked by the silent conflict in his heart. For an account of his career in Edinburgh University I am largely indebted to Dr. D. M. Ross, who from University days was his intimate friend. There were brilliant men at Edinburgh in these days, both among the students and the professors. Among the notable figures in the chairs was John Stuart Blackie, the Professor of Greek. Blackie was picturesque and so eccentric that many took him to be a mere harlequin. Those who knew him, however, claimed that, though he was eminently discursive in his teaching, he gave freely of his garnered wisdom of life, and widened their intellectual and religious horizons. He dealt freely with theology, and persistently recommended the divinity students in his classes to draw their theology from the fountain-head, the Greek New Testament. 'Yesterday,' he once said, 'I listened to the most evangelical sermon I have ever heard from a pulpit. Evangelical because it kept so close to the teaching of Christ in the Gospels.' Other teachers were Sellar, the ripe and finished Latinist; Campbell Fraser, the philosopher who imbued many students with the genuine metaphysical spirit; P. G. Tait, the eminent physicist, the friend and colleague of Lord Kelvin; David Masson, the strong, manly, inspiring teacher of English literature; and Henry Calderwood, the solid and practical teacher. Mr. Barrie has written about some of these in his little book *An Edinburgh Eleven*. It could hardly be said that any of these roused Watson to enthusiasm. He did not join in the strife for prizes; he was content with passing examinations and taking his degree in the regular course. But as his writings afterwards showed, he watched very closely the play of life among his fellow-students, and especially the sacrifices made for intellectual eminence by many whose means were straitened. He did not by personal experience know what poverty was, but he had among his fellows many who did. As Dr. Ross says, the Scottish peasants with their passion for education and for seeing their children 'getting on,' will readily pinch themselves to send a clever lad to college. With his parents' savings, eked out by a bursary or by his own private tutoring of schoolboys in the evening, such a lad manages to scrape along on scanty fare—sometimes with tragic results. Eager for intellectual distinction, and for the rewards which will enable him to repay the sacrifices made in his humble home, he is reckless of his bodily health, and the end comes speedily. Watson did not miss the broad culture which is to be won from the social life and atmosphere of the University. He took from it the intellectual stimulus, the widened horizon, and the lifelong friendships which are among the choicest gains of college years.

In after years he would talk chiefly about Blackie, and give imitations of the class-room and of the professor on the slightest excuse, breaking into wild Gaelic songs. But his memories of his teachers were very tender and very loving, and he did not blame them for any deficiency in his scholarship. For his time was not wasted. He was a diligent reader, and in after years never expressed the slightest regret for the time thus spent on acquiring great stores of general information. It was always said of him: 'No matter where you put him down, he will be at home with the man at his elbow.' He never envied the cleverer men of his time, and often remarked in later years when his name was famous: 'I have been a very fortunate man. Everything has always been in my favour. My friends were all cleverer than I was.'

Among his fellow-students were men who rose to eminence. Sir John Murray, of *Challenger* Expedition fame; Dr. Sorley, the present Professor of Moral Philosophy in Cambridge University; Professor Pringle Pattison, who occupies the chair of Logic and Metaphysics in the University of which he was once a student, were all his contemporaries. In the English Literature Class sat Robert Louis Stevenson. It does not appear that Watson ever spoke to Stevenson, but he remembered that his attendance was very occasional, and that when he entered the class-room with his velvet jacket and bohemian air, he was usually greeted with a round of cheers.

It was not in English Literature but in mental

philosophy that Watson first distinguished himself. Dr. Ross writes that the students of the Moral Philosophy Class were keenly interested in the discussion of Utilitarianism and Free Will. Professor Calderwood, who had several times found a group of the students after the class was over engaged in such discussions in the quadrangle, suggested that they should establish a society and thrash out their questions in circumstances of greater comfort. From that suggestion originated the Philosophical Society, which had an honourable and useful career. Robert Adamson, who had already passed through the philosophical classes and proved his pre-eminence as a philosophical student, was one of the four presidents for the first year, and the secretary was James Walter Ferrier, son of Professor Ferrier, and friend of Robert Louis Stevenson, who has described him with infinite love and pity.

The subject of discussion at our first meeting in the Associated Societies' Room was 'Protoplasm: the physical basis of life'—suggested by Huxley's famous address and Hutchison Stirling's reply: 'As regards Protoplasm.' Towards the close of this discussion, a tall, spare, pale-looking student, who was unknown to most of us, made a short speech and wound up his criticism of the attempt to explain the origin of life by mere physical processes with this sentence: 'Mr. Chairman, we heard of the dance of death, this is surely the dance of life.' The speaker, we discovered, was a student in his first year at the New College, a cousin of one of our class-fellows, and his name

John Watson. In a later year, he was Secretary of our Society, and afterwards President. That he thus associated himself with a society whose members were his juniors in academic standing indicates the strength of his interest in the intellectual problems which engaged his attention in after years to the profit of his hearers.

To this I may add that Watson retained to the end his interest in philosophy, and generally found time to read any new philosophical book which was attracting general attention.

His own somewhat severe and shadowed judgment of these early years was given in one of his last writings:—

When my readers know that the whole instruction I received at schools was in classics, and (much less so) in mathematics, and that I went to the University of Edinburgh at the age of sixteen, they can imagine how likely I was to profit by philosophy and literature. I was at home in Horace and Homer, and knew my Euclid fairly well, but I might as well have remained outside the classes of that great and venerable teacher, Professor Fraser, the modern father of philosophy in Scotland, and an honourable name far beyond his own country. It was only after I had graduated that my mind awoke to philosophy, and very largely through the influence of the University Philosophical Society, which contained many distinguished men, and of which, through patient continuance in well-doing, I became a president. If I had only entered that eminent man's class at the age of twenty! One hopes that the day has come when no university anywhere will admit students without a matriculation examination, and when they will refuse to do the work of secondary schools. So far as I now can understand, I was simply a schoolboy at the University.

When Watson was passing through the University he did not think of becoming a minister. His mother, who chiefly directed his life, would have put him in the Army if she had judged the means of the family sufficient. She allowed her son to learn farming and to follow the pursuits of a country life till he was much more at home in the saddle than in the study. He had to take his degree in order to satisfy his father and rank as a moderately educated person. But once that had been done, he hoped either to join a relative who was farming on a large scale, or to prepare himself for a post as a land agent. His sympathy was with the scenes, occupations, pleasures and people of the country, with all of which he was familiar. His love of the country was kept alive in these days by his vacation visits to his uncles. He had ample room, for his uncles—all bachelors but one—rented or, in some cases, owned quite a number of the largest and best farms in eastern Perthshire. The brothers Maclaren were widely known in Strathmore for their worth as men and their ability as agriculturists. Watson's college holidays were largely spent at Gormack Grange, or some other of the hospitable farms, where the quick, sprightly lad with his endless drolleries of speech was ever welcome. It was there as the years passed on that he gained his full initiation into rural life. In the portraiture of Burnbrae and Drumsheugh there are recognisable many characteristics of the bachelor uncles. He had many stories to tell of these days. He stayed chiefly with an aunt and uncle, both unmarried, at Kinloch, near Blairgowrie. The three sat in a prominent position in the little kirk, and it was his aunt's terror that his uncle would drop asleep at the other end of the seat. For this purpose she placed an umbrella along the intervening space, and at the slightest nod of the head, without altering the pious and thoughtful expression of her face, her left arm grasped the umbrella firmly, and in a moment attention was assured. His imitation of his aunt inserting a peppermint into her mouth with the general appearance of one following a train of theological thought was irresistible. For these friends of early days he had a great and enduring love. In after years he always paid a visit with great regularity to the Kirkyard where they lie, to assure himself that the graves were in repair, and if he was too busy he sent instructions to a trusted friend. For him there were few sadder sights than a neglected grave, especially some little child's grave hidden by a riot of weeds. In his last years he showed a desire to see again the scenes which were associated with the recollections of other years, and a longing to roll back the mist which was gathering between him and the past.

These bachelor uncles were men of powerful build, but they took such risks and hazards that they did not live their full time. Once late at night during a snowstorm one of them coming home shouted to the man on the other side of the river to bring the boat across. But the river was running too high on that wild night, and the man refused to risk his life. At that Maclaren calmly wrapped himself up in his plaid and slept soundly under a bush till dawn, when he crossed and returned home none the worse. In fact so ordinary an occurrence was never mentioned by him. It only became known through the boatman. It was from this stock that Watson inherited his iron constitution, for in spite of what has been said to the contrary, a man who could lecture often three times a day, and travel at night for weeks at a stretch, must have had quite exceptional physical strength.

It may seem that his University days were partly wasted. But wise observers of life have noted that there is a time when intellectual young men are sure to idle if they have the opportunity. Though such times are often bitterly regretted in after life as lost days and years, the probability is that they have special value and contribute an element not otherwise obtainable to the ultimate development of the man. Toffper says: 'A year of downright loitering is a desirable element in a liberal education.'

In after years he became intimate with some of his old teachers, and particularly with Professor Blackie, the best loved of all. Among the very few papers he kept I found a treasured certificate from Blackie dated April 1868 and containing the words, 'He displayed a knowledge of the Greek language that distinguished him highly among his fellow students; he was an excellent student and gave me great satisfaction.' Along with it is a letter from Mrs. Blackie which tells its own story:—

Feb. 28, 1895.
9 *Douglas Crescent, Edinburgh.*

DEAR MR. WATSON,—I must not wait longer without acknowledging and thanking you for your photograph. It arrived too late to be more than recognised by my Dear who since you were here has been too ill to see letters or even to hear them read. It is a failure of the whole system. He slept night and day for 4 days this week, only awaking for a few intervals. Yesterday he sunk very low, and his mind, up till then perfectly acute, began to wander. He never gave much trouble in health and he continues true still to his instincts, and is simple and sweet when lucid moments come.

It was a true pleasure to him to see you, and he and I have often spoken briefly of that pleasure. I hope you will like the enclosed photo. It is the one we like. He looks such a happy sage there.

With my sincere regards,—I am, yours,

E. H. S. BLACKIE.

CHAPTER III

NEW COLLEGE, EDINBURGH

TOWARDS the end of his college days he was faced with one of the determining questions of life. He had to choose his profession. On this, as on all others connected with him, my business is to give the facts as he gave them. It is fair to say that the impression of some who knew him at that period contradicts his own in some points. But Watson was reticent on the deepest matters, and no doubt his friends misunderstood. For every sentence of this chapter I have his own authority either in printed articles or in manuscript.

He did not intend and did not wish to become a minister. He was not closely associated with religious circles. 'While I attended Church and lived a moral life, I had not the remotest contact with Church work, and was an absolute stranger to what may be called the religious circle. I did not know one word of their language then, and now, although I know it fairly, I have never acquired the accent; it is with me as with an

Englishman brought up in France.' One day he was informed by his father that he must enter the Church. He was allowed the alternative of the Bar, if he had an insuperable objection to a clerical career. But it was plainly indicated that such a choice would be a disappointment to his mother and to his father. So little had he thought of his future profession that he was not a communicant in the Christian Church, and he became one in order to fulfil a condition of entrance into the Theological College. He dwelt upon this almost painfully after he had resigned his charge.

> If sometimes I have been almost choked in the atmosphere of ecclesiastical courts, it was because my lungs were accustomed to the wind blowing over the moors or across a field of ripe, golden wheat; and if I have not understood the subtleties or the phraseology of esoteric piety, it was because I had been so much at home with open-air folk. It has, therefore, come to pass that I have always been slightly nervous, and more than slightly ill at ease in religious circles, not, I hope, because I do not hold with all my heart the Christian faith, but because in my youth I was never within the circle of professional religion. Jesuits, who are in some ways the wisest men I have ever known, are careful to frame the novice's whole nature for his future work, so that all its powers be gathered in and consecrated to the priestly office. This one thing he sees and thinks and loves.

It was by no means a foregone conclusion that he should become a minister of the Free Church. He might have entered the Established Church, and through nearly all of his clerical life it was his opinion that he would have been more at home within its bounds. He was an Established Churchman in theory, and he passionately maintained that he was a Moderate in theology. It was among Nonconformists that he was to spend his life, and he loved them more as life went on. Still he writes in 1905:—

While I have never seen cause to repent either of my Churchmanship or of my theology, I gratefully acknowledge the inspiration which came to me from the warm piety and self-sacrificing ideals of the Free Church, and I hope that I have not been unfaithful to my Church. I wish also, in passing, to acknowledge the courtesy and kindness I have received from English Nonconformists who have welcomed a Scottish foreigner to their pulpits, and for whose historical love of liberty, religious and political, I have a respectful admiration. But it is always better that one should live in his native country rather than in a strange land, however fairly the sun may shine and delightful the people may be. It fetters a man's speech, and perhaps even his soul, when he is not in thorough-going sympathy with his colleagues; it brings a man to his height, and calls forth all his energies when he is working with the same method and thinking on the same principles as the man beside him. I should like to record my conviction that so long as there are different schools in the Christian Church, a minister will do his work after the best fashion when he is placed in the most congenial atmosphere. And, therefore, let a man choose his natural church, the one for which he was born.

It will be seen then that he became a student

for the Free Church ministry with a certain reluctance and hesitation. But there can be no doubt that he found himself far more at home in the Divinity Hall than he had been in the University. His powers were maturing. Most young men with a similar experience look back on their theological course as one of the happiest times of their life. There is a freedom from responsibility; there is a widening sphere of knowledge and interest; above all, there is the inspiring contact of fresh minds with the same interests and the same end in view. Henry Drummond was his fellow-student, and in his life of Drummond, Professor George Adam Smith has given a graphic account of the College life. The Divinity course occupied four winter sessions. There were about a hundred regular students, and twenty or thirty others from America, Ireland, and the Continent. During Watson's time at New College the bond of fellowship was strengthened by the institution of a common dinner-table. The atmosphere of the College was genial and stimulating. 'One remembers not only greater maturity, but more buoyancy, more humour, and more *camaraderie* than in the University.' Among the students there was a good proportion of able men. Robertson Smith had just left the College, but in Watson's picturesque phrase 'the white track behind the vessel was still on the water.' Smith carried on a tutorial class in Hebrew, and when he left Edinburgh Watson and others who had been indebted to his help presented him with an illuminated address expressive of regret at his departure, and gratitude for his services. Andrew Harper, now Professor of Hebrew at Melbourne, and David Patrick, now editor of *Chambers's Encyclopædia*, were in their third year. W. G. Elmslie, afterwards Professor of Hebrew in the Presbyterian College of London, was in his second year. In his own year were James Stalker, Henry Drummond, and John F. Ewing, who fulfilled a brief but memorable ministry in Melbourne. There were other men of note, and they educated each other with great zest in the Theological Society which met on Friday evenings. Watson's social gifts made room for him. It is impossible to conceive that he could have been sullen under any circumstances, and in a measure he yielded to the atmosphere. But he was more distinguished as a brilliant talker and speaker than as a laborious student. The determined orthodoxy of the Free Church was beginning to yield. The new generation of students were eagerly discussing Biblical criticism, evolution, Hegelianism. These acted as solvents on traditional views of the Bible and on current Calvinistic theology. Watson was caught in the newer theological movement. Clement of Alexandria was a greater favourite with him than St. Augustine. He was a close student of Frederick Robertson and Horace

Bushnell, and he gave himself freely to such writers as Ruskin, Emerson, Tennyson, Longfellow, Matthew Arnold, and Russell Lowell. In fact there were few men in the College more intent on finding their theological bearings. One of the books that fascinated him at that time was a little volume containing two of T. H. Green's sermons to undergraduates—'Faith' and 'The Witness of God.' This had been privately printed and was handed eagerly about as if it had been the revelation of a prophet. But Watson was mainly distinguished by his social vivacity and mental alertness. 'No one could approach him,' says Dr. Ross, 'in his power of hitting off good-humouredly the peculiarities of his classmates, or, be it said with bated breath, of his class professor. Many a New College student is best remembered by some of us to-day through a phrase or story of Watson's. At the College dinner-table his stories and sallies were an endless source of wonderment to the graver students; and in the after-dinner walks in Princes Street Gardens, across the Meadows, or round the noble crags of Arthur's Seat, in the company of his more intimate friends, Watson was a perennial fountain alike of *camaraderie* and intellectual stimulus.' He gave and he also received, for it was ever in bright and animating society that he found a tonic and a stimulus.

It cannot be said that he judged favourably

the teaching in the College. It was one of his dominating beliefs that Churches generally do far too little to secure the efficient training of their ministers. He held that a mistaken tenderness in retaining professors who could not instruct was at the root of much weakness in the Christianity of to-day. He held that five out of his seven professors, though excellent men in different ways, were absolutely useless as teachers. No freedom of choice was allowed. The students had to attend every class whether the subject or the teacher profited them or not. As the training of Divinity students was a subject which always interested Watson very keenly, it is worth while to give his ripe judgment on the subject:—

Were one recasting arrangements from his practical experience, there are several changes he would make in the system of theological colleges. For one thing, the Chairs should be filled by men at the height of their power, and who are acknowledged experts in their subject; the professors should hold their Chairs for a certain number of years, and then, if they be efficient, be re-elected; certain subjects such as Old and New Testament languages and criticism, and possibly dogma, should be compulsory, and a man should be obliged to choose, in addition, one or two more subjects out of Church History, Apologetic, Christian Ethics, Social Economy, Palæography, and suchlike. He should have liberty to go from college to college where he can find the best teachers. And before he leaves his college, the student should be carefully trained in pastoral theology. It is not just and it is not moral that a man should be sent forth to the work of the holy ministry who does not know how to preach, who has never been trained to conduct a service, who has not been instructed in pastoral work, who has no idea what to say to men when they come with their doubts or with their sins, and who is not in contact with the living thought of the day. Until lately theological colleges were the most inefficient institutions in the world of education, and the sufferers from this sin are scattered up and down the ministry of the Christian Church.

But there was one at least of his theological professors whom he regarded with peculiar and abiding reverence. Perhaps no theological teacher of this time or any time has succeeded so well in dominating successive companies of students as the late Dr. A. B. Davidson, the distinguished Professor of Hebrew in the New College. Davidson, who was professor from 1863 to 1903, was for forty years regarded in the New College as its most famous man and its singular glory. A scholar of the first rank, a man singularly unobtrusive and modest, but with formidable powers of sarcasm, endowed with a deep and passionate nature severely held in command, Davidson was the ideal scholar and teacher. I quote a large part of the tribute which Watson paid to his old master when Davidson died, for it reveals much of the author as well as of the subject:—

Dr. Davidson taught, in the seventies at least, in a dingy room on the highest floor at the back of New College; and his class, even with strangers from various quarters of the world, would seldom exceed thirty. He was obliged to spend a lamentable proportion of his priceless time in teaching grammar to young lads who, in many cases, only learned as much as would pass the exit examination, and then afterwards forgot it all. He was only able to give a certain portion of his time to those lectures on the Hebrew Literature and Spirit which are an inspiration across the lapse of years. If he preached—and each sermon was an event—his coming might not be advertised nor even announced; and latterly he would not preach at all, declaring either that his sermons were so bad that he had burned them, or that preaching was a bad habit into which a man might fall if he did not take care. No one ever heard of his attending a public meeting or moving a resolution; he went very little into society, and took no part in Church Courts, where, curious to say, he was never formally prosecuted, although the pioneer of modern Hebrew scholarship; no one turned to look at him as he went along Princes Street, and his face was unknown to the people. Yet this retiring and modest man, who simply loathed publicity and sensationalism, who would rather any day have been silent than speak, and would have given his year's stipend rather than mount a public platform, who was always endeavouring to escape notice, and who flushed red if suddenly addressed in a room, changed the face of theological thought in Scotland, put a new spirit into the preaching of the Bible, affected the people through a thousand pulpits, and was the most powerful intellectual influence in the Scots Church, and, through the men whom he taught and through the work he did, a pervasive light throughout the whole English-speaking Christian Church.

There was an instant hush in the class when the door of the retiring-room opened and the Professor entered in gown and bands, and the keenest intellectual face some of us have ever seen—thin, clean-cut, crowned with iron-grey hair—looked at the men for a brief instant before prayer. No one could hear anywhere else such a prayer—short and slow, with slight pauses and hesitations, but reverent and individual. The petitions were those of a scholar, and perhaps the most characteristic was 'Lord, grant us teachableness.' If a man were called up to read and translated with care, the Professor heard him with approval, and the man was content when Davidson was satisfied. If the student showed scholarship by some felicitous turn of speech or touch of grammatical accuracy, then Davidson gave him a brief word of praise, and the man was not to be spoken to on equal terms for the rest of the day, since praise from Davidson was a decoration. If the man were an idler, and could not even read the Hebrew correctly, then, after a few mysterious words suggesting Hebrew sounds had fallen from the unhappy reader's lips, Davidson would suggest that he should proceed to translation, and when the translation was an exact repetition of the accepted version, Davidson would blandly congratulate him on the correspondence between his work and that of King James's scholars, and ask him to sit down without censure. But the way in which Davidson used to say 'That will do, Mr. Tomkins,' was like the cut of a whip. If a working student by some accident broke the stillness while the Professor was lecturing, he would give him a quick, reproachful glance, which brought the man into the retiring-room afterwards to explain the conduct of his ink-bottle with abject apologies; but if it were only some idler at the back who had been amusing himself by making a pyramid of hats, then the sudden flush of anger would fade from the Professor's brow, as he recognised the cause, and he would say, as it were to himself, 'It's only Mr. Tomkins.' Only Mr. Tomkins! There was no man living in Edinburgh who could administer such punishment.

When the Professor lectured, the men toiled after him, writing at top speed and fearing lest they should lose a sentence, and there were days when they could not write because they required every power to appreciate. And there were lectures so perfect, final, fascinating, inspiring, that when their time came again in the course of after years, men left other classes for the day to hear Davidson once more on Saul.

It must be left to scholars to declare the value of his work, scattered throughout many theological journals, and contained in his handbooks on the Epistle to the Hebrews and the Book of Job, and the Hebrew Grammar, and no doubt a capable and generous tribute will be paid to the departed scholar in many high quarters. But it is open for any one to point out that perhaps his greatest achievement was the creation of scholars and the inspiration of ordinary men. He was the master of Robertson Smith and George Adam Smith, and with them of almost every one of the young Hebraists who have brought such distinction to the Free Church and to Scots theological learning. And I suppose the New Testament and the dogmatic students would also confess how much they owe to the love of learning, and the enthusiasm for theology and the principles of study which they learned from Davidson. But his influence was not exhausted upon scholars; it has reached to every working minister who ever sat in his class-room and had soul enough to appreciate the man. If a New College man has learned to come to the Bible with an open mind, and to place himself in its original environment; if one strives to reach the soul of the Book, and has felt the power of its spiritual message, and indeed if one loves learning at all and good books, and is moved to serve truth and do righteousness in his calling, he finds out more clearly as the years come and go that, while he has debts to pay to many men, his chief debt is due to Dr. Davidson. What Professor Davidson was to his distinguished pupils the writer does not know; but he can tell what he was to pupils who had no special claim upon his interest and goodness. He did not lay himself out to pet his students, and encompass them with social observances. He kept himself aloof, and was always somewhat of a mystery to them. His manner could not be called genial and affectionate; it was reserved and silent, with a flavour of cynicism. The students never complained of that; on that account they rather respected him the more. What students ask is not that a professor should be a social philanthropist or a person of jocose manners, and patronage of every kind and fulsome attentions they will deeply resent. They demand that a man shall know his subject through and through, and that, if possible, he shall be able to teach them what he knows. That he shall work hard for his class, and compel them to work, that he shall do justly by every man both in praise and in blame, and if, in addition, he also takes an unaffected interest in the men who do their best, however poor that best may be, then they will honour that professor, and hang upon his lips, and declare the honour of his name, and take his most sarcastic criticism with secret pride, and cherish a single word of approbation for all the days of their life. And though they would never say it to their most intimate friends, and the professor himself would laugh the idea to scorn, they will love that man.

Davidson's power of speech when he criticised a man's Exegesis, and the writer had taken refuge from a difficulty in pleasant fancy, or from honest exposition in Evangelical twaddle, was as a razor working swiftly and surely; while the things he could say in private to reduce a man's swollen self-conceit or to prune his eccentricity were distinctly memorable. And although he was not easily provoked in society, and did not care for the clash of words, yet when an ignorant minister challenged Dr. Davidson at a dinner-table, boldly and rudely saying, 'I count myself fortunate never to have learned Hebrew,' the reply of the Professor was described to me as swift and sufficient. 'And I count that Professor also fortunate who might have had to teach you.' One, indeed, did not envy the man who tried to cross swords with Dr. Davidson, nor the student who fell under his displeasure. But if he believed that you had used the brains the Almighty had been pleased to give you, and if you had carried yourself in a becoming manner while under his charge, he would neither forget nor be indifferent to you in after years. He would walk the length of Princes Street with you—an honour now to be deeply cherished: he would show an unexpected acquaintance with your difficulties and duties: he would make a shy allusion to some little success you had had—a tremendous success after he had acknowledged it—and you would learn, to your utter surprise, that behind your back he said the friendliest things of you, and spoke of you almost as if you had been a Hebrew scholar, so kind a heart and so generous a temper were hidden behind a reserved disposition and a scholar's severe mask.

As often as two New College men met after an interval, they talked sooner or later of their master, and complained bitterly that he wrote so little, and that there was no word of his great book—which some said would be on Old Testament Theology: that he refused to preach, and hid himself more and more from sight. Their complaints were a veiled tribute to his scholarly fastidiousness, his loyalty to truth, his contempt for raw work, his dislike for notoriety, and his strong individuality. It was hoped that in his years of rest, Dr. Davidson would have made the world partaker of his stored treasures; but one fears that the ripest and sanest Old Testament teacher of our day has left his chief monument in the work and lives of his pupils, and the rare combination of the finest scholarship with the fear of God.

> Yea, this in him was the peculiar grace,
> (Hearten our chorus!)
> That before living he'd learn how to live,
> No end to learning.
> That low man seeks a little thing to do,
> Sees it and does it;
> This high man, with a great thing to pursue,
> Dies ere he knows it.

Another teacher not less famous, but famous after a different fashion, was Principal Rainy. Nobody who knew Rainy could doubt that he ranked with the greatest statesmen of the Scottish Church, with Knox, Henderson, and Carstares. He was also a powerful and subtle lecturer, and a man of the noblest Christian character. As a teacher he did not attain to the greatness of Davidson. Watson wrote:—

Principal Rainy was teaching Church history, and it were an impertinence for me to criticise his lectures. His is the subtlest mind of our time with which I ever came in contact; possibly because it was so subtle, and his manner was so perfectly cleansed from enthusiasm, that students of weaker capacity did not receive the full benefit of his instruction, or feel, as they have afterwards felt, the fascination which gathers round the long evolution of Church life and doctrine.

But when Rainy died some time after, Watson wrote:—

From a suggestion of superciliousness in his manner—due to his habit of half-closed eyes, and from the subtlety of his style, due to the caution of his mind, a section of the public imagined Dr. Rainy to be the conventional ecclesiastic of the Roman type—haughty, crafty, ambitious, and not too scrupulous. There never was a more shallow or more unjust reading of his character. He did not give his mind to every acquaintance, and if he had it would not have been understood; he saw far ahead of the average man, and had plans which the average man grasps slowly. But there was nothing cunning or double, nothing ungenerous or unchivalrous in Rainy. He was lifted above the jealousies, private ends, personal grudges, unworthy prejudices which blind and fetter even able men. His eyes were ever fixed on the lofty ideals and broad enterprises of the Kingdom of God in Scotland. It was his, besides much patient labour over the affairs of the Church, to prepare the way for the complete and final union of the Kirk, and he lived to see the first step taken, and to secure freedom for believing criticism in the Church, and he could have proudly said that no Church, in proportion to her size, has produced a larger number of Biblical scholars. At a great cost he did this service, and coming generations will do him honour.

Watson liked to illustrate Rainy's ways. Once in lecturing he turned from his manuscript and leaning back in his chair he said, 'The fact is, gentlemen, Archbishop Sharp was a great rascal.' The students gave a unanimous cheer, and the Principal caught the point, and concealing a smile with difficulty, went on with his lecture. Rainy's style was perfectly lucid when he was at his keenest, but was apt to be over-careful in its qualifications, and he would deliver himself at a time after this fashion: 'There are in this theologian certain tendencies which, unless you consider them balanced by other leanings in the opposite direction which do not certainly obtrude themselves, might lead an impartial student to entertain the fear that our author might ultimately find himself in a position which could not be very clearly distinguished from semi-Pelagianism.' No one could say that this was a rash statement. Watson did full justice to Rainy's extraordinary ascendancy over the Free Church Assembly. Every year, during the Assembly sittings, Dr. Rainy had his 'great fortnight.' This was the fortnight during which his Assembly met to discuss the affairs of the Church. No one described him better than Watson:—

His head is thrown back and through his half-closed eyes he is watching his opponent. His commanding forehead, clear-cut profile, firm chin, his air of culture, and his aristocratic bearing, mark him out as a member of the ruling caste, who are born to direct and command. When one looks down at the face of Rameses the Great, lying in his coffin, he recognises in an instant that between that Egyptian monarch and the multitude of peasants who toiled in the steaming valley of the Nile, there was a great gulf fixed. They were created to obey, and he to govern. Dr. Rainy sits among able and distinguished men on that bench, and around him are laymen and clergymen who may be fairly called the flower of the people, but one feels that this man has a place by himself. Behind that face of perfect lines and inscrutable expression are thoughts which few in that Assembly share, and a will with which they cannot compete.

Towards the close of Watson's time at the New College in 1873 an extraordinary religious movement began in Edinburgh, and spread over Scotland and England. This was the revival associated with the names of Messrs. Moody and Sankey. Nearly all the Divinity students caught the fire and flung themselves into the work. In particular, Henry Drummond devoted himself to evangelisation for some two years. Dr. George Adam Smith gives a history of the work and says that the effect of the great revival was extremely helpful to the students, and prepared them to face the questions raised by Professor Robertson Smith upon scholarly and strenuously religious lines.

The practical and theological thus developed in close co-operation with inestimable benefit to both. The strong intellectual activities of the College were in the healthiest possible touch with real life. At the same time the College was full of happy play, and there was a good deal of joking. Watson does not seem to have taken any special part in the revival. He was always in respectful sympathy with such movements, but it was on the normal work of the Church that he always relied. He characterised Moody as 'the most capable, honest, and unselfish evangelist of our day.' But his judgment is probably summed up in the sentence: 'Religion is without doubt the better for the popular evangelist, although there be times when quiet folk think that he needs chastening; religion also requires in every generation one representative at least of the higher evangelism, and if any one should ask what manner of man he ought to be, the answer is to his hand—Henry Drummond.

Dr. Smith, referring to the testing controversy connected with Professor Robertson Smith, says:—

> The great Mission of 1873-75 had quickened the practical use of the Bible, and the Church was studying her sacred books in the congregation and in the Bible-class with a freshness and a thoroughness hardly seen before. But now came the necessary complement to all that, in the critical study of the Scriptures; and by those who believe in God's Providence of His Church it has always been a matter of praise that the revival of the experimental study of the Scriptures in Scotland preceded that of the critical.

An episode which ought not to be omitted is Watson's connection with a little society known as the Gaiety Club. During the winter of 1876 Drummond engaged the Gaiety Music Hall in Chambers Street for a number of Sunday evenings, for meetings of men. From these meetings came the name of the Gaiety Club which still exists. Among its members were some of the more brilliant young men of the times. They arranged to meet every spring for a week at some country inn, and it is amusing to learn that at first they set apart some evenings for criticising each other's growth or decline during the year. This passed away, but the comradeship became closer, and Watson's meetings with the Gaiety Club had a large part in his conversations. On the whole, I cannot but feel that his time at the New College was exceedingly profitable, and he gained more than he fancied from the teaching. Undoubtedly, however, he gained most from brotherly comradeships. A freshness of vivid sensation acting upon the vigorous energies of youth produced that condition of the feelings which elevates men to the best enthusiasms. There was a delightful combination of religious life with intellectual activity. There was a buoyancy of untried strength.

> Whether we lay in the cave or shed,
> Our sleep fell soft on the hardest bed.
>
> . . . .
>
> Fresh we awoke on the morrow,
> All our thoughts and words had scope;
> We had health and we had hope,
> Toil and travail but no sorrow.

This was the period when Watson's spirit awakened to independent life and thought.

As was the custom among the best students, Watson spent a few months in Germany. He chose the University of Tübingen, favoured by Scotsmen on account of the venerable and pious Beck, who was then perhaps the chief theological influence in the University. Though Beck spoke broad Swabian, the warmth of his Christian feeling, his argumentative power, his learning and his mysticism attracted and moved young men. Drummond was also a pupil, and so was the late gifted R. W. Barbour, who contributed an appreciation of Beck to the *British and Foreign Evangelical Review.* From a little note-book it appears that Watson lived with great economy, and indulged in prodigious walking tours with college companions. But in later life he seldom alluded to this episode. Dr. D. M. Ross writes:—

Twenty-five years ago, Tübingen was a favourite resort, not so much perhaps for the Christian eloquence of Professor Beck and the New Testament scholarship of Professor Weizsäcker, as for the beauty of the Swabian Alps, in the midst of whose charming scenery and picturesque country life the little town of Tübingen is built, on the banks of the swift-flowing Neckar. As a member of the Wingolf Club, Mr. Watson threw himself with zest into the social life of the Tübingen *burschen.* He may have learned something of the synoptic problem and of Pentateuchal criticism in the University class-room, but one may be pardoned for suggesting that the insight he gained into German life in the "kneipes" at the Schottei, or Mullerei, in the Whitsuntide excursion into the Black Forest, and in summer evening strolls to Waldhörnle, Bebenhausen, or the Wurmlinger Kapelle may have been the most valuable advantage he reaped from the semester at Tübingen.

Now came the time for entering the ministry. It will be admitted that Watson had gone through an elaborate preparation — four years at the University, four years at the New College, and a semester at Tübingen. Though he had not distinguished himself in examinations, he had done well in everything; he had been an assiduous reader and latterly an eager speculative thinker. He had moved in the atmosphere of intellectual life and free discussion, and he had associated on terms of comradeship with some of the brightest young Scotsmen of his time.

CHAPTER IV

THE MINISTRY—LOGIEALMOND AND GLASGOW

WHEN a Scotch divinity student concludes his course, he is examined by his Presbytery and licensed to preach. If he is popular he is soon called by a vacant congregation, and after that he is ordained and settled in a charge. The intervening period is trying enough to many. Men have been 'probationers,' licensed to preach but not called to a particular parish, for as many as twenty years. Some have never been called, and these are described as 'stickit ministers.' Watson's time as a probationer was very brief, though not altogether bright. He became assistant to the Rev. Dr. J. H. Wilson in the Barclay Free Church, Edinburgh. Wilson was a man of the highest character and the most generous heart, but in some respects his thoughts and methods were opposed to those of his assistant, and they did not find each other. Watson said later on:—

When I returned from Germany in the autumn of 1874 I had no idea where I would work, and had no fitness except quite moderate scholarship for working anywhere.

One day walking along Princes Street I met one of my College friends, who is now a distinguished professor and writer in theology, and he asked me my plans. When I told him that I had none, he suggested that I should succeed him as assistant in one of the largest Edinburgh churches. As the assistantship in the Barclay Church was the blue ribbon for men leaving College, and as it was usually given to men of large experience and pronounced Evangelical views, I judged myself quite unsuitable, and I am of the same opinion to-day. Upon his strong recommendation, however, I was appointed, and I am afraid was a perplexity to my chief, one of the most devoted and single-minded of Scots ministers. He did not conceal from me that I was a poor preacher, and I was perfectly aware of that myself. He entrusted me, however, with a large amount of pastoral visitation, and an elder who was good enough to bid me good-bye when I left—there were only three or four elders knew me—cheered me with the thought that though I had not the gift of preaching I might yet have a useful ministry in my little country charge.

The three months which Watson spent as assistant at the Barclay Church were the most miserable period of his whole life. The pulpit nearly lost him for the Bar. As assistant he said:

I was reserved for the work of visiting elderly ladies and trying to bring young men into Church who did not attend. On rare occasions I was allowed to enter the pulpit. The crisis in my life came when on a Friday I was told my chief was suffering from a sore throat, and that I should have to prepare to preach the following Sunday. What should I do? I had usually consumed two weeks in preparing a sermon from Hodge. As I had recently lost my mother the miracle of Nain appealed to me, and I preached about a man's relation to his mother. I know it was real, for I felt what I said. But my chief told me he had had a bad report of me—I did not preach conversion.

This was a trying time for Watson—for the mother who had pleaded with him to enter the Church was gone, and he wavered for a while. He thought much about the comparatively monotonous and commonplace career that lay before him. It was in one of these moods, no doubt, that he sketched the brown beaten path in which many a Scottish minister travels.

Nothing can be more conventional than the career of the average Presbyterian minister who comes from a respectable religious family, and has the pulpit held up before him as the ambition of a good Scots lad; who is held in the way thereto by various traditional and prudential considerations, and better still—as is the case with most honest lads—by his mother's wishes; who works his laborious, enduring way through the Divinity Hall, and is yearly examined by the local Presbytery; who at last emerges into the butterfly life of a Probationer, and is freely mentioned, to his mother's anxious delight, in connection with 'vacancies'; who is at last chosen by a majority to a pastorate—his mother being amazed at the blindness of the minority—and settles down to the routine of the ministry in some Scotch parish with the hope of Glasgow before him as a land of promise. His only variations in the harmless years might be an outburst on the historical reality of the Book of Jonah—ah me! Did that stout, middle-aged gentleman ever hint that Jonah was a drama?—which would be much talked of in the common room and it was whispered, reached the Professor's ears; and afterwards he might propose a revolutionary motion on the distribution of the Sustentation Fund. Add a handbook for Bible classes on the Prophecy of Malachi, and you have summed up the adventures of his life.

But it was with real delight that he accepted a call which came in 1874 to the parish of Logiealmond in Perthshire, which he was to make known through the world under the style of Drumtochty. His uncle, the Rev. Hiram Watson of Ratho, had been minister there from 1841 to 1853, coming out at the Disruption. Watson's predecessor was the Rev. W. A. Gray, latterly of Elgin, an able and cultured minister. Watson writes:—

My idea was to remain as assistant in Edinburgh for some time if my chief was willing to keep me, but it happened—these happenings are very instructive in the afterlook—that I had once taken duty in the Free Church of Logiealmond because its young minister was my friend. When he was promoted shortly afterwards, the people immediately and unanimously elected me not because of my gifts, but again because a friend had recommended me—what would I have been without my friends!—and because my uncle, a fine scholar and most excellent parish clergyman, was minister of Logiealmond from about 1840 to somewhere in the fifties, and did much for the people!

Watson as usual underestimated his gifts. The young man who came to the Free Church Manse of Logiealmond was anything but commonplace, and this was speedily recognised by not a few.

In the Scottish Church it was once thought wise that ministers should begin their work in small country charges, and thus prepare themselves for wider opportunities if these came. It was wise no doubt, provided the leisure of a country charge was put to good use. Goethe said in his play of *Tasso*, 'A talent moulds itself in stillness but a character in the great current of the world.' It might perhaps be said with equal truth that talents are moulded by the great current of the world, and that characters are formed in stillness. John Watson was anything but a trifler. He took hold of his work with strong resolutions to do his best. It is now known that during the early years of his ministry he adopted much of the Roman Catholic discipline. He observed the fasts; he wore a hair shirt; he aimed strenuously at self-conquest and self-knowledge as well as at knowledge of books and men. All this was done in the strictest privacy. He gave over these methods, but he always maintained that moderate asceticism as a discipline of character and as a means of training men to master themselves is of the highest value. Another conviction of a Catholic mind was that worship and adoration ought to be a far more substantial part of Christian life than is usual in Protestant Churches. He began his preaching with an enthusiastic love for Christ, and this love kept running and gleaming through all his years like a thread of gold. He had little polemical ardour, and took small part in theological controversy, but he never at any time wavered on the central facts of Christianity. Dr. Ross writes: 'Robertson of Brighton was his master in these days, and he shared the spiritual earnestness of his master. . . . In the years of his ministry at Logiealmond he was the liberal theologian as we all knew him when he was at the height of his influence as a preacher.' He was wont to illustrate the reconciliation between dogma and religion by a reference to a picture of the meeting of St. Dominic representing dogma, and St. Francis representing religion. When they met they flung their arms around one another and kissed each other; and so he was wont to say in the end would the religion of the soul embrace the reverent dogma of the intellect. He held fast to the life and death and resurrection of Christ, and the gift of the Holy Spirit to the Church. In his view all doctrinal theology was the product of reflection on these facts, and the attempt to hold them intelligently and coherently. He would have claimed that the essence of unity in a Church is what it believes concerning God's mind and character and active manifestation in history, concerning the Divine sacrifice and suffering on our behalf—in short concerning the secrets of the Divine nature as far as they affect our standards of life and duty.

He determined to be a preacher, and spared no

labour towards this end. He persevered with extraordinary determination in the art of preaching without manuscript; although he sometimes wondered in after years whether the practice had not overstrained his brain, he seldom entered the pulpit with anything but a page of notes and heads. Sometimes in these early days his memory would fail. 'Friends,' he would say, 'that is not very clear. It was clear in my study on Saturday, but now I will begin again.' These good country people never showed impatience, and a gaunt Highland elder came to him after service one Sunday and said, 'When you are not remembering your sermon just give out a psalm and we will be singing that while you are taking a rest, for we all are loving you and praying for you.' Watson once said, 'I am in the ministry to-day because of the tenderness and charity of those country folk, those perfect gentlemen and Christians.' It was in this way that he learned his convincing method of delivery and his great freedom of speech, but he always admitted the cost of the attainment.

The Logiealmond days were days of real happiness. He looked back to them with constant tenderness. He loved the country, and he knew the country folk. He amazed the parishioners with his knowledge of crops, cattle, and corn markets, and all the details of their life. He knew the grit, the endurance, the shrewdness, the dry humour, the sinewy character of the people, and he had an extraordinary faculty of getting inside their minds. Though he always denied that save in a very few cases the originals of his characters could be identified, there is no doubt that Logiealmond gave him much. Mr. Mackenzie writes that afterwards 'it was a great pleasure to revisit with him his old haunts and see how warmly welcomed he was by his old parishioners. I never liked to bother him with questions, but sometimes as we went over the old ground he would point out to me where Flora Campbell came back or show me Donald Menzies's farm. He had always been on the most friendly terms with his brother ministers in the Glen, and also with the Warden and masters of Trinity College, Glenalmond. When he last visited me he joined our party to Commemoration at the College, and I think none who were present, especially the boys, will ever forget his speech or his story of the boy who was a "beggar to cheer."'

Happily, I am able to give a letter written by him to his friend Mr. Henry Drummond, senior, of Stirling, the father of Professor Drummond:—

May 9th, 1875.

My dear Sir,—I feel certain you will be interested to know how things are moving with me in my retired corner of the Vineyard, and send you this short letter of intelligence.

In the success of mere organisation, I have reason to be

encouraged. You can judge of the numbers in proportion for yourself. Our proportions are very small in comparison with a large Church. What I may call our internal proportions are I think somewhat encouraging.

Total membership 116. Attendance 150. We have a few adherents, and about a dozen Established Church people attend daily.

Y.M.C.U. Society meets at 10.30 on Sunday morning, and once a fortnight through the week. 18 Bible-class after service. 19 Sunday-school, after service. 25 Prayer-meeting on Wednesday night. About 50 as an average. The distances are very great.

District meetings vary according to place. Last Sunday night at Buchants, a very thinly peopled place, had over a hundred. This was, however, exceptional. Sometimes we have them in a room. My own work is attendance at Y.M. Meeting from 10.30 to 11.15, and taking a small part, public service at 11.30 to 1.30. Bible-class, a few words at Sunday-school, in evening sometimes a meeting.

Last Sunday I preached to the children, and I monthly address them. In the service I have a prayer or part of one for them. The order of service is as follows: Prayer which is short. Praise. Prayer. Reading or exposition. Praise. Prayer. Sermon. Praise. Prayer. Praise. Benediction. In a month we shall have double service.

In prayer-meeting we sing hymns and consider a portion of the Psalms. The Elders take part one each evening in prayer.

This you see is all form, all means, and can be of no service unless used for the Holy Ghost. It is but the sod, and before blessing any must blossom.

I will say nothing of fruit, it is too soon, and I cannot speak surely. The responsibility of preaching and the oversight of the people weighs me down. They are few perhaps, almost the smallest flock in our Church, but too many for me. Had I not been called as I believe by the Head of the Church to the work, I could not go on. But He is faithful and to all who are faithful giveth grace by the laying on of hands. The living present Lord is the only hope of His weak and foolish ministers. 'I am with you.' In some ways I have been cheered by an attention such as I have scarcely seen, and more than once there have been signs of feeling that were manifest and twice, cold and unemotional as you know me by nature to be, and hard of heart as I know myself to be, I have with the greatest difficulty continued my sermon, being deeply moved. Surely the Spirit working, and I am the more persuaded it was so, because there seemed neither intellectual nor spiritual power of any high order in the sermon. May God have all the praise! My visiting is most extensive and requires more than one entire day. Exclusive of sick and funerals. This is interesting but most delicate work. I write to you as you see frankly as I do to few.

With kindest regards to all and much respect for yourself.—Yours very sincerely, JOHN WATSON.

PS.—Give my love to Henry, and you may mention we remember his work, daily in intercession. Surely the Lord has arisen to bless our land. It is a day for strong prayer. It is a day for pressing in. Is not the gathering at last unto Shiloh?

But the true story of his Logiealmond ministry is to be found in his Scottish sketches. He continued his watchfulness over the parish, and messages passed frequently between him and one of his successors, the Rev. D. M. Tod. On receiving congratulations from the Logiealmond church

Dr. Watson wrote to Mr. Tod on the semi-jubilee of his ministry :—

May 18th, 1900.

Dear Mr. Tod,—It was like the glen to think of me and to send that address in which I detect the hand of a certain young accomplished minister of the Free Kirk. I enclose a reply which you will convey in the way which is most convenient, but my reply is really in my heart. If it be possible I will come up and take a Sunday in the Autumn, and I will let you know the date in good time, that you may go away and have a holiday, which even the minister of the glen needs at a time. At present, however, with my duties as Moderator I cannot be quite sure of my plans.

May 18th, 1900.

My dear Friends,—It was with a warm heart that I received and read the address which you sent me in connection with the twenty-fifth anniversary of my ordination, an address so kindly conceived and so beautifully expressed.

Nothing could be more encouraging to a minister than to know that after the lapse of a quarter of a century his ordination day is still remembered in the Glen where he began his work.

From a great city and from very different scenes my thoughts turn with fondness to the slope of the Grampians, and the parish which was then so much secluded from the outer world, and where on that account the hearts were so true and deep.

When wearied with the din of the city and hard-driven by its many demands, I often wish that I were again in the Manse garden, or by the side of the Almond, or on the hill below the quarry where the wind is blowing free and clean, or in the little Kirk with the familiar faces of the past, old and young, looking at me. . . . Oh! the days that have been and shall be no more, but love remaineth.

As I go up and down England in the discharge of my duty as Moderator of our Church, it will strengthen me to know that friendly eyes follow me from the North, and that I am still sustained by the prayers of those to whom I ministered, with many imperfections but with lasting affection, in the days of the past.—Believe me ever, your faithful friend, JOHN WATSON.

Later on, wrote :—

January 12*th,* 1901.

DEAR MR. TOD,—It gives me much pleasure to know that the Free Church in the Glen—I ought to have said United, but it is hard to learn new names in your old age—is about to express in a tangible form the gratitude which for many years its members must have felt to Mrs. —— for her services in the choir.

My interest is greater in one way than that of any other person, for my ministry in the pulpit and Mrs. ——'s in the choir began, I think, about the same time, and we have both completed our semi-jubilee. I am sometimes ashamed as I think of my imperfect work, but I can bear testimony to the diligence and ability and real devotion with which my colleague in the choir discharged her duties in the former days, and I have good reason to believe in the days following. How loyal and true was the little choir of 1875, some of whom now sing the new song of Moses and the Lamb where they serve God without ceasing in the Heavenly places.

Please add my name to the list of subscribers, and as I cannot get North to the presentation, let my letter speak for me, and let my name be sometimes mentioned in the prayers of those who remember me in the Glen.

My love to the friends of former days, and may grace, mercy and peace be with you all in your worship and in your work.—Yours faithfully, JOHN WATSON.

It will be seen that though his ministry at Logiealmond lasted for less than three years, it was a momentous period in his life. He was a friend of all, and was particularly popular among his brother ministers. He showed in the Presbytery some liking and aptitude for ecclesiastical affairs. The tact and skill with which he guided the business of his congregation were observed, although it was only in a larger sphere that his administrative and strategical talents found full play. Above all his tolerant and sympathetic nature ripened. He was one who felt as much sympathy for the dull as for the sickly. Sharp and acute himself, he suffered fools, if not patiently yet gladly, holding that the feeble in mind often made as gallant an effort to carry on the business of life in adverse circumstances as the feeble in body. He was gradually acquiring a Scottish reputation as a preacher, though, if I am rightly informed, he was even more unequal than most young ministers are. Much depended on his mood at the time. I remember one very competent judge who told me that the chief impression he gave was one of singular and wistful goodness. Watson was never an ambitious man, but it was almost inevitable that he should find his way to a more prominent place. It was his wont neither to ask for positions nor to decline them if they were offered to him, and if they seemed to give him an opportunity. So in 1877, in less than three years from his settlement at Logiealmond, he was called to Free St. Matthew's Church, Glasgow, as colleague and successor to Dr. Samuel Miller.

Of his ministry in Glasgow I have very little information. The congregation to which he was called was at one time one of the most powerful in the whole city. It was presided over by Dr. Samuel Miller, whom Watson characterised as 'one of the most effective and faithful ministers, and one of the noblest men God had ever given to the Free Church of Scotland.' Dr. Miller was a strong theological preacher with a full measure of the Disruption orthodoxy. He had vehemently opposed a union between the Free Church and the United Presbyterian Church. In consequence of this there had been dissension among his people, and a considerable number had seceded. But though thus weakened, the congregation was still large and influential. I imagine that Watson was chosen as colleague because he was supposed to be in sympathy with Dr. Miller's views. He was certainly in sympathy with Miller's opposition to Disestablishment. Whenever the question of Disestablishment was raised in a church court, Watson walked out. It seems also that, owing no doubt to the impression of his environment, Watson reverted in Glasgow to the orthodoxy of his early years, or rather of the teachers of his early years, John Milne and Horatius Bonar. That the congregation increased during his brief ministry of three years is certain, but he does not seem to have made a very marked or striking impression. This at least was his own view. But one of his people who knew all the circumstances wrote after his death as follows:—

I heard his first sermon there, from Rev. xiv. 6, 'The Everlasting Gospel.' There were touches in it which made me even then think that it had been preached at Logiealmond—for example, he said if the Gospel ceased to be preached by its accredited representatives, the Spirit of the Lord might come upon some shepherd on the hills and send him forth to proclaim the glad tidings.

I do not think I ever heard what first directed the attention of St. Matthew's to him, but it was by something which, repeated to Dr. Miller, drew from him the remark, 'That cock will fight.'

A year or so afterwards I was constrained to connect myself with his congregation. He was admired and loved by his people as few ministers have been, and if he happened to preach in other churches in the city, one had only to look round and they would see some of his regular hearers. His preaching was eminently Christological, and one was struck by the loftiness and spirituality of his prayers. He took a special interest in, and always presided at, the Sabbath-school teachers' prayer meeting, and was genial and kindly to all with whom he came in contact.

The senior colleague, Dr. Samuel Miller, had in his day been a powerful preacher of the doctrine of grace, and put an imprint on the congregation which lasted for almost two generations. There was a strong bond of affection between the two, as none who heard Mr. Watson's funeral sermon at Dr. Miller's death will forget. Yet, while there was large and substantial agreement, sometimes they differed. Once Mr. Watson happened to preach in the morning from Hebrews, and expressed a doubt whether Paul was the writer. In the afternoon Dr. Miller also preached from Hebrews, and gave an elaborate defence of its Pauline authorship, and closed by saying that they were but 'babes and sucklings in Christ' who thought otherwise!

Mr. Watson also took a lively interest in an additional mission that had been taken over by St. Matthew's, and in consequence of that he said he never passed a group of open-air preachers without stopping for a few minutes to listen, and then on leaving he would say, 'God bless you.' Once in private conversation he said on one occasion a young man was handing out tracts, but did not give Mr. Watson one till he asked for it. The young fellow then invited him to say a few words, which Mr. Watson at once did. At an undenominational institute I heard him give an admirable address on 'Paul's Ambition: I must see Rome,' and was amused at the heartiness with which Dr. Andrew Bonar went up to him and clapped him repeatedly on the shoulder.

When in St. Matthew's he was a believer in the personal premillennial advent. I have an idea that he was led to adopt those views by his early training under Mr. Milne of Perth, the intimate associate of M'Cheyne, the Bonars, and men of that school, and they gave a certain tone to his preaching.

When the call from Liverpool came I wrote urging him to be patient and remain, and outward success was assured. He had not full scope in a collegiate charge, and perhaps a small—very small—section of the congregation was more in sympathy with the old minister's preaching. The first Sunday after, he seemed quite perturbed, but by the following Sunday he had recovered himself and preached a splendid sermon on 'Rejoice in the Lord alway; and again I say Rejoice.'

When in St. Matthew's we did not think him a strong man physically, and often when looking at him I used to fear that he would not be a long liver. He was very hollow in the chest.

His farewell sermon in St. Matthew's was, 'I am not ashamed of the Gospel of Christ, for it is the power of God unto salvation.' And he punctuated the text as has been done with Milton's line:

> 'Eyeless-in Gaza-at the mill-with slaves,'

and took as heads—'Power' 'of God' 'unto salvation' 'to every one that believeth.' This was also his first sermon in Sefton Park, and a St. Matthew's elder who was present, was asked by a gentleman at the close if Mr. Watson always preached like that, and on being told it was just an ordinary sermon, exclaimed, 'Then the half has not been told!' It was Mr. Watson's custom then, when preaching from home, always to take the sermon he had last preached to his own people. He learned that, he said, from an old minister.

Some of us in St. Matthew's held that his 'high-water' mark in preaching was when he was with us. On one of the few occasions on which he afterwards preached in St. Matthew's, I remember making a remark of this nature to one of the elders, and he at once said, 'He is not half so good.'

His style of preaching changed to some extent, probably with a view of appealing to a wider circle of hearers. A writer has said, 'trammelled by his association with influential Conservative Presbyterians.' That I doubt, and think he would have developed all his powers in Scotland just as well. He was a man who could not be hid, and was bound to come to his own anywhere. He was a Conservative in most things. Some of his later stories, notably *The Minister of St. Jude's*, relate to his experiences in Glasgow. He describes St. Matthew's as 'a congregation that contains a few rich people and thinks not a little of itself.' 'John Carmichael' is just 'John Watson' altered and adapted.

There can be little doubt that Watson was not happy in Glasgow, though he always drew a good congregation and was supported by the younger members. He used to recite two verdicts on his preaching which should perhaps be accepted with reserve. One elder on being asked his opinion of Watson answered, 'Ah, weel, a nice enough young man, but there 's nae future in his heid.' When he was leaving St. Matthew's another elder, desiring to cheer him on his way, shook him warmly by the hand saying, 'Well, Mr. Watson, I wish you all success. You may be a pastor, but you 'll never be a preacher.'

In 1880 Watson was appointed by the Free Church to accompany their Moderator to the English Presbyterian Synod in May. He says: 'I addressed the Synod in Marylebone Church, giving an account of the Robertson Smith case, which I considered most impartial, but which, I believe, revealed to people of insight that I had too much sympathy with the unfortunate scholar.' He was told that evening that the special preacher who was to officiate at Sefton Park Church, Liverpool, had broken down, and urged to help in the emergency. 'Against my own will, and against the counsel of my colleague in Glasgow, I preached, and as a result was offered the charge by the committee.' When Watson took farewell of the Glasgow Presbytery, he frankly said that he had a desire to assume again the undivided charge and responsibility which belonged to the sole ministry of a congregation. This was so, although he acknowledged warmly the consideration, courtesy, and kindness with which Dr. Miller had always treated a comparatively young and most inexperienced man. At this crisis of his life Watson was not quite thirty years of age. As he always judged, the real work of his life began when he came to Liverpool. The rest had been preparation.

During his ministry in Glasgow Mr. Watson was married to Miss Jane Burnie Ferguson, daughter of a well-known business man in the city and nearly related to Sir Samuel Ferguson, the Irish poet and scholar. Mrs. Watson, as all his friends know, was the inspiration of his life, 'companion of many journeys,' and the tender watcher in his last illness. Like Richard Baxter, Watson had spoken and written in favour of clerical celibacy when there was no temptation to be a Benedick. But perhaps the supreme good fortune of his life was that he, unlike Baxter, did not survive his wife.

CHAPTER V

HIS MINISTRY IN LIVERPOOL—PREACHING

JOHN WATSON now commenced what he always considered to be the real work of his life—his twenty-five years of ministry in Liverpool. Nothing could have been more complete and felicitous than the accord between him and his sphere. He was made for Liverpool; Liverpool was made for him. It is impossible to exaggerate his love for Liverpool. The name of the city was written upon his heart. As will be seen, Liverpool returned his love.

He came in the full freshness of his youth to be the first minister of a new congregation in the Presbyterian Church of England. It was fortunate that he had to create his own audience. Like most Celts he needed the inspiration of growth for his full happiness and efficiency. He would have faced adverse circumstances, but he was stimulated even more than most by the signs of progress, and to the end of his Liverpool ministry there was no ebbing of the tide. Again, he was a man who needed sympathy, and was disheartened by coldness or by enmity. In Liverpool he had for a congregation men and women whom he had personally attracted, and with whom he was perfectly at home. The Presbyterian Church of England is comparatively small when measured with other religious communities, but it has been for many years progressive, and it has a character of its own as it were midway between the Church of England and the powerful Nonconformist bodies. Watson was perfectly at home among the English Presbyterians, and his loyalty to them and his conviction that they had a work to do in England never faltered. They were largely Scotch either by birth or by descent, but a very considerable number were connected with them who found themselves not quite at home either in the Church or in Nonconformity. They were by no means uniform in their political convictions, and their comparative paucity in point of numbers allowed a great measure of independence to separate congregations, much more than could be realised in Scotland. Among them Watson sprang at once to his full stature. He threw aside the opinions that were merely prejudices, and applied his many-sided nature in all its force to the attraction and instruction of his people. His ministry was successful from the very first, and in no long time he was one of the most prominent personalities in the city.

Here it is right that I should say something

about the religious history and conditions of Liverpool, and I can find no better guide than Sir Edward Russell, who has been for many years part of the life of the city, who was also for so long one of the most attached and trusted of John Watson's friends.

The distinguished men in the religious life of Liverpool were Hugh M'Neile, Dr. Raffles, Hugh Stowell Brown, C. M. Birrell, Dr. James Martineau, John Hamilton Thom, and Charles Beard, and later on Father Nugent and Charles Garrett. The Orange Protestants and the Irish Roman Catholics were strongly represented, and came into frequent conflict. Canon M'Neile was a leader of the Evangelical party, and the religious leader of the Liverpool people. He did not rule the Nonconformists nor the Liberals, but he always secured by religious influence the Tory majority. A pronounced Protestant, he manned the pulpits of Liverpool with men like-minded. He was even more concerned for Evangelical religion than for Protestant political zeal, and it was in the elucidation of the Scriptures, not otherwise, that he exercised as preacher his religious powers. It was perhaps upon the platform that his magnificent oratorical powers were displayed most effectively. Sir Edward Russell tells of a speech he delivered on Governor Eyre's action in Jamaica. The audience was hotly divided, but M'Neile, who was the chief orator, showed his usual impassive dignity. He surveyed unperturbed the vast audience. Every one heard easily the familiar, deep tones which without apparent effort filled any building in the world. In an opening sentence or two he said that as there was so much legitimate difference of opinion, he would state each of the two cases separately. The audience was half-amused, and altogether soothed. Amid a deep silence he detailed in deliberate accents and with unsparing truth the things that had been done in Jamaica. The silence was absolute—almost painful. Suddenly, as the fatal indictment was coming to an end, a dog that had somehow got into the meeting set up horrible squeals and howls. There was great confusion while the disturber was got at and ejected, a proceeding which took quite a time. M'Neile stood motionless for all this interval waiting for perfect silence. When it came he slowly waved his arm, and in his deepest tragedy voice said, 'The very dogs bark at it.' 'Never was there a more splendid *coup*. Simple as it now seems, it was quite unexpected, and its effect was irresistible. I have often thought the dog saved the meeting.' Among M'Neile's allies was Archdeacon Jones. Of him it is told that he brought the Gladstones over to the Church of England. Mr. Gladstone's father was a substantial and active Presbyterian. He became inclined to go over to the Church of England, but was deterred by the disinclination of his wife, who was not satisfied with the Anglican preaching. Her husband took her round the churches, and at last brought her to Mr. Jones. Both were pleased, and the husband proposed to the wife that he should build a church for Mr. Jones, and that they should attend it. The bargain was struck, and this is how Mr. Gladstone was brought up in the Church of England. He was born a Presbyterian, and was six years old when his father passed from the Scotch to the English Establishment bringing his wife with him. Dr. Raffles, who for many years led the Congregationalists, was a great orator, a man of the warmest affection and the largest charity. It was said of him that he could not speak unkindly of a mad dog. Hugh Stowell Brown and C. M. Birrell (the father of Mr. Augustine Birrell) were Baptists differing exceedingly in their ways of preaching, but warmly attached as friends, and in full inner harmony. It is needless to say that Martineau, Thom, and Beard were Unitarians. John Watson used to maintain, however, that Thom and Beard were not Unitarians, but Arians, and in common with the whole city he regarded with admiration and pride their unquestioned gifts of sanctity and intellect. It may be doubted whether in any city of England Unitarians were better represented than they had been in Liverpool.

Watson had very little part in the Protestant

controversy. With many of the Evangelical clergy, including Bishop Ryle and Bishop Chavasse, he was on terms of cordial friendship. There was in him a deep and passionate Evangelicalism, and to Evangelical teaching as shown in spiritual earnestness he always responded eagerly. His relations with the Roman Catholic priests, and to a lesser extent with the High Church clergy, were even more cordial. There was a side of his nature that turned their way. But he was also very much drawn by the literary culture, the piety, and the noble ethical teaching of the Unitarians. While he maintained the best relations with the Evangelical Nonconformists, he was for long less intimate with them than with others of the Liverpool ministers.

His strength lay in the many-sidedness of his sympathies. He could preach sermons which pleased the Evangelicals; sermons which pleased the Unitarians; sermons indicating great breadth, and sermons of such intensity and urgent appeal that they might have come from a flaming evangelist in the great revival. Thus he was able to draw round him a congregation of very various constituents. They might not be all equally well pleased on any Sunday, but very soon they heard a sermon to which they could listen with perfect satisfaction. I need hardly say that there was not the faintest touch of insincerity or unreality in all this range of method. Watson was simply expressing his mood, and the largeness of his comprehension enabled him to understand the spiritual needs of men who in their training and in their dogmatic convictions were far apart. There were very few congregations in England made up of recruits from so many armies as Sefton Park Church. He said himself three years before his death: 'Not only have we members of every shade of Presbyterianism—Scots, Irish, English, Canadian, Established Church, Free Church, and United Presbyterian—but we have had people of many nations—French, Germans, Swiss, Danes, North Americans, South Americans, Russians, Greeks, Austrians, Belgians—and as many creeds, high and low, narrow and broad, and no creed at all. I have taken a section of fourteen pews, and I find, so far as I know, that the following is its ecclesiastical ancestry: four Presbyterian families, six Episcopalian, four Congregationalist, three Baptist, two Welsh, two Unitarian, two German, one Swiss.' Liverpool is a large cosmopolitan world, and Watson's singular adaptability had a most congenial outlet there. Liverpool was always responsive. But there was never any doubt as to the real drift of the preaching. Watson was always a convinced Evangelical of broad sympathies which perhaps grew broader and broader. He understood them all—the mystic, the Catholic, the Evangelical, the revivalist, the moralist, the sceptic, and for each as the time came round he had a living message. He said at the close of his first sermon in Sefton Park Church :—

Brethren, I feel sure that these words have made my aim as a preacher clear to you all. I shall not try to astonish you with any display of learning, nor attract you by the mere eloquence of words, but I promise by the grace of God and according to my ability to preach the Cross of Christ. The Cross as I understand it combines both the doctrine of forgiveness and the doctrine of holiness, and I trust to be able also to show that a Christ Who is our sacrifice is also our ideal. Some of you may prefer one doctrine, some the other, I am sure you will all see both are necessary. If I seem unpractical, ask yourselves if the fault be altogether mine, if personal do not suppose this intentional, do not weary when I ask your faith, do not be angry when I point out duty, but always search the Scriptures and see whether these things are not so, and so we will be blessed.

Beloved brethren, the double responsibility of work and prayer lies on me, the responsibility of prayer lies also on you. Pray that I may be led into the truth myself, and so be able to lead you. Pray that I may be able to deal honestly with intellectual difficulties and wisely with cases of conscience. Pray that I may have grace to speak tenderly to mourners and simply to the children. Pray that I may ever be found offering a full and free Christ to sinners, and exhorting the saints to follow Him more closely. Pray I beseech you that the messenger may be lost in his message, that if any good results should come of his preaching the glory may be all given unto the Father, the Son, and the Holy Ghost, one God now and for ever. Amen.

In this key he continued and ended his ministry.

The outward results of his work were very remarkable. He began with 133 members, but among them were many strong and wise men prepared to back their minister, and both generous and loyal. The population of the district was rapidly increasing. A beautiful church had been erected, and at the opening more than £1000 was subscribed. Everything was favourable, and in a few years the church was full. The congregation numbered some 700 members; every seat was let; and the contributions amounted to more than £5000 a year, while there were 1200 children in the Sunday-schools. Branch churches were erected at Earle Road and Smithdown Road, and the Balfour Institute for social work was opened in 1889. This was built in recognition of the late Mr. Alexander Balfour's unwearied efforts for the social and moral elevation of his fellow-citizens. In short, every department of Church work was steadily prosperous. Watson said himself in 1900: 'If you ask me what have been the conditions of the success God has given us, or in other words the salient features of our history, they may be stated in order of importance from the least to the greatest thus: A good site, no debt, hearty liberality, a cheerful service, making strangers welcome, active work, no drones, wise office-bearers, internal peace, external charity, Wednesday service, and a desire to do God's will.' This was his own modest reckoning, but unquestionably the prosperity of the church was mainly due to the brilliant abilities and the unstinted devotion of the minister.

The late James Ashcroft Noble, himself a Liverpool man, summed up his impressions of a Sefton Park service as follows:—

> He addressed his hearers not from some platform of scholastic thinking and hypothetical experience, but from a homely stable ground, common to him and to them and to the whole world of men and women. . . . When on that Sunday night I looked round upon the congregation which densely packed both floor and galleries, I knew from common rumour that I was looking upon a crowd in which were representatives of all that was finest in thought and noblest in character among the men and women of the great city of Liverpool. The simple Presbyterian service relieved of its primal northern baldness, but unspoiled by florid and incongruous adornment, had a peculiar impressiveness. For the first few moments of the preacher's discourse it could be said that this impressiveness was preserved, but hardly that it was intensified, for Mr. Watson's manner in the pulpit is as free from prepared effectiveness as his manner in the study—it has no *ad captandum* quality, no rhetorical trick. But before five minutes had passed I became aware that I and the hundreds by whom I was surrounded were listening to an utterance of quite exceptional grasp and weight.

Watson on various occasions, and particularly in his book *The Cure of Souls,* which contains the lectures on Practical Theology delivered by him at Yale University in 1896, has carefully explained his views on preaching. In what follows I borrow first from him; next from those who were familiar with his pulpit work; and I also incorporate my own impressions of the occasions when I heard him preach both in his own church and in others.

He held that the critical and influential event in the religious week is the sermon. Whenever preaching falls into low esteem, the Church becomes weak and corrupt. It is impossible to exaggerate the opportunity given to the preacher when he ascends the pulpit and faces his congregation. There his business is not so much to teach or define as to stimulate and encourage. This work cannot be done rightly without inspiration, but this inspiration only rests on the outcome of hard, honest work.

Among the elements of the work the first is Selection, and the text should select the man rather than the man the text. 'As the minister was busy with study, or as he sat by the bedside of the sick, or as he walked the crowded street, or as he wandered over the purple heather, or—such things have happened, the grace of God being sovereign—as he endured in a Church Court, the truth, clad in a text, which is the more or less perfect dress of the Spirit, suddenly appeared and claimed his acquaintance.' Such an experience means the pre-established harmony between a particular truth and the soul of a minister.

The second process is Separation, and this means that the sermon should be a monograph and not an encyclopædia. The handling of one idea is sufficient. 'He's a good preacher'—a Highland gamekeeper was describing his minister,—'but he scatters terribly.' The sermon should be like a single rifle-bullet which, if it hits, kills, not a charge of small shot which only peppers. The next process is Illumination. It is the setting of the bare, cold, lifeless idea in the light of all he has read, has seen, has felt, has suffered. Here it is that culture comes in. The student has an invaluable advantage over the ablest Philistine. 'Those mornings given to Plato, that visit to Florence where he got an insight into Italian art, that hard-won trip to Egypt, the birthplace of civilisation, his sustained acquaintance with Virgil, his by-study of physical science, his taste in music, the subtlest and most religious of the arts, all now rally to his aid.' The fourth process is Meditation. The idea must be removed from the light, where reason and imagination have their sphere, and be hidden away in the dark chambers of the soul. Many masterly sermons fail because they have never had the benefit of this process. They are clear, interesting, eloquent, but helpless. The brooding over a spiritual experience where the subject is hidden in the soul as leaven in three measures of meal till all be leavened gives preaching the greater qualities of the past, depth of experience, and an atmosphere of peace.

Then comes Elaboration, the placing, reviewing,

transposing, till the way stands fair and open from Alpha to Omega—a clean, straight furrow from end to end of the field. There should be no introduction; nothing more certainly takes the edge off the appetite than the laborious preface. The latest results of the criticism on the book from which the text is taken should be severely left alone. Elaborate perorations are also to be put aside.

When a speaker is pleading a great cause, and sees hard-headed men glaring before them with such ferocity that every one knows they are afraid of breaking down, let him stop in the middle of a paragraph and take the collection, and if he be declaring the Evangel, and a certain tenderness comes over the faces of the people, let him close his words to them and call them to prayer. Speech can be too lengthy, too formal, too eloquent, too grammatical. For one to lose his toilsome introduction, in which he happened to mention two Germans, with quotations, and his twice-written conclusion, in which he had that pretty fancy from Tennyson, is hard to flesh and blood. . . . But in those sacrifices of self the preacher's strength lies, on them the blessing of God rests.

Revision comes last, and that should be done with an earnest consideration of those who are to hear the sermon.

A well-turned epigram, which cost much toil: but that white-haired saint will misunderstand it. Our St. John must not be grieved. So it must go. A very impressive word of the new scientific coinage: what can yon sempstress make of it? Rich people have many pleasures, she has only her church. Well, she shall have it without rebate : the big word is erased—half a line in mourning. A shrewd hit at a certain weakness: but that dear old mother, whose house is a refuge for orphans and all kinds of miserables, it is just possible she may be hurt. The minister had not thought of her till he said the words with Dorcas sitting in her corner. Another black line in the fair manuscript. This exposure of narrowness is at any rate justified: but the minister sees one face redden, and its owner is as true a man as God ever made. It is left out too. Somewhat strong that statement: an adjective shall be omitted: some people have a delicate sense of words. This quip may excite a laugh: better not—it may hinder the force of the next passage on Jesus. The sermon seems to be losing at every turn in harmony, vivacity, richness, ease; it is gaining in persuasiveness, understanding, sympathy, love: it is losing what is human and gaining what is divine; and after that sermon is delivered, and has passed into men's lives, the preacher will bless God for every word he removed.

Of Watson himself it may be said without fear that he did not shirk the labour involved in these counsels. He was one of the most patient and persistent of students, and the fruit of all his labour went into his sermons. It was for this that he read, observed, travelled, thought and prayed. Though not an omnivorous reader, he carefully accumulated a well-selected library of the best books in theology, in history, and in English literature generally. He did not care to read inferior or ephemeral books except as an occasional relief, and he found no room for them on his shelves. But he was especially careful to have the latest authoritative works on Biblical criticism and theology, though he read few sermons. His preference was for historical reading, especially the history of Scotland, and in the department of history few modern books of weight were absent from his collection. I well remember the enthusiasm with which he hailed the beginning of the Cambridge Modern History. He delighted in the fine editions of the English classics, and his chief favourites were perhaps Shakespeare, Thackeray, and Charles Lamb. With these and a few others he was so familiar that he might have said that their books had passed like iron atoms into his mental constitution. Among theologians he was wont to mention Fairbairn, Gore, and Martineau. From theological writers who had no style he turned away. The Puritan divines gave him little, and he often expatiated in private on the absence of the great antiseptic from their productions. Every morning was set aside for hard study. He spent the week in meditating over his subjects and in gathering together his material. Many notes would be made in this process. Towards the end of the week he wrote his two sermons. There was rarely a slovenly sentence in them, and never a tedious and laboured conclusion. On Sunday morning he wrote out a final list of heads, and with the sermon committed to memory entered the pulpit. Although an excellent extempore speaker, he still preferred to write out everything beforehand if possible, and then commit it to memory. He never preached old sermons without great changes, usually rewriting and reconstructing the entire manuscript, building up a new discourse on the old framework, and giving if necessary more suitable illustrations. 'You outgrow sermons,' he once said, 'as you outgrow clothes.' The level of his preaching was thus singularly even. A member of the congregation says he only heard him once preach a poor sermon. He was greatly astonished, but some time afterwards he learned that Watson sat with a dying elder of his church through the whole of Saturday night, and had reached his pulpit on the Sunday weary and depressed. But his hearers never knew. They only wondered why he faltered and looked worn out.

Before most of his contemporaries Watson learned that preaching had to adapt itself to the new conditions. He would often refer half satirically, half regretfully to the tranquil old days.

There are moments when the calmness and regularity of the worthies of last generation drive us to despair, as when one reads from the diary of the Rev. Joseph Tomlinson, in the memorial volume issued after his death, and much valued by his congregation:—

'*December* 10 (Monday).—Rose at 5.30, although tempted to remain in bed owing to the darkness and cold. Completed the first head of my seventh sermon in the course on Sanctification before breakfast. Have now sermons prepared for the next three months, and note with thankfulness that I can produce three sheets hourly without fail.'

The good man died in the fifties, at the age of eighty-six, having preached till ten days before his death, and never having been once out of his pulpit through sickness; and one has a distinct vision of him moving about with great authority and dignity among his people, and a vague recollection of his thundering in a sermon against those who denied creation in six literal days,—'which showed to what a height of insolent audacity infidelity was rising in those days.'

This early rising, which is a marked feature in such biographies, and a needless irritation unto the generations following—this turning out of sermons by machinery, in longhand writing without an erasure, and sometimes on pink paper—this immunity from perplexing questions—this infallibility in doctrine, as well as the fixed, smooth untroubled face at the beginning of the book, suggest an atmosphere very different from that in which we think and labour.

Watson himself had begun to live in a time when people knew what to expect and the minister said what was to be expected. He keenly realised that the atmospheric conditions had changed, and that a minister had to find truths which held him if he was to hold the people. A modern audience is sensitive and detects the difference between reality and unreality without fail. This created difficulties, and these were increased by the fact that preachers have now to attract an audience. They cannot hope any more that people will come from a sense of duty. In Watson's view sensationalism, eccentricity, anecdotage were all to be deprecated. 'Against religious sensationalism, *outré* sayings, startling advertisements, profane words and irreverent prayers, the younger ministry must make an unflinching stand, for the sake of the Church and the world, for the sake of our profession and ourselves.' But he believed that what could be done to make style and manner winsome ought to be done. The demands of the age must be met, as far as might be. The preacher had to recognise that the Gospel now addresses itself to the masses. 'When tides meet there is broken water, and many are tossed in their minds as to whether the pulpit ought to give its strength to the regeneration of the individual or of society.' On this point he held that while the Church must labour to bring heaven here, that heaven is long of coming, and meanwhile the Church must comfort the oppressed, the suffering, and the beaten with the vision of the City of God. But if in any critical conflict between the poor and the rich, the minister of Jesus sides with the strongest, he has broken his commission and forsaken his Master. The preacher must acknowledge and welcome the large and solid contribution made by criticism to our knowledge of the Bible. At the same time the introduction of details of Biblical criticism into the pulpit would be tiresome and irritating as well as arid and unedifying to the last degree. What the minister should do is to give careful and systematic instruction in the literary and historical circumstances of the Bible to classes where the pupils can have the full benefit of his knowledge. What is wanted above everything is positive preaching by men who believe with all their mind and heart in Jesus Christ. Theology has its great value, but it is only a theory of religion, and theology which has not been in the main current of letters is invariably stranded in some creek and forgotten. The minister ought to leaven his preaching with theology, and while in other departments of knowledge one must know to love, in Christian theology one must love to know.

He held in substance that religion has three places of abode—in the reason, which is Theology; in the conscience, which is Ethics; and in the heart, which is Quietism. His belief was that the Church was returning to Christ, to a true and sane mysticism. The work of the immediate future was the reconstruction of dogma commenced by writers like Gore and Fairbairn, but still needing to be carried through. He looked forward passionately to the glorious day when the theology of the Christian Church should rise again, having lost nothing that was good and true in the past, and be reconstructed on the double foundation of the divine Fatherhood and the Incarnation of our Lord Jesus Christ. These were the truths which he preached with surpassing power and unshaken faith.

There is some difference of opinion about Watson's oratorical powers. No doubt there have been greater orators, but in his later period at least there were very few to match him. His tall and commanding figure, his resonant voice, his power of adaptation, and his intense earnestness enabled him to arrest, captivate, and influence an audience as few have ever done. He himself judged his gift of speech very humbly. He always regretted that he had never studied elocution, which he regarded as extremely important. His manner was rarely rhetorical or dramatic. As a young man he was inclined to vehemence in the pulpit, but in later years he became calmer. Zealot as he was, he had learned to hold himself well in hand. His gestures were natural and never exaggerated—an occasional lift of the hand to command attention, very rarely more. The inflections of his voice and his great command of facial expression riveted his hearers. His voice would sometimes be a trifle harsh, and sometimes sink into an inaudible whisper, especially at the end of sentences. When I first heard him he preached on the character of Jacob. He stated the case for and the case against like an accomplished lawyer, and then summed up as an impartial judge. It was intensely interesting, but the real effect was produced by a few electric sentences at the end. He seemed to me most successful when he was in his own pulpit. I have known him elsewhere somewhat impair the effect of his sermons by sustained irony or by needless witticisms. But from the pulpit of Sefton Park he spoke as one master of himself, his subject, and his audience. Sir Edward Russell, who had many opportunities of hearing him, is decidedly of opinion that when he resigned his charge he was at his very best as a preacher, having distinctly advanced and ripened in melody, and ease, and eloquence. At first there was something of the Scottish tone and manner which Englishmen find difficult of assimilation. 'In recent years, and more especially in recent months, the feeling has been distinctly lessened, and a facility, a rich pouring forth of natural thought in natural words without any diminution of profundity or keenness have convinced me that just at the time when he unhappily felt bound to retire from his work, John Watson had reached the zenith of his oratorical efficiency.' To others who knew his preaching well, he seemed to combine a dauntless ministry of righteousness with a wide and subtle knowledge of men's lives, and a mysticism which helped him to receive spiritual truth by intuition as well as by exertion of thought and faithfulness to reason. He was indeed an interpreter of the divine providence and in particular of complex human experience. His work was not so much to expose the defects of society, though he could do that on occasion, but to place constructive ideals before men. But here I am much helped by the admirable sketch sent to me by a lady who was a member of his church from 1884 to 1896.

I well remember the Sunday evening on which I first heard him preach. When contemplating a removal to the neighbourhood of Sefton Park, it had been decided to attend a certain Church of England, when on this particular day a member of the family mentioned there was a fine preacher at Sefton Park Presbyterian Church, and suggested attending the evening service. We sallied forth, a large family party, and were accommodated with seats in different parts of the church. The subject of the sermon was 'John Mark'—one of those wonderful biographical sketches in which Dr. Watson excelled ; full of insight, of understanding, of gallant, uplifting thought. Before that sermon was half over I had come to a decision, and had braced myself to defy opposition. When the scattered family met once more on the way home I launched my bolt:—'I am going to join Sefton Park Church!' when behold the expected opposition came in a simultaneous chorus of 'So am I!' and from that moment there was no talk of another church.

It was, I think, a somewhat unusual experience to fall under the spell of Dr. Watson's preaching at a first hearing. Many people went away disappointed after a first visit to the church, but I have never met one whose disappointment was not changed into warmest admiration at the end of a month. His delivery was somewhat difficult to follow, and strangers found his voice a trifle hard, but they soon discovered that it had a wonderful eloquence of its own, and—on occasions—a quite irresistible pathos.

I have never seen a preacher whose demeanour in the pulpit was more dignified and impressive. His people will recall the quiet lift of the right hand with which he would invoke instant, intense stillness in a crowded congregation, and which was the summons to the simple prayer which began the service; and one of the moments in which I most love to recall him was while the hymn before the sermon was being sung. He would join heartily in the first few verses, but before the end would cease singing, and stand silently, bending slightly forward, turning his head from side to side with quick, intent glances—as if noting the different members of his congregation, calling to remembrance their separate trials and sorrows, and bracing himself to meet them. Every Sunday afresh I was reminded of the words—'as one who girdeth himself to run a race.' Dr. Watson's prayers had a dignity not often noticeable in extempore utterances, and withal a most widespread remembrance of different members of the community. He would pray not only for the sick, but for 'those who wait upon them'; for 'the little children at home'; 'for the boys and girls at school'; for 'those bereft of the kindly light of reason'; 'for those who have fallen into sin, and for whom the help of man is vain'; and continuously, and with most tender emphasis, '*for lonely people.*' This last prayer to my knowledge endeared him greatly to many who came under that sad category, but who left the church heartened to find that they were not forgotten.

Dr. Watson's preaching was extempore in effect, for though a manuscript was always before him for reference, a quick turn to of the leaves now and then, was the only sign of its presence. He never read, yet as the following anecdote will show, his memory was wonderfully accurate. His sermons were so original and striking that it was impossible to forget them, yet he bravely repeated several of their number from time to time; sometimes at the request of a member of the congregation, always, I think, to the pleasure of his hearers. My own memory—sadly deficient in some directions, is tenacious of *words*, and in listening to these repeated sermons I used to wait in a sort of tremor to hear whether at certain telling passages, the right word would come in the right place. I once said to him—'I knew that that illustration about the pool was coming, and waited to see if you would call it "the *sullen* pool," as you did before. If you had said "the turgid pool," or "the muddy pool," I think I should almost have been obliged to correct you!' He asked eagerly, 'And *did* I say "sullen"?' and on receiving an affirmative answer, 'That's very interesting!' he said, 'very interesting. I did not know I repeated myself so exactly. I suppose the original idea was so vivid, that it remains imprinted in my mind.'

One Sunday evening as a very rare exception I elected to stay at home, and on my sister's return from church questioned her about the service. She looked at me in a sympathetic manner, and said quietly, 'He preached on, "The Peace of God."' I had heard that sermon twice before, but after all these years the intense disappointment of that moment remains with me. The opportunity of hearing that most beautiful message a third time had been mine, and I had wilfully thrown it away. I could not forgive myself, and the entire family circle condoled with me on my loss. Of how many preachers could such an incident be recorded?

Dr. Watson was fond of preaching short series of sermons, announcing in advance the general subject and the points to be taken up in sequence, and these were always of intense interest. He had a great gift of character study, and of reading between the lines in the Bible narrative many things which escaped the ordinary student. At the end of such sermons he would often give a clever and humorous sketch of the Bible character as it would appear in the present day, which sketch drove home his point in irresistible fashion. It is safe to say that after his series of sermons on the women of the Old Testament, few of the matrons in Sefton Park Church escaped being christened by a new name by their husbands and families!

His sermons to young men on Sunday evenings were largely attended by the class whom he most wished to attract, and I had it on the authority of a young girl that one sermon on 'Chivalry' was the talk of many of her partners at a ball, and that one of them told her that on the Monday morning groups of young men were to be found eagerly discussing it on the Exchange. 'He gave it us straight,' said one, 'and we deserved it.'

Before his illness in 1889 Dr. Watson had no assistant and took all the services himself, including various classes during the week, notably one for the ladies of the congregation which is still remembered gratefully by those who were fortunate enough to have the benefit of his teaching. More than any one I have ever met he seemed to have the gift of putting himself in the place of another, and no woman could have dealt more sympathetically or wisely with the trials and irritations which beset the life of the mistress of a household.

Fine as was Dr. Watson's pulpit oratory, it always seemed to one that it was on the quieter and more intimate occasions that he rose to his highest level. When, for instance, he stood beside the desk in the lecture hall on Wednesday evenings, 'talking' rather than preaching to an audience packed to overflowing; or after the quarterly Communion Service, when he rose to his feet and spoke the few beautiful, moving words which made a fitting ending to the service.

His appearance at such times was very striking, especially before his illness in 1889, when an air of intense fragility added to the spirituality of his expression.

When he came to sum up his impressions of preaching he lamented that he had not made his sermons shorter.

Years ago a minister came into my vestry after evening service and said he should like to have a word with me. It was winter time and he was an old man, so I wheeled my most comfortable chair to the fireplace and besought him to be seated, also to deliver his mind, for it is always a privilege to have a word in season from a man who has grown old in the ministry. He told me that he was a country minister in the north of Scotland, and I think he said a clerk of his Presbytery, which at least proved that he had the reputation for sound judgment, and that he was liked by his brethren.

'I happened,' he went on to say, 'to be in Liverpool this Sabbath without duty, and I determined to worship once in your church, because'—and now he smiled at me good-naturedly—'I did not hear a good account of you or of your church.'

'The rumour went'—and everything was touched with his pleasant smile—'that you were too broad and your service too high for a Presbyterian Church; and so I horrified my hosts, who are of the straitest set, by coming out to Sefton Park Church. I saw nothing,' he concluded, 'and I heard nothing, of which I could disapprove, and I wish you well. Mine has been a long ministry, and it is drawing to its close; and this I can truly say, of its later period at least, every year I have been growing broader and preaching shorter.' He gave me his blessing, and I judge that he has now rendered in a good account of his stewardship.

He also came to think that he had spent too little time on the form of his sermons. The want of distinction in the case of a speaker dealing with the most majestic ideas he thought a crime. 'It is a species of profanity. It is an act of intellectual indecency.' He said that if he went back he would seek more earnestly a becoming dress for the message of God. 'Evangelistic preaching has seemed to me to be, as a rule, careless to a scandal, and almost squalid in style, with vain repetitions of hackneyed words by way of exhortation and with incredible anecdotes by way of illustration.' But he thought the time would come when the preacher would be held responsible not only for the truth which he declared, but for the dress in which he clothed it. He also held that the chief end of preaching was comfort. He had no faith in sermons on Biblical criticism and philosophy. 'Never can I forget what a distinguished scholar, who used to sit in my church, once said to me. "Your best work in the pulpit has been to put heart into men for the coming week." I wish I had put more. And when I have in my day, like us all, attempted to reconcile science and religion, one of the greatest men of science who used also to be a hearer in my church, never seemed to be interested, but when I dealt with the deep affairs of the soul, he would come round in the afternoon to talk it out.' He held specially that the preacher should be a preacher of Christ. 'I now clearly see every sentence should suggest Christ, and every sermon, even though His name had not been mentioned, nor His words quoted, should leave the hearer at the feet of Christ.' He recalled a story told him 'by an eminent and saintly Roman ecclesiastic, who was my dear friend, about Faber. Shortly before the poet died, he had visited my friend, and was asked to address the senior pupils in a certain school. Faber explained that he was now too weak to speak, but he consented to give them his blessing. Before doing so he said he would like to say one word to them, and as it could only be a word, it must be about Christ. Whereupon he began to give the titles of the Lord Jesus from the beginning of the Bible, as the mystics found them, on to the Book of Revelation, and when he ceased he had spoken for five-and-twenty minutes singing the high praise of the Lord. "Faber was a great lover of the Lord," said my friend, "and in Him we are all one." As it now appears to me, the chief effort of every sermon should be to unveil Christ, and the chief art of the preacher to conceal himself.'

As might have been expected Watson attached great importance to public worship. He held that those who depreciate the service and those who depreciate the sermon are alike in error, because sermon and service are not rivals but auxiliaries. He believed that there was a case for a liturgy. A liturgy had a certain stateliness of thought and charm of style; it lifted its children out of sectarian and provincial ideas of religion; it expressed not individual moods or experiences, but the ordinary wants of all kinds and conditions of men. It made the worshippers independent of the officiating clergyman; it bound the members of a church, both old and young, to one fellowship and loyalty. Along, however, with a liturgy there ought to be free prayer, giving the service a certain life and freshness, and giving also opportunities for fit thanksgiving and supplication prompted by the need of the time. Without disparaging the real gift of prayer bestowed on certain ministers under whose charge worship combines a perfect form of a liturgy with the loveliness and spontaneity of spoken prayer, Watson had a keen sense of the dangers of committing the conduct of divine service to the absolute discretion of one man. He thought it wise for ministers in Free Churches to form a liturgy for themselves with much care and pains, choosing from the liturgies of the early Church, and the choice books of Christian devotion. Services should also be prepared for the administration of the Sacraments. Public worship should be comforting, joyful, enthusiastic, beautiful, the flower of all the week, but its chief note should be reverence and godly fear. 'Praise and prayer, the reading of Holy Scripture, and the preaching of the Evangel, should conspire to lift the congregation above the present world and the sensible atmosphere in which they have been living, and bring them face to face with the Eternal. . . . Nothing is more urgently needed in this day, which knows how to doubt and jest, but is forgetting how to revere and adore, when the great function of worship has become pleasing and amusing, a performance and a comedy.' To the order of divine worship in his church Watson gave the most scrupulous care. His own prayers were largely liturgical. He made conscience of every detail, studying to make the whole service from beginning to end an impressive unity. It was a matter of grief to him that among so many of the Protestant Churches public worship without a sermon was thought to be unattractive. While, as we have seen, he gave a great place to the sermon, he yet believed that there ought to be solemn services of praise and prayer, of devout worship and communion where no sermon was needed.

Nothing called forth his great powers of sarcasm as did the degrading and debasing of public worship. He was perhaps hardly quite just to those who were trying in England to make

Church life really popular. He loathed the idea of 'running' a church upon modern lines. He conceived that the type of minister required for such a purpose would not be a man of learning and insight and devotion and charity. The teacher who expounded the Bible after a thorough and edifying fashion, the pastor who watched over and trained the character of his people would hardly be needed, and certainly would not be much appreciated. 'The chief demand is a sharp little man with the gifts of an impresario, a commercial traveller, and an auctioneer combined, with the slightest flavour of a peripatetic evangelist. Instead of a study lined with books of grave divinity and classical literature, let him have an office with pigeon-holes for his programmes, circulars, and endless correspondence, and cupboards for huge books with cuttings from newspapers and reports of other organisations, and a telephone ever tingling, and a set of handbooks, *How to Make a Sermon in Thirty Minutes*, *Splinters of Ice and Scraps of Coral; or, One Thousand Racy Anecdotes from the Mission Field*, *The Secrets of a Happy Social*, and suchlike practical works for the modern minister.' That such ways would be successful even as their promoters desired he did not believe. Christianity would not have existed if the Apostles had been 'pleasing preachers' and 'bright men.' The Church was not a place of second-rate entertainments or a cheap business concern, but the witness to immortality, the spiritual home of souls, the servant of the poor, and the protector of the friendless.

FROM SIR OLIVER LODGE

February 18*th*, 1899.

My dear Watson,—Over here for the Sunday I read your *Ageless Life* aloud with the greatest interest, admiration, and enthusiasm.

As you know your Christ-drawn conception of life now as a bit of life always, no discontinuity except one of body and of physical memory, the Platonic idea, is the one to which as I think science is arriving by a slow and groping method of its own.

If it does so arrive the information would gradually be forced upon the uninspired and average man, with results I should hope of a useful and helpful kind.—Very truly yours,

Oliver Lodge.

CHAPTER VI

PASTORAL WORK

WATSON'S pastoral work was, in some respects, even more remarkable than his preaching. As his friend Dr. Oswald Dykes has said, the pulpit offers attractions for artistic natures like his sufficient to outweigh any fastidious shrinking from those vulgar accessories which attend a popular preacher in these days of advertising. But quiet pastoral duty with its absorbing demands upon the spiritual as well as the physical resources of a minister is done out of sight of the public, and promises nothing to the lover either of sensationalism or notoriety. The ends it seeks and the rewards it gains are such as only a true lover of souls will value. 'John Watson,' he says, 'never stood so high in my eyes as when I came to know how assiduous was his visitation of his flock, and with what keenness he had studied the problems and the methods of pastoral care.' He made it a point to visit each member of his great congregation every year. This was by no means the whole of his pastoral labour.

He was tenderly watchful in times of joy, and especially in times of sorrow. He comforted assiduously the sick, the dying, the bereaved. It was much more by his presence than by letters that he did his work, though every member of his flock was made conscious that at no turn or epoch of his life was he forgotten by his pastor. It has to be remembered that in all probability he added very little to the outward strength of his church by this toil. Hardly any minister in his position would consider it necessary. His congregation for many years taxed the limits of his church, and would have been more numerous still if he had not refused to have a larger building. He found his reward in the strong ties that bound himself to his people, and also in the consciousness of having done his duty, for he would often repeat the saying, 'Duty done is the soul's fireside.'

Dr. Oswald Dykes remarks that the chapter on this subject in his book, *The Cure of Souls*, is the most open window we have, letting light into the inner secrets of his own heart, and revealing what manner of man he really was. Watson thought that the ideal way was that a great congregation should have two ministers, one to be the preacher and the other the pastor. Many men combine the two gifts of the shepherd, to feed and to watch, but as Nature specialises on her higher levels, it is rare that one should excel both in the pulpit and in the house. One man rejoices in preaching, another longs to be planning a round of visits. One man rejoices in forty minutes' intellectual conflict with a crowd of human souls, but afterwards does not wish to see the face of man. Another has that in the grip of his hand and the sound of his voice which sends people on their way rejoicing. 'When he enters a house there is a general stir and an adhesion of the whole household; sick people declare with solemnity that he does more for them than the doctor, and in the hour of trial the thoughts of a family turn by instinct to this man. Between these men there should be no comparison, for the two are the piers of the arch.' But Watson was a true shepherd of souls. His people were always in his heart. He claimed identity with them in the joys and sorrows and endless vicissitudes of life. No friend was blessed with any good gift of God but he was also richer. No household suffered but he was poorer; no one resisted temptation but he was stronger; no one failed but he was weaker. He inquired and planned about all his young men, trying to find spheres for them or to stimulate them in their work, or to protect them from temptation.

One thing he cannot do: criticise his people or make distinctions among them. Others, with no shepherd heart, may miss the hidden goodness: he searches for it as for fine gold. Others may judge people for faults and sins;

he takes them for his own. Others may make people's foibles the subject of their raillery; the pastor cannot because he loves. Does this interest on the part of one not related by blood or long friendship seem an impertinence? It ought to be pardoned, for it is the only one of the kind that is likely to be offered. Is it a sentiment? Assuredly, the same sublime devotion which has made Jesus the Good Shepherd of the soul. If the pastoral instinct be crushed out of existence between the upper and lower millstones of raging sensationalism and ecclesiastical worldliness, then the Christian Church will sink into a theological club or a society for social reform: if it had full play we might see a revival of religion more spiritual and lasting than any since the Reformation.

He divided his work as pastor into the departments of visitation and consultation, and this is how he spoke of them:—

With the true pastor, visitation is a spiritual labour, intense and arduous, beside which reading and study are light and easy. When he has been with ten families, and done his best by each, he comes home trembling in his very limbs and worn-out in soul. Consider what he has come through, what he has attempted, what, so far as it can be said of a frail human creature, this man has done. He has tasted joy in one home, where the husband has been restored to his wife from the dust of death; he has shared sorrow with another family where pet Marjorie has died; he has consulted with a mother about a son in some far country, whose letters fill the anxious heart with dread; he has heard a letter of twelve pages of good news and overflowing love which another son has sent to his mother; he has carried God's comfort to Darby and Joan reduced suddenly to poverty, and God's invitation to two young people beginning life together in great prosperity. He has to adjust himself to a new situation in each house, and to cast himself with utter abandonment into another experience of life. Before evening he has been a father, a mother, a husband, a wife, a child, a friend; he has been young, middle-aged, old, lifted up, cast down, a sinner, a saint, all sorts and conditions of life. . . . It is exhausting to rejoice or to sorrow, but to taste both sensations in succession is disabling; yet this man has passed through ten moods since midday, and each with all his strength. His experiences have not all been wiped out as a child's exercise from a slate; they have become strata in his soul.

This labour of visitation was conducted in a most careful and methodical fashion. Whenever a family came to his church he obtained from them the names of the household, and the ages of all below sixteen, and also particulars about those who were communicants and had done church work. All these he wrote into a large book in which he had his congregation before him at any moment. From it he reminded himself who ought to become communicants, who ought to take part in the church work, where recruits could be found for the guilds and classes. He also made careful secret notes on the spiritual history and character of his people. Thus his yearly visitation was no formality. The visits were brief, generally fifteen minutes. Gossip was left out, and it was understood that business had to be done. When conversation moved onward till it reached the brink of prayer, the visit culminated and completed itself in a few earnest petitions. Whenever a message came from a house of sickness no time was lost on the way. He read to all in trouble the fourteenth chapter of St. John's Gospel. It was his experience that every man and woman wanted to hear it in great sorrow or when the shadow was falling. With every reading he noticed that it yielded some new revelation of the Divine Love and the Kingdom of Heaven. 'If one is sinking into unconsciousness, and you read, "In My Father's house are many mansions," he will come back and whisper "mansions," and he will wait till you finish: "where I am ye may be also," before he dies in peace.'

Much of his time and strength were given to consultation, and this he ever considered a primary department of his work. His Roman Catholic affinities partly fitted and prepared him for this.

It is the custom (he said) of Protestants to denounce the confessional, and not without reason—for the claim of a priest to hear confessions and absolve is a profane interference between the soul and Christ—but it would be wise to remember that there are times and moods and circumstances when every person desires to open his heart to some brother-man, when some persons cannot otherwise get relief. To whom are these persons to go? What they want is one who has a wide experience of life, who is versed in human nature, who is accustomed to keep secrets, who has faith in God and man, whose office invites and sanctions confidence. Who fulfils those conditions so perfectly as the minister of Christ? and is it not good that there is within reach one ordained to be a friend unto every one who is lonely and in distress of mind?

His rules for consultation were well thought out and strictly adhered to. He only received such confidences as were freely offered. He hated anything like prying into people's private affairs and pursuing a clue to the end. Curiosity and meddlesomeness were forbidden to a true pastor. Neither should he encourage the revelation of anything more than was necessary to enable him to give his advice. For example, if a woman states that she has a heavy sin on her conscience, and indicates that her husband has no idea of it, then the pastor should suggest that they should speak of the matter in general terms, and, if he knows the goodness of her husband, that she ought to confess the sin, whatever it may be, to him. Afterwards the pastor advises her how to meet and overcome this sin if it should rise again, and so this human soul has not been put to shame, but has gained help without losing self-respect. The pastor, though he has taken no oath of secrecy, must regard every confidence as absolutely sacred, and will on no account, except at the command of the law, reveal what has been told him in consultation.

This was a rule on which Watson specially insisted, and to which he most closely adhered. It may be safely said that he never broke a confidence. The very thought of such treason seemed to fill him with horror. He betrayed, I remember, considerable excitement when he heard that many of the letters addressed to Henry Drummond by those in straits had been preserved. Drummond, like Watson, was one to whom men laid bare their hearts and their lives, and he was ready to give himself to their help without stint. Drummond, too, was never known to break a secret of the confessional. Watson was careful to destroy at once any letter recording the sad secrets of humanity. He did not fear so much that pastors might be consciously dishonourable. What he dreaded was mere leakiness. 'The pastor does not consider his own wife a privileged person in this matter, for though she might be the most prudent and reticent of women, yet it would embarrass his people to know that their secrets were shared with her. The high honour of doctors, who carry in their breasts so many social tragedies, is an example to be followed by the clerical profession.' The pastor should direct all those who consult him to accept Christ as Saviour and Friend, giving also such practical counsel as he can, especially urging restitution, reformation, watchfulness, as the case might be. I know that very many who were in trouble went to him. I know that as time passed scarcely any phase of suffering and anxiety and sin was unfamiliar to him. He found many precedents as he grew older, and was furnished with many aids for emergency. But sometimes he was overwhelmed by the misery of it all.

Watson had many who consulted him about the difficulties of faith. Here his quick insight served him well. He could distinguish between the earnest sceptic and the man who was playing with doubt. He had fought his own way and knew the conditions of the struggle. There was no trouble he would not take for those whose perplexities were real. His large and liberal conception of Christianity, his sharp discrimination between the essential and the non-essential, his vivid belief in Christ as the centre of his creed, all came out in such dealings. But for those who were merely trying to puzzle him he had small tolerance, and on occasion, though rarely, he would use his wit and sarcasm on their vanity. The result of it all may be summed up in his favourite motto, 'Be kind, for every one is fighting a hard battle.' He was never meddlesome, censorious, unsympathetic. Every year he saw more of the temptations of life and the goodness of human nature. For the innocent gaiety and lighter follies of youth he had a vast toleration, for the sudden disasters of manhood an unfailing charity, for the unredeemed tragedies of age a great sorrow. Life was a hard fight for every one, and it was not his to judge or condemn; his it was to understand, to help, to comfort, for these people were his children, his pupils, his patients; they were the sheep Christ had given him, for whom Christ died.

When he came to review his career, he confessed that pastoral work had not been easy to him. He knew the full attraction of the study, and it was irksome for him to leave it. He thought himself by nature a student rather than a pastor. It was also difficult for him to exchange the attitude of a friend for the attitude of a pastor. He had a sincere and continued joy in human life in all its ways, also in dogs and horses and every living thing. He was naturally a humanist, observant, but also tolerant, kind-hearted, and easy-going. He loved the comedy and the tragedy of life. He shrank from oversight as a wanton intrusion upon other men's affairs. He found it his business to concentrate upon the spiritual concerns of the people, and he toiled very hard in this department. But he did not disguise the difficulties. Some homes were attractive, and others were antipathetic. It was often difficult to speak directly about the deepest affairs of life. He counted himself not a priest among his people, but a fellow-pilgrim with them on life's perilous journey. Still he continued to believe in the work, and he refused to criticise the Roman confessional with the high spirit of many Protestant writers. 'Many are my regrets for unpaid visits to people who alienated me, and for tardy visits when trouble called for attention. Many also are my regrets for foolish words I have spoken in jest, and for the words which died away upon my lip, and which I ought to have spoken. I reproach myself for impatience with chronic invalids, and impracticable faddists, and bigoted people, and tiresome talkers. Who has not his own weaknesses and his own prejudices? and therefore he ought to be charitable. But I am thankful that, so far as I know, I have never deserted any fellow-creature in black distress, however awful was the tragedy, and I can also claim that I have never betrayed a professional secret, nor kept in my possession a compromising letter.' It deserves to be noted that he was specially careful never to poach on the congregations of other ministers, or to do anything to take away their people. He thought that ministers ought in this matter to copy very closely the etiquette of the medical profession, which insists that a doctor shall not meddle with another man's practice nor criticise another man's work. For a minister to visit a family belonging to another congregation unless on the understood ground of private friendship, or in some very exceptional circumstances, he thought was less than moral, and certainly was not honourable.

The truth is, however, that Watson's visiting

greatly strengthened his preaching, just as his preaching gave value to his visits. This was observed by every one who really knew him and his work. In any case his pastoral work would have been fruitful. As it was, it gave him the power of putting himself alongside the personal experience of his people with brotherly humanity and longing to help. He pressed home his message with personal force—that is, he had always in his mind, not merely ideas, but persons. He saw sin and pain not in the mass, but by their real tokens in the souls they bow down. The characters, the dangers, and the sorrows of his people were ever in his mind. More than once after his death he was called an interpreter. He knew men so well that he spoke home to them. He knew life so well that he understood the Bible, and could make it a living book. His familiarity with life's tragedy and comedy saved him from cynicism and caricature, and kept him sound and sweet at heart. He exercised a priesthood of love as well as a priesthood of truth. That priesthood of love was fulfilled with constant vigilance, with unsparing labour, and with such a severe self-denial as gave dignity to his whole character.

Nor must I forget to touch on his courage, wisdom, and fidelity in the training of the young. 'We must accept,' he said, 'the age into which Providence has cast us, and enter into its spirit.

One can hardly imagine any more honourable task than to meet its wants and guide its inquiries. There are ages which have been saved from sin by evangelism; this is an age which must be saved from scepticism by knowledge.' And again: 'We come now to the mind of the congregation, and it must be felt by every one that at present an enormous responsibility lies on the Church with regard to the instruction of the young (and others) in the Christian faith. For this purpose there ought to be an educational ladder constructed in every congregation which will receive the young child into the infant-class of the Sunday-school at the foot and, as a man, give him the latest results of Biblical research at the top.' He realised these ideals in his organisation of the Sunday-school, the senior classes, and the guilds in his own congregation. While he did not profess to be a specialist, his acquirements in scholarship, in theology, and in philosophy were very considerable, and all of them were humbly, faithfully, fearlessly and reverently used in the conveying of religious truth to his people.

The outward monument of his successful ministry is to be found in the great, liberal, influential, and devoted church which he built up year by year. Of individual instances in which souls were touched and helped by his ministry, there are not a few records, but for the most part they are too sacred for publication. One of the most widely known incidents in his ministry is the fact that Matthew Arnold heard Watson preach on the day he died. Mr. Arnold was staying with his brother-in-law, Mr. Edward Cropper, who was a worshipper in Sefton Park Church. Arnold accompanied his sister and his brother-in-law to the morning service. He was deeply impressed by the sermon on the Cross of Christ, and remarked that he had rarely been so affected by any preacher as by Dr. Watson. One of the hymns sung was:

> When I survey the wondrous Cross
> On which the Prince of Glory died.

Arnold when he came home repeated the lines, and said that the hymn was the finest in the English language. 'Yes,' he went on, 'the Cross remaineth, and in the straits of the soul makes its ancient appeal.' In the afternoon he walked with his relatives and was in the highest spirits. He vaulted lightly over a stile, but the effort was too great, and he died very suddenly from disease of the heart. The Sefton Park Church *Magazine* of May 1888 has the following:—

> Mr. Arnold worshipped with us at morning service on Communion Sunday, and before evening we were all the poorer for his loss. Death by a sudden stroke deprived English literature of a most delightful critic, a most fascinating essayist, and a poet of classical purity and beauty. Our nation has also lost a life which elevated as much as it

interested us, a life devoted to 'sustaining the course of noble conduct and to exalting the elation of duty, the rapture of righteousness.' He showed us an example of splendid service and high thinking, and by his kindliness and culture reconciled sweetness and light. We can never forget that distinguished man of letters whose last public act was to attend divine service in this church, and who died as it were under the shadow of the Cross.

His beloved friend and brother minister, the Rev. William Watson of Claughton, wrote a letter to him which he permits me to quote.

October 31st, 1903.

Here is an incident full of interest and cheer for you. A lady in this neighbourhood, unknown to me, met with a great sorrow some months ago. She lost a much-loved daughter, she has been quite inconsolable; so stunned as to be unable to weep. She was agonised in prayer, calling on God for comfort and rest of mind. No response seemed to come. She could find no alleviation in the teaching of her own Church. Her distress has been terrible. She heard you were to be here last Sunday evening. For two or three days before the burden of her longing had been, that God would put it into your heart to speak about prayer; its power and comfort. So eager was she that this should be your message, that the medical attendant, an intimate friend of the family's, was almost on the point of writing to you and making a suggestion. You came, preached on prayer, she was present, she could scarcely believe her ears when you announced your subject. She went home from Church to a new world of peace. The tears long checked, came. She let her poor wounded life down on the Divine Compassion of the Christ, and has been marvellously strengthened. The Doctor told me the story last night, and I give you it very much as he gave it me. It is impressive, and he a busy but kindly man has been much moved by it, and like me sees that it cannot be explained on human grounds alone. Your words have saved and uplifted a broken heart. May the Master's blessing for ever be upon them when you utter them, and may this little incident give you heartening for to-morrow's toil.

Watson was indefatigable in writing pastoral letters of counsel and consolation to those in his charge. Of these a very few specimens must suffice. The first is to a young officer about whom he was a little anxious :—

My dear A.,—There is a matter on which I feel a little anxious and on which I want to give you a word of advice. You are young, a great blessing by the way, and I want you to form not only good habits, but the best, so that your future may be without shadow and crowned with success. What I want to suggest to you is to take great care that among those older officers you do not fall into the way of drinking wine and whisky freely.

I do not ask you to be a total abstainer, although some good fellows are so with no loss to themselves, but I have no hesitation in asking that you leave whisky alone, which I never touched until I was a middle-aged man, and to take very little else. A glass of beer is all right if you want it. Your mother, I know, takes nothing, your father very little indeed. I want you to be like them all the more that you are still a lad. If a habit of drinking ever grew upon you, little by little it would ruin your life, and break your parents' hearts.

Now, my dear boy, you will accept this as a letter of warning from an older man anxious that you should make the most of your life; remember you are your father's son carrying a good name and having before you, as I trust, a long and happy life.—Your affectionate friend, J. W.

The next was written on the anniversary of a little child's death.

My dear Friend,—Have you read *The Blessed Damozel*? 'They are safe who are with Jesus where they follow the Lamb to Living Fountains of Water.' And the day has now broken.

But I am writing in the train to send you a quotation from that Scots saint Archbishop Leighton. In a letter of his to his sister on the loss of her little boy: 'Sweet thing, and is he so quickly laid to sleep? Happy he. Though we shall have no more the pleasure of his lisping and laughing, he shall have no more the pain of crying or of dying, or of being sick: And hath wholely escaped the trouble of schooling, and all other sufferings of boys, and the riper and deeper griefs of riper years. This poor life being all along nothing but many sorrows and many deaths. John is but gone an hour or two sooner to bed, and we are undressing to follow. The more we put off the love of this present world and all things superfluous beforehand, we shall have the less to do when we lie down.'—Yours affectionately, John Watson.

The following accompanied a gift to his friend and physician:—

My dear Doctor,—Will you accept a copy of *À Kempis* for your study table. The longer I live the more I value those brief words I read at a glance between work, and that sweeten the soul. Every moment I need to be reminded of the Cross through which we live.

Accept my deep gratitude also for your great and patient kindness to the least worthy of your patients. May God fill the empty place in your heart.—Your friend,

JOHN WATSON.

This letter is one out of many which show the care and labour with which he attended to the requests of his friends. No man could have done more to obtain situations for the unemployed and to help men in business difficulties.

July 5th, 1901.

DEAR MRS. A.,—I put the case of the man in whom you are interested before a very able shipowner who has French connections, who I thought might be of some service. I am sorry to say that he holds out no hope, and I quote a passage from his letter for your information. 'I know that young man, the probabilities are that he has no business training and that his friends imagine that a knowledge of French without any other equipment makes him of use. These young men come to Liverpool in scores and want to enter offices as volunteers without pay, and expect to be taught business.'

As this is a very able man and has taken the trouble, a busy man, to write the note with his own hand, and at considerable length, I am afraid there is no chance for the Frenchman.

Will you accept this expression of regret that I can do no more and that in consequence of my very heavy work at present I was unable to call at offices myself?—With kind regards, Believe me, Yours faithfully, JOHN WATSON.

I give three more letters of comfort.

My dear Mrs. ——,—Your letter has come, and made me very anxious and sad. All day I have had you in my thoughts and my prayers, and now I am going to preach with heads, and you must listen just as if you were in church, for indeed you cannot answer, and

1. You are not well, and I know that you are hiding suffering every day with splendid bravery. I hope the other profession may be able to help you, and that you may be long spared in health to your dear man, and us all who love you. But remember how closely the mind and body are related, and how John Baptist himself lost heart in the dungeon.

2. You have had exceptional trials, and I am often full of self-reproach that we have not all the more sympathy with you. Never was woman more tried, and more patient. But this must tell on your mind, and you are in the trough of the wave now.

3. You must not talk or think of leaving us, and imagine that this is the will of God. Consider what you are to your husband, how close and beautiful and loyal is the tie. What would his life be without you? If God did call you home before him, and I was spared, you may be sure that I would stand by him to the end, for I love and honour him. I do think that we understand one another, but you may not go, there is need of you, and as St. Paul argued in his Philippian Epistle, as there is need here life will be continued here. May God comfort and cheer you.—Ever your faithful friend, John Watson.

March 15*th*, 1892.

Dear Miss ——,—It is laid upon me to send you these

—amid a morning of business—it is *not* laid on you to answer.

(a) ‘A sea below
The throne is spread; its pure still glass
Pictures all earth scenes as they pass.
We on its shore
Share, in the bosom of our rest,
God's knowledge and are blest.’

(b) ‘Shall I forget on this side of the grave?
I promise nothing: you must wait and see,
Patient and brave.
(O my soul, watch with him and he with me.)

Shall I forget in peace of Paradise?
I promise nothing: follow, friend, and see,
Faithful and wise.
(O my soul, lead the way he walks with me.)’

My kind regards to your father.—Yours faithfully,

John Watson.

November 19*th,* 1906

My dear Friend,—It was good of you to send me those letters to read; I think them both admirable in everything. Alas! that such a felicity of insight should be wet with tears. I thought I had realised the bitterness of your sorrow, so far as a friend walking among the trees of the garden could; but your letter has in some way told me more than I knew or rather imagined. Yours has been a bitter cup, but you are the more in the fellowship of His sufferings, and the nearer you are to Him in the order of suffering, the warmer is the touch of His Hand on the cup. There is a quiet sanctuary in the heart of the storm, and the Lord with every kind of trouble encompassing Him, spoke of Peace, My Peace, and this was because He had entered into and hidden Himself in the Will of God. 'In His Will,' as Dante says, 'is our tranquillity.' Upon the first day of the week your sweet girl was with the Lord, and entered into the Fullness of life. Then do not sorrow overmuch because your arms are empty, for so were the Mothers' arms in Galilee when they brought their children to Jesus. His strong, kindly Arms were fuller, and by and by He restored His charge with His Blessing. This also He will do for you, and in that day I feel certain you will not reproach the Saviour for His guardianship, when in the dawning of the morning you see your child coming to meet you. We have been walking among the gray gnarled olive-trees in the cold light of the moon, but she has been in the garden city where they follow the Lamb to living fountains of water, and have no need even of the sun, for the Lord God and the Lamb are the light thereof.

But the wind is in my sails, and I am making for the open sea, where the sun coming out from behind a cloud is shining on the shimmering water, and Cambridge calls.—Your faithful and affectionate friend, JOHN WATSON.

Among those who attended Sefton Park Church were several of the Liverpool Professors. Among these Watson had many close friends. Sir Oliver Lodge kindly allows me to print the following extracts from Watson's letters to him:—

October 19*th*, 1891.

You call me Mr., but I fancy that is the dignity of an F.R.S. keeping an ignorant person in his own place. It is no use, our impudence is invincible. I thank you for the invitation for the 23rd. Alas! I am on duty, and it is a great grief I cannot come. I feel your kindness in asking me.

PS.—You are a better disciple of Jesus than I am, why don't you stay to the Sacrament?

November 24th, 1891.

I am so busy that I cannot get round to ask you a question. Am I right in my idea that you as a Physicist see no difficulty about prayer being answered, allowing for changes in natural sphere? You made a distinction between force and will, I think; can you give it me on a post-card, it will be a favour.

November 28th, 1891.

It was very kind to leave a Christmas gift for me to-day, and I shall value it for that kind word you wrote on it. It strengthens me that you should have anything like affectionate regard for a man so far below you as I am, but when you give that you do your best for me.

December 19th, 1892.

It was a greater disappointment for *me* on Saturday. Let us post-card time on Friday evening, for I can't afford to miss you. My heart's thanks for that book, *Copernik and Blake,* done with much satisfaction, a most timely and lucid book, but I must have the name on it for generations to come. My *friends* are not many, some six true men, so I hold them very dear.

With the warmest wishes of the season for you and yours.

CHAPTER VII

PUBLIC WORK

DR. WATSON was not merely a minister of Sefton Park; he was also a great citizen of Liverpool. As such he took a very active part in public life. He was strongly disposed at first to concern himself with ecclesiastical affairs, with the business in Synod and in Presbytery of the Presbyterian Church of England. But he fancied, rightly or wrongly, that his efforts in that way were discouraged, and for long he stood aside. But he found another sphere. He was not an active politician, though his views on politics were never concealed. They were in the main decidedly Conservative. He was not a strict party man, and differed from the Unionists in their educational policy, and in their attitude to social reform. But his favourite politicians were Mr. Balfour and Mr. Chamberlain. Mr. Balfour he would speak of as the prince of courtesy, and he would tell how on the occasion of a dinner in London when he himself had arrived rather late, and the guests were already seated, he found

Mr. Balfour sitting opposite him on the other side of the table. Watson was introduced to him, and Mr. Balfour, instead of bowing across the table, rose and walked round and shook hands very warmly. For Mr. Chamberlain's debating and administrative powers he had an unbounded admiration, and he considered that as a debater he surpassed easily all other politicians. However, these opinions were not spoken in public. Watson considered that it was the duty of a minister, unless in exceptional circumstances, to maintain neutrality in politics in so far as his public actions were concerned. He also disliked the habit of discussing political questions in ecclesiastical courts. But no one had more of the civic conscience, and few equalled him in the energy of patriotism. One of his great ambitions —and it was largely realised—was to train young men in his church to care for the life of the community, and to take when the opportunity came, an active part in municipal affairs. He never ceased to glorify municipal work. It was his deliberate conviction that the worth of such work was seriously and dangerously underrated in our country. He sometimes incurred censure for the vehemence with which he expressed himself on this subject. He held that among the various influences which make for the good of the common life, none ought to be more carefully fostered than the pride in the city—local patriotism as distinguished from the Imperial patriotism into which the other flows as a river into the ocean. He held that no honour was too generous to be paid to men who with every qualification of intelligence and integrity, with every private reason to safeguard their leisure and to gratify their honourable tastes, had entered the City Council and worked to make the city more like the City of God. He dreaded the passing of local politics into the hands of professional managers manipulating affairs for their own aggrandisement, and the shadow of the calamity which has fallen largely on American municipal life often oppressed and grieved him. While deprecating the idea that the Church as an organisation should take a direct part in politics or interfere directly in trade disputes, he pleaded that she should use her whole influence through her children in working for the happiness of the people. He believed that the Church could help the Kingdom best in this way, and he hoped that long before the twentieth century ended, every man would have a home of some kind where he lived in peace and decency with his wife and his children, that the gross temptations of the city—the public-houses at every corner, and the scenes in Piccadilly Circus at night, would be brought to an end, and that every man would be willing to work, and work honestly, and receive a fair wage to keep himself and his family. He longed to see an end of the alienation between the people and the Church, and he believed that the time was coming when the poor and miserable would know that Christ by His Body the Church was their best friend. He also frankly expressed his desire for the day when every young man in the country in ordinary circumstances would be invited in an extremely pressing manner to become a member of one of the armed forces of the country, whether military or naval. When that day came, not only would the country be impregnable against foreign attack, but a very great benefit would be conferred on the young men. They would get bodies erect instead of slouching, and they would be taught obedience and subordination as well as courage and loyalty.

I shall have occasion to deal with his profound interest in University College, Liverpool, now the University of Liverpool. In the whole subject of education his interest was constant. In an address to the Federation of Head Teachers which met in Liverpool in 1903, Dr. Watson urged upon the teachers that it lay with them to make intelligent and loyal English citizens. He would have the children to understand what the flag meant, and he held that they should be drilled in the history of the nation. They should be prepared to take a share in the government of the country, and should be instructed in the history of politics. They should be taught that they must work hard, quickly, skilfully, and honestly, if it was to be well with England in the competition before her. The people could only be raised in proportion as their character was raised. The chief forces in the world were not physical but spiritual, and the most successful method for the elevation of the individual was not repressing evil, but replacing it by goodness.

From his pulpit he constantly stimulated the civic conscience, and taught a large view of the State. He repudiated wholly the notion that the State was nothing but a night-watchman to protect the property and person of the lieges. The business of the State was so to regulate the corporate life that every member of the commonwealth should come to his full height, and have his full opportunity of living. That was a happy State which maintained a just balance between justice and benevolence. Few things were more disheartening to him than to see the very different attitudes of obligation which the ordinary man had to his family and to the State. He would sink himself in the interests of the family, but he was indifferent or neutral to the State. Especially he was cold to the municipal State, and had never come within a thousand miles of believing that the government of the State was a divine ordinance, or that the local State was the nurse of character, and the sphere where citizens could rise to the stature of moral independence. Whatever might be the benefits of the party system, party should never be served at the expense of the community.

His success in his deliberate aim was very marked. During his pastorate six members of his church became Mayors or Lord Mayors of Liverpool. The Mayors were—Thomas Holder, 1883-4; James de Bels Adam, 1891-2: the Lord Mayors were Sir Charles Petrie, 1901-2; W. W. Rutherford, 1902-3; John Lea, 1904-5; and John Japp, 1906-7. Many others were prominent in the City Council. He was wont to recount these facts with infinite pride, giving each man his municipal title and reciting their services to the community. He would say that during his residence in Liverpool he had seen twenty-five Mayors and Lord Mayors, and every one of them was animated with an earnest desire to maintain the high reputation of the city and to do his duty by the citizens of Liverpool. During his years in Liverpool, one of the most severe and triumphant fights for purity and reform ever known in any municipality was carried through. The late Mr. Samuel Smith, M.P., in his autobiography gives an account of the facts. Watson was the friend and colleague of these reformers. It is in vain to attempt a history of these services. To give it would be to summarise the public life of Liverpool for a quarter of a century.

Suffice it to say that every good cause found an advocate in John Watson. At all the chief public functions he was a prominent and honoured guest, and for all righteous ends a most efficient worker.

CHAPTER VIII

HOME LIFE AND FOREIGN TRAVEL

AMIDST these strenuous labours, Watson's life went on happily and peacefully for years. He confined himself to the work of his congregation and his city. He was not much known outside, but in Liverpool his fame and power steadily grew. Four sons were born to him, and the atmosphere of his home was sweet and sunny. He was able to be much with his wife and children, and he had also many opportunities of cultivating the society of his friends. Among these he numbered many of the best men and women in Liverpool. Children had a great love for him, and he was the comrade of his own boys. Father Day once took Watson to visit the Jesuit schools in Liverpool. The boys gathered round him much to his delight, holding his hands, and searching for the peppermints he was accustomed to carry in his coat pockets. 'Don't leave us, Father,' they cried, as the superintendent tried to take him away. Watson often spoke of the great joy given to him that afternoon. The following story from a lady in the South of England will show how he understood the heart of a child :—

He wrote to my husband offering to preach for him, and gave us a memorable day both at Church and at home. During dinner on Sunday, our six-year-old boy, who was sitting next to Dr. Watson, upset his glass of water, and overcome with shame, took refuge under the table weeping and saying 'I can't come out, I'm far too ashamed.' Watson, seizing the pepper-pot and a broken piece of bread for purposes of illustration said, 'Athol, here 's a shipwreck! Look how the waves are creeping over the vessel.—Ah ! it 's going to be wrecked. See, there 's a lighthouse, come and see if we can't save this poor ship,'—and by degrees the sobs ceased, and a tearful but deeply interested face appeared from under the table. Not a glance was cast in the boy's direction, and the rescue of the vessel proceeded, till all was peace and joy. He understood the boy's nature so well even during that short visit, and urged us not to let him work too hard when he went to school.

At home he was the soul of good humour and kindliness. He possessed the habits of a business man, and nothing fretted him like casualness. Morning prayers over, he read the paper and his letters either before or during breakfast. At nine he was ready for his study. He typed answers to his correspondence, and then worked on till lunch. The afternoon was spent in visiting the congregation, or in fulfilling some business engagement. His evenings latterly were almost always occupied, but in the earlier part of his ministry many were free. He loved to see his young men, and he was especially successful in winning their confidence. He used to say: 'If you get young men into your study, let them smoke. It is as a man lights his pipe that he gives you his confidence.' In his library he was perfectly happy. He loved books, and he bought them. He had some dozen or so valuable first editions, and a fine collection of beautiful art books, though he was never extravagant in his hobby. He had the book-collector's reverence for books. He never marked a book all his life, and could not bear to see one ill-used, ill-cut, or in danger of getting soiled. He could not read a dirty library book; in fact he was altogether æsthetic as a reader or collector. He never tired of imploring young men to read, and regarded systematic reading as a great factor of success. His own general knowledge was extraordinary. I have heard him at one dinner-party speak of stocks and shares, the Italian Renascence, the East, the Highland Regiments, with a perfect grasp of each different subject, and with each department include a perfect shower of appropriate stories. His love of animals was very marked. He would not pass a cat in the street without 'passing the time of day,' as he called it. His house was always the home of numerous creatures of all sizes and varieties, mostly dogs, for he was devoted to dogs and horses, and as a young man found his chief companions in books, horses, and dogs. He told many humorous stories of dogs, especially when on visiting they came in a solid mass to sit on his knee, and of one bulldog of more than usually repulsive appearance and colossal weight whom he feared to remove, and over whose back he was compelled to write all the morning.

As a Highlander, he suffered very greatly from curious fits of depression which did not seem in any way to be connected with bodily health. But he never inflicted his melancholy moods on his family, and was only very quiet and absorbed, and kept more closely to his study. In a day or two he would emerge again as a man coming out into the sunshine.

He was highly strung, and in spite of his strong build and calm exterior, was very nervous, and extremely sensitive to noise. It actually seemed to pain him, and he would jump and cry out if anything dropped suddenly beside him. Schopenhauer in his essay on Noise writes: 'In the biographies of almost all writers or wherever else their personal utterances are recorded, I find complaints about it . . . and if it should happen that any writer has omitted to express himself on the matter, it is only for want of an opportunity.' His very walk was that of a nervous man absorbed in mental work. It was quick, then slow; often he would stop altogether and scrape a figure in the dust with his walking-stick. Otherwise, he was continually clinking a chain or coins in his hands, tossing them backwards and forwards, pausing suddenly and staring straight before him saying nothing, then again the rapid, unceasing working of his hands. The chain he carried was a horse's curb, and he said that on many occasions after playing with it in a railway carriage he was relieved to find himself deserted by the other travellers.

He was always moving some part of his body. When reading he waved one foot without ceasing. His was a nervous temper—a short, quick temper—and when aroused over some mean act or something underhand, his Celtic nature carried him sometimes rather too far. But he knew his weakness and was very careful to keep calm as much as possible.

On holiday time he was fond of walking and sitting in the sun. With no covering on his face he would sit for hours in blazing sunshine with great enjoyment, and no sun from the Nile to Perthshire ever made him feel ill. He also drove, but in latter days was so lost in thought that the corners were apt to be taken sharply. It was his great joy to go to the livery stables, and as an experienced judge of a horse, to renew his old acquaintance with the country. Once he had entered a stable and was looking at a fine black horse with a view to hiring him for the summer holidays.

'Is he sound?'

'Oh, ay, he 's quite sound.'

'Is he quiet ?'

'Oh, ay, he 's quiet enough.'

Then followed a long pause.

'Look here,' said Watson, 'what 's the matter with him ?'

'Oh, there 's naething the matter with him, naething at all, but'—and this with a burst of confidence—'supposing that ye were in a narrow road with a dyke, and ye met a motor, weel I 'm no saying so ye ken, but may be he 'd just gae porp.'

'Ay,' said Watson, 'let us get along. I 'm wondering where we 'd porp to, possibly over the hedge. No, let us have the other one with the broken knees.'

The first prolonged break in his Liverpool life was in October 1889. One Friday morning Watson, when at work in his study, was struck down with serious illness. The news came with a shock upon the congregation, and caused a feeling akin to consternation. Day by day information was sought, and as there was no return of the symptoms by which his illness was first manifested, the alarm was somewhat allayed. The fact is that one of his lungs seemed to give way, but he had gone through many examinations at the hands of doctors, and was considered by them absolutely sound, while his family history was perfect. The doctors prescribed an absence of six months, and this holiday was one of the happiest times of his life. He went with his wife to the Riviera and to Egypt, and some of his cheerful letters to his people and his friends may be quoted.

Mentone, November 26th, 1889.

MY DEAR MRS. P.,—You have doubtless heard how it has fared with us since that forenoon when you and other true friends saw us leave for this long absence, how we made a most favourable journey and had fine weather at Cannes. Perhaps you may also have heard that somehow, we cannot say exactly how, I had the slightest relapse, and now I write to assure you that I am again prospering. The doctor at Cannes, a Liverpool man, a most skilful and kindly man, agreed exactly with my own doctor in their diagnosis. There is nothing wrong but what care and rest should cure, but he thinks that I have not been quite so careful of my body those last years, as I should have been, and this particular trouble is always a sign that nature is in arms. He insists on great care and quietness, and I mean to follow every direction and do all in my power to regain strength. But you must not think I plead guilty to carelessness in the past: really it is a mistake to say so, for I always thought myself rather hypochondriac—so much are men misunderstood. Before leaving Liverpool I was much hurt by the doctor's directions which concluded, 'and no public work.' It seemed hard, but he was inexorable. 'If I must do something and could not in fact hold my tongue, I might have singing lessons.' After that I felt how useless it was to fight against popular delusions. We met at Cannes a very agreeable London lawyer, and we were thrown a good deal together. He told capital stories about our cleverest judges, and he also tasted some of my anecdotes, and so either through much speaking or otherwise I got a warning. We laid it to heart and made a plan in the trains. You may be interested to have the outlines of the safeguards of silence. Mrs. Watson to sit on my right preserving a stolid face and making one remark of course to show that we are happy tho' married. If the person on my left was a German I must listen to the past participle rattling past like the brake van at the end of a luggage-train, telling one that that marvel of engineering and constructive skill the German sentence is finished—then I was to gently clear my throat and this would be understood to be a German remark in concurrence. After which he would dig the foundations of another edifice. If my neighbour happened to be French then I was at once to attempt that imbecile smile with which an Englishman listens to a Frenchman, it being taken for granted that anything said in such a language must be more or less childish, and to be heard with indulgence, and then when he had made the last flourish I was to say 'oui,' but with reserve, as of one who wishes to take the matter into consideration, and after a little add with emphasis 'oui, oui,' which would ensure another shower of rhetoric. But every plan has to be judged by its success, and ours has only been a partial success. Mrs. Watson and I hardly exchange a word, except outside, when she states her impressions of the scenery and I look. The 'oui' policy succeeded admirably with my neighbour who was an old French doctor, and a trial to his compatriots above him. He was one of those exasperating people who pronounce every word slowly and complete every sentence perfectly, and is didactic from beginning to end. His theme is the climate of the Riviera, and on this he has been expatiating for three days, and there are one or two points still to be taken up. But you can imagine that he is a nice soothing man to be with. His only drawback is that he is stout and at intervals sighs, a real sigh I mean, which affects his neighbourhood. His other neighbour, a German lady, has changed her place, and told me 'I have heart disease, and could not hear those sighs all winter.' I like a quiet, thoughtful man and don't mind. My trial has been with an English widow, touring about with two daughters, who is my *vis-à-vis* and will speak. 'Just think of me here for days, and not one English person to speak to.' It has been as the bursting of a reservoir, and I lie in the track. Her two subjects for choice are Mr. Spurgeon, who lives beside her, and the remarkable and solemn fact that she is the mother of seventeen children. When she announced this one evening in the drawing-room, several foreigners, who just knew what she said, were permanently impressed. They regard her with admiring interest, and the more thoughtful have got sidelight on the secret of our success as a Colonising nation. Personally, however, I have never shared that reverence for population statistics which Mr. Arnold declares a characteristic of the British Philistine. So I chose Mr. Spurgeon and know all about him now, his carriages, homes, top-coats with fur cuffs, and his average diet. Thus I combined pleasure to the mind with profit to the body, and gathered the harvest of a quiet tongue. Our plan, you see, has points, and we made it up between Cannes and Nice, and from Nice we returned and gave ourselves to scenery. By the way, I may mention, altho' I hope not ostentatiously, that we have homes all over the Continent and all in charming places. We have a Schloss on the Rhine, looking down on the bend of the river where the midday sun lights up the sea-green water: a Casa at Florence: upon the Arno from whose upper windows one gets a glimpse of the street where Romola lived and not ten minutes from the Pitti. Then we have a Lodge buried in firs with a background of purple heather at the head of one of the Scotch Lochs, and thence can see the sun go down red behind the Skye hills—when we grow Jacobitish, and Mrs. Watson sings 'Over the Sea to Skye,' and we think of Prince Charlie. Nor must I forget an old Spanish Castle at San-Sebastian to which I rode across from France one spring day, and found to let. It was not in my heart to resist an appeal directed so significantly to English hearts, and so we took possession there and then, and lay in the sun on its tower, with the lizards playing round us as we meditated on the 'grandeur that was Spain.' You envy me, which is natural, but you must not accuse me of extravagance. Those houses are kept up for me without costing us a penny, except the Spanish Castle which is in want of repair. One enjoys without owning. Both art and nature and higher ranges still belong to him who sees their beauty and loves them. I wish I had more meekness, but still I find I do inherit much of the goodness of life and better men go up and down the Promised Land.

But there is one beautiful spot on this Riviera the wrong people possess, and that is Monte Carlo. The situation is most picturesque and the climate warm and genial, and I suppose there is not on earth a fountain of greater misery. One knows when you are coming near the place by the people who come into your carriage. One man travelled from Cannes with us who gave us grave concern. He pulled down the blinds that he might not be disturbed by the scenery: then he sat alternately every thirty seconds on two sides of his door: he sometimes stood for a change. He did sums in his head and then on paper: he forgot some rule and then worried with his hair till he had it again. Had all this happened on the L. and N.-W., we should have left the carriage in order to give him more freedom. But as it was, we only whispered, he is going to Monte Carlo and he is doing his calculations. He was as anxious as if he had been going in for the Indian C.S. Very likely he was cleaned out before we sat down to dinner: I was never so moved to give a tract in my life: 'The Gambler of Monte Carlo: a true story,' or some such thing. As far as one can gather, the upper-class rascaldom of Europe seems to come to a focus there, and unfortunately the place has an unholy attraction for quite respectable people. The German lady with heart disease has just been working a roulette machine in the drawing-room, and showing how you stake your money. She goes to the concerts twice a week, which are very fine and free, and feels bound to gamble a few minutes in return. To-day she lost thirty francs.

Mentone is the other extreme from Monte Carlo. It is, indeed, very different from Cannes or Nice. The place is not countrified: it is simple and homelike. How amusing it is to notice the rivalry between those health resorts. Each depreciates the other and exalts itself. The Cannes hotelkeeper said Mentone was well enough if we must go on. 'Warmer than Cannes? Well, it was, that is why people don't go there. The worst cases only are sent there.' He gave you to understand that Mentone was simply a hospital for incurables. The Mentone man congratulated us on having got away from Cannes. 'Was it not healthy?' 'Well, strong people born and bred there might be able to stand it, but strangers should insure their lives.' Recently we have had fiercely cold weather here: I hinted at the Mistral, the opprobrium of this district, but he repudiated the idea, spoke as if he hardly knew the word, but on my repeating Mistral, recollected there was such a wind, and excused his stupidity, because it did not blow at Mentone. It was a Cannes and Nice wind. As regards the east wind which we now have, he simply denies it—it is a west wind. I expect to hear that it is one of the advantages of Mentone that the east wind is taken round by the west to be modified.

I hope those hotelkeepers may be forgiven: I think they will. It is partly because they have hard, anxious work to get any profit out of a five months' season, with their enormous expenses, and partly out of sheer good nature to cheer invalids. 'Everybody gets well here,' said my man; 'oh, yes, they go home fat and laughing.' I am afraid hardly, but God bless the man's kind heart, for he wanted to cheer up a pale-faced and dejected Englishman. People do progress here, I fancy, for I have seen one or two faces looking better on the promenade since we came. One young man whom we saw in a chair on Tuesday is now fairly on his legs, and we have made up 'The Invalid's Progress: a brief view of Mentone.'

1. Emaciated figure arrives at Station in rugs.
2. He is hurled in bath-chair.
3. Sits on seat on Promenade, shawled and shaded.
4. Walks wrapped up, with stick.
5. Takes two promenades a day with light top-coat.
6. Sits in café hearing band, and drinking Munich beer.
7. Obese figure forces himself into railway carriage and goes home. *Voilà.*

But I see Mr. P., the kindest and most courageous of hearers ever placed by Providence just before the pulpit, looking at the clock. No wonder, I have sadly transgressed, and the worst of it is that I have half a dozen points still untouched. The situation of Mentone—the nature of Italian goats, which is a chapter in natural history—the sardine-fishers landing their nets, one of our day-studies. But I am merciful to those who, in the pathetic phrase of our fathers, 'sit under me.' (Was that intended for humour or was it sheer tragedy?)

Mr. B. considered my last letter as what we call a general epistle, and he read it to the 'saints scattered abroad.' Should you desire to take a good-natured revenge on him, then I have placed a weapon in your hand still longer than his.

We are now looking towards the East, and are planning after a few weeks more here to start for Naples; this must depend on my strength and also confidence that I can make something of the visit to Egypt. It is a little hard to be quiet, but in quietness for a few weeks still is my strength.

But East or West we ever remember with warm heart the friends of that circle round which the last letter went, and from which it would receive that indulgence which has been extended to greater faults than so slight an epistle could contain.—With our warmest regards, believe me, yours most faithfully,

JOHN WATSON.

From Mentone he went to Alassio, from which he writes to a brother-minister who had formerly assisted him at Sefton Park:—

January 4th, 1890.

Your very handwriting raised my spirits, and much more was I cheered by your welcome news and kind words. There are so many letters I must write, and when they are off my hands, I rest from pen and ink. I have never loved them, though they are the marks of my trade, but I would have been writing you if you had not forestalled me. As regards my health, to clear away that disagreeable but inevitable subject, I am holding my own in spite of most trying weather. My general health is good, and there is no active mischief in the lung, but it remains weak and will only very slowly improve. Its condition is that of a healed scar—that must ever be there, but once I am strong will give no trouble, only a clever doctor will always be able to find it. What would now completely cure would be warm weather and fresh air. This I had to some extent up to Christmas. Since then the weather has been so cold and wet, I have been almost confined to the house; now that is how the matter stands. My hope and belief is, that God will allow me to resume work sooner or later; if not, my strength has been given to His service, and all is well. What has done it all, the doctors say, is overwork and laborious public speaking. So. Your account of yourself is most interesting, and everything that concerns you, will ever concern me. You must not be too much cast down by either the intellectual or spiritual deficiencies of your flock. Out of a comparatively small congregation in a manufacturing town, you cannot expect many leaders. Here is a work to do, to teach your young people to love books. You might form a reading society with meetings to speak about books, and help one another. The more informal the better. If you will allow me to compare great things and small, I had one such club in my kitchen at Logiealmond! It did first-rate. 'Tis harder to create spiritual life. We must preach Christ, especially His love and death on the Cross, and pray for the Spirit. My feeling is that a number of our Scots congregations in England are dull and dead. Held together not so much by the Spirit of Christ as by prejudices and 'isms.' But you will be the means of bringing about better things, I do not fear. It is a matter of sincere regret that I cannot officiate at your marriage to one whom I so esteem as your future wife. It had been a very happy day for me as well as you. We shall think of you that day, and beseech for your united lives God's best blessings. If some small token of our friendship should reach Miss ——, I hope it may prove acceptable. I wish we had been at home to choose it.

They are managing wonderfully at Sefton Park, they are so well fed that it will seem short commons when they land in the old pastorate. Mr. —— has shown his entire fitness for his position as Premier and has been well supported. You will sometimes see a trace of an old hand in the magazine.

We are now living in our former home and feel thankful to be here in such bad weather. We spent a quiet Christmas, but received even here upwards of a hundred cards and letters. People are so kind, some of the letters are most touching. One of the best came from Mrs. M., the doorkeeper of the south gallery. It was a charming letter, and told how the servants there had been asking for me; is not that nice? Professor —— of Liverpool and his wife are with us. He is a most interesting man and most modest; I believe he is considered one of the future Faradays of science. Then we have also a young doctor, very nice too, in the house. So we are very learned—not to mention that a Scots Professor, and a Fellow of Trinity College, Cambridge, have been with us for a short time. They are gone. Influenza, I am sorry to say, is now here, and I hope we shall escape it. It would be rather serious for me, I fear, otherwise it is not alarming, but I begin to drive—talking about influenza, I had better stop in time, so with every good wish for the New Year and warmest united regards.—Yours affectionately, JOHN WATSON.

PS.—You did as much good to me as I ever did to you. Alas, no orange blossom now!

He came home in April much refreshed, and resumed his labours with a happy heart. The holiday had done its work. For years after his strength was never seriously impaired. His retrospect of this incident may be seen in a letter which he addressed later to his friend, the Rev. Dr. Aked, then of Pembroke Baptist Church, now of New York. Dr. Aked was then ordered abroad for the same malady:—

TO DR. AKED

May 8*th*, 1893.

Dear Dr. Aked,—When you left for the Riviera I imagined that you were on the high road to complete recovery, and I trust that you were on that way, but I learned with regret and some anxiety from this morning's paper that you are not making that rapid progress which we all desire.

As I cannot call at your foreign residence, tho' I should dearly love to do so, for selfish as well as friendly reasons I must fall back upon a letter, and since I cannot write a long letter without my hand trembling and my writing is bad enough at any time, I am falling back on the machine, which really fills my friends with gratitude. First let me begin with exhortation, for as Professor Davidson used to say, 'preaching is a bad habit, and if you once get into it you may never be able to get out of it,' but on this occasion mine is to be like the speech of Barnabas, 'comfortable exhortation.' Do not consider that a strange thing has befallen you, for no man can do as much as you have done, and put yourself so thoroughly into your work, without suffering both in body and in soul. So far as I can judge watching your career in Liverpool, you have done what every man has not, you have given yourself, and it is one thing to make speeches and preach sermons in a state of safe detachment from the subject, and another to speak from the marrow of your bones. A man pays a price who does this, and doubtless also he obtains his reward as you have done, in the impression you have produced upon so large a multitude, and the confidence with which they follow you.

My next head is, that this breakdown will not, please God, do you any permanent injury, but be rather in the end a help. Some fourteen years ago I had myself a sudden and unexpected breakdown of a serious character, and in an unexpected direction. Having passed many examinations at the hands of doctors, and being considered an absolutely sound man, and having also a perfect family history, and having come to the age of thirty-nine, one of my lungs gave way. I had not many symptoms as they call it, nor did I suffer much, but things looked rather bad, and I went from home for six months. Since that time I have done harder work than at any other period in my working career, and except a brief attack of influenza I have never been ill since in any shape or form, till in a moment of inexcusable folly I took an office, the Moderatorship of our Church, for which I was absolutely unsuited, and since then I have been suffering from insomnia, nervousness, and an enormous access of stupidity, in which I have discovered resources of dullness which even my past experiences never prepared me for. Still that attack passed off and left no disability.

Wherefore cheer up, and take courage.

Passing on, as the old preachers used to say (it was a weary passing often) consider what a great work you have done in Liverpool. You have proved that an empty building in an unpromising quarter can be filled to the doors, and kept filled from year to year by preaching, and this is an instructive achievement in the present day. You sometimes take a position with which I do not agree, just as I on my part belong very largely to that middle school, which used to be called the Moderate School in Scotland, which I have no doubt you would be tempted to criticise, but I have ever believed that you have delivered a true and kindly message from God on the greatest questions of life and righteousness, and I have regarded with admiration the thoroughness of your teaching and the masculine vigour of your style. In ordinary circumstances I would not say such things, for they would be in doubtful taste, but I do not see why in time of sickness, one should not offer to his brother such poor cordial of respect and esteem as it is in his power to bring.

And now to bring the sermon to a close with practical advice, let me speak faithfully to two classes. First to Mrs. Aked, exhorting her to keep jealous watch over you, and to secure you in a state of absolute idleness, to insist upon you eating and drinking to a shameful extent, to prevent you bothering about letters, whether they be taxes or sermons (from doddering old ministers), and to be prouder than ever of her husband, who has come back for a little wounded from the front.

Next, and finally to yourself, that you be quite sure your illness is in the plan of God, and that it is an immense opportunity not for reading nor even thinking, but simply absolute resting, that you have deserved your furlough, and that after the doctors have passed you again (desperate rascals but going to take a front seat in the next world in spite of us all) you will join the regiment again, where they are keeping up the good fight, in which victors and vanquished rejoice together.

'One word more,' as those gray-haired deceivers used to say, when we thought the sermon was done, let no answer be sent to this letter, which is written simply to assure you that a fellow-minister in Liverpool is thinking about you and praying that you may be soon restored to health, and that in the meantime, the grace of God be exceeding abundant in your experience.—Believe me, with sincere regard, yours faithfully, JOHN WATSON.

CHAPTER IX

BESIDE THE BONNIE BRIER BUSH

For fifteen years Watson had been steadily building up his congregation and his influence in the city of Liverpool. Though he had been in the highest degree successful, he was not much known outside of Liverpool and his own church and denomination. He had made no attempt at authorship. The only article he had published was a brief biographical sketch of his friend and neighbour, the late Dr. Alexander Macleod of Birkenhead. This appeared in the *Sunday Magazine*. I must say something about the circumstances under which he began to write for the press, especially as he, with his habitual generosity, has greatly exaggerated my share in the matter. As editor of the *Expositor*, I wrote to Watson somewhere about 1890 asking for an occasional contribution. At that time my acquaintance with him was extremely slight. He replied saying that he was a hard-working preacher and pastor, and had no time for learned research, but that he had thought of publishing some religious booklets similar to *The Greatest Thing in the World* and other very popular little volumes issued by Professor Henry Drummond. Nothing came of this, however, and the subject was not renewed till two or three years later, when I wrote to Watson again, and suggested that he should write some papers for the *Expositor* on the Leading Ideas of Jesus.

This interested him, and he came up to London and stayed a few days at my house. The *Expositor* articles were arranged for, and were afterwards published in a volume entitled *The Mind of the Master*. I was so much struck with the racy stories and character-sketches with which Watson regaled us, that I suggested he should make some articles out of them. The idea had never struck him, and was at first unwelcome. But I kept on persuading him. I had no success till I was accompanying him to the station, when I pressed the matter on him. Just before he said good-bye he promised to try, and in a few days the first sketch arrived. It was clever, but disappointing. It told how the schoolmaster went to Drumsheugh with the purpose of inducing him to support a promising boy at the University. It described how, under the influence of succeeding tumblers of toddy, Drumsheugh's heart gradually warmed to the idea, till at last he gave his promise. I returned this to Watson stating objections. He sent a second sketch, also more or less unsatisfactory. Then he sent the first four chapters of what is now known as *The Bonnie Brier Bush* complete, and I knew on reading them that his popularity was assured. The first was published in the *British Weekly* of November 2, 1893, under the title, 'How we Carried the News to Whinnie Knowe.' It attracted attention at once, and the impression was deepened as the stories were continued. Almost immediately the *nom-de-plume* which he selected, Ian Maclaren, was widely recognised. He took the Gaelic form of his own Christian name John, and the surname of his mother. There was very little mystification about the authorship. His own friends knew the tales they had heard from him. Dr. George Adam Smith sent him a post-card on the appearance of the first sketch, 'Bravo, Ian Maclaren!' and was answered by another post-card containing the words, 'Bravo, Higher Criticism!' Watson gave extraordinary care and labour to the construction of his first short stories. He said himself:—

Each one was turned over in my mind for months before I put pen to paper. It took a prodigious amount of labour before I even had a story formed in my head. Then I blocked it out at one sitting. Then the thing was put aside while I went over and over in my mind each detail, each line of dialogue, each touch of description, determining on the proper place, attitude, share, colour, and quality of each bit, so that the whole might in the end be a unit, and not a bundle of parts. By and by came the actual writing with the revision and the correction which accompanies and follows. The actual composition of the *Brier Bush* occupied fifteen months. They were the more difficult because in every case the character is revealed in dialogue exclusively. It is different when the writer has a plot, because then there is something definite to hold the attention, and one can dash ahead, but I was compelled to make slow progress.

In his later work he did not take such pains. His life was too much crowded for careful preparation and revision. But in *Beside the Bonnie Brier Bush*, and the volume that followed it, he was at his very best, drawing upon the fresh fountain of his recollections, and sparing no pains with his style. The sketches were published under the title *Beside the Bonnie Brier Bush* in October 1894. They were instantly welcomed, both in this country and in America, as very few first books have been welcomed. My friend, Mr. Frank Dodd, the head of the great firm of Messrs. Dodd, Mead and Co., in New York, was persuaded by me during a long afternoon to publish the book (the contents of which he had not seen), but he had no expectation that it would have a large American sale. The public, however, was ready. The great success of Mr. J. M. Barrie's stories—success achieved against a combination of difficulties which some of the shrewdest publishers judged to be insuperable—had paved the way for others. Along with Mr. Barrie and Mr. Crockett, Ian Maclaren was dubbed a member of the Kailyard School. There was in reality hardly anything in common among these writers save that they all wrote on Scottish life and character, and also on Scottish religion.

A few figures will best indicate the popularity of *Beside the Bonnie Brier Bush.* In Great Britain 256,000 copies have been sold in various editions; in America the sale has amounted to 484,000, and this exclusive of an incomplete pirated edition which was circulated in enormous numbers at a low price. The critics of *Beside the Bonnie Brier Bush* were friendly, and even enthusiastic. I have not been able to trace a single unfavourable review. The *Spectator* published a second review because the first was not cordial enough. Queen Victoria was an admiring reader. I have before me letters from many of the most eminent men of the day expressing their admiration. Those from medical men are particularly striking, and I may venture to quote a few lines from Sir Dyce Duckworth :—

December 27th, 1894.

Ian Maclaren's book is most touching and interesting. If you know the writer you may tell him his writings pull at my heart-strings, and there is an atmosphere of Heaven in them, which is very refreshing in these days when good men are wasting so much time over trifles. This man is a modern prophet, and I have hardly read anything I have liked better since I was steeped in Charles Kingsley's writings. One needs one's Scottish blood to enjoy it properly. The pure Englishman will take it in with more difficulty. DYCE DUCKWORTH.

Ian Maclaren, as we may now call him, had a very hearty friendship for the then Bishop of Liverpool, the stout-minded English Evangelical, better known as J. C. Ryle. Ryle, who was himself master of a powerful and interesting style, wrote as follows:—

FROM THE BISHOP OF LIVERPOOL

December 29th, 1894.

DEAR MR. WATSON,—You must let an old minister thank you very much for 'Ian Maclaren's' book; it has touched my heart, and brought more tears to my eyes than anything I have read for a long time. May God bless your pen, and make use of it for His own glory.

Accept every good wish for 1895.—Yours most sincerely,

J. C. LIVERPOOL.

TO MRS. STEPHEN WILLIAMSON

November 1st, 1894.

DEAR MRS. WILLIAMSON,—From a letter this morning I learn that the book cannot be obtained in Edinburgh for love or money. This is nonsense, for the new edition is out, but it shows how good a thing it is to have the head of a Salon on one's side, as used to happen in France. Hope the book will not make Mr. Gladstone weep for his eye's sake. The *Daily Chronicle* reviewer locked himself into a room.—Your affectionately, JOHN WATSON.

I am permitted by Mrs. Stephen Williamson to give a letter in which she records Mr. Gladstone's talk about the book.

FROM MRS. STEPHEN WILLIAMSON

December 28th, 1894.

My dear Mr. Watson,—I was at Hawarden yesterday at luncheon. I was in the library of the house where Mr. Gladstone was busily correcting proofs for America, and had heartily welcomed me in, saying, 'you will excuse and I shall not know you are in the room.' This with a genial smile and merry twinkle of his splendid eyes. I ventured among the books to ask Mrs. Drew if her father had begun the *Brier Bush* yet? 'Oh! dear yes, here it is all marked over with pencil, he is perfectly enchanted with it and has so much enjoyed it, I can't tell you how much.' At the same moment, taking up the well-known book, and then saying, 'Ah, this is another copy which some one has sent him and he has given it to me; this is mine.' I took it up and found the paper inside saying it came from Hodder and Stoughton. We could not lay our hands on the original without making a fuss, but I would like to get back that marked copy I gave him. Before we came away he came into the drawing-room to ask me about two Scots ministers, their histories, etc., and I then put in my word, and asked if he liked the *Bonnie Brier Bush.* He was a little perplexed at first, and very politely but gravely said, 'I am sorry, I am afraid I have not yet found time for the pleasure of reading it, but there is a book by a countryman of yours that I have been immensely delighted with. There are several sketches in it, many of them very beautiful, but one in particular about a country doctor.' 'Oh, that's my book,' said I. 'Ah, is it really? I am so glad: of course I have read it with great delight. I did not recognise the name, pardon me, but I have had very great enjoyment in that book. The papers are not all equal, but it is a very fine book, and there has never been anything written finer than the sketch of that country doctor.'

'Don't you also like the "Lad o' Pairts"?'

'Oh, very much, very much, most touching, most true and beautiful.'

We told him about your big rich congregation, the mission churches begun, continued, and flourishing. Also adopted the language of . . . as to Mr. Watson as a man. 'I can well believe it all, he must be a fine man indeed who can write like that. Is he Free Church or Established or U.P.?' I explained as well as I could the mystery of the English Presbyterian Church, but I did not tell him you were a Tory. Wasn't that kind of me now? —Ever yours most truly, ANNIE WILLIAMSON.

TO MRS. STEPHEN WILLIAMSON

December 29th, 1894.

DEAR MRS. WILLIAMSON,—Many thanks for your kind note with Mr. Gladstone's welcome approbation. It is wonderful that he finds time for reading stories.

By the same post had letter from working man, whose sweetheart had given the book to him on Christmas Eve with a pair of socks. Also a note praying that on their marriage they might live like the people in the Glen.

My best wishes for you all at this time.

JOHN WATSON.

I add other letters addressed to Mrs. Stephen Williamson at this time.

TO MRS. STEPHEN WILLIAMSON

May 28th, 1894.

MY DEAR MRS. WILLIAMSON,—I can only imagine what some obscure poet of the third order may have felt when he got favourable notice from Browning, but that is something like my state of exaltation at receiving so kind a note about my trifles from one of the experts in Scottish art.

If my efforts to represent Scottish life please you, I have some hope.

Dr. Nicoll insists on a book in Autumn: I hope L. will order copies for the Liverpool Presbytery: With such help of charitable people it may succeed.

The 'Sermon-Taster' will be followed up by the 'Collapse of Mrs. MacFadyen' this week. One of the Highland brethren was too much for her. Unless Dr. Nicoll be afraid.

I often think of you, and if I had one hour to myself when in London would do myself the pleasure of calling. But I have to drudge all the day, and half the night.—Yours faithfully,
JOHN WATSON.

TO THE SAME

January 11th, 1895.

DEAR MRS. WILLIAMSON,—The success of the book will be divided between two, you for Great Britain and Colonies, and Mr. Andrew Carnegie for the United States.

Yesterday I had an enthusiastic letter from the famous ironmaster, inviting me to Cluny where he occupies the fastness of the MacPhersons: To-day yours comes with the staff of *Punch* at your heels. Well, well, it is good to have friends: I wish I deserved them.

All this trouble on your part is most friendly and I feel

it very deeply. Le Gallienne, Ashcroft Noble, and Lucy all have asked to see me in London, and another set have put up my name for the Savile Club. Don't tell dear Mrs. G., for I'm really the doucest of men.

TO THE SAME

January 29th, 1895.

DEAR MRS. WILLIAMSON,—The thought of Rhodes Africanus planting the *Brier Bush* over the new South African Empire is inspiring. Instead of the (fill in African Botany) shall come up the Brier, and 'instead of Matabele shall be Drumsheugh.' Sounds well. I have always regarded Rhodes as a hero—an Elizabethan Englishman: This willingness to read classical literature convinces me that I was right. Can anything be done with the Czar? He is a well-intentioned young man and ought to be encouraged. But these are matters I must leave in your hands.—Yours faithfully,

JOHN WATSON.

For a special reason I give a letter from the late James Ashcroft Noble, a critic whom many of us still remember with affection and esteem. It was the beginning of a friendship between Noble and Watson.

FROM MR. JAMES ASHCROFT NOBLE

October 10th, 1894.

MY DEAR SIR,—Although I am a stranger to you I think real gratitude or rather the expression of it may be reckoned among the few rights of strangerhood, and therefore I make no apology at all for telling you how largely I am your debtor, for the high and rare delight given me by the

Brier Bush. I read the book more than a week ago, and felt impelled to write at once and express my profound obligation, but just then I was simply overwhelmed with work, and found myself unable to write anything in addition to the review which appears in the *Daily Chronicle*, and which you will probably see before you receive this note. Of the inadequacy of that review as a rendering of the total impression stamped by the volume no one can be more conscious than myself. It deals merely with its more obvious qualities of pathos and humour and leaves untouched, or all but untouched, the penetrating, spiritual and imaginative insight which gives to the work so much of its momentum. Only one disturbing thought mingles with my delight. In 1892 I lived for nine months in Upper Parliament Street, Liverpool, and I believe that some friends of mine were friends or acquaintances of yours also. I shall never cease to regret the ignorance which prevented me from seeking the pleasure of meeting and conversing with you, but I hope that some happy day may bring me this gratification.—Yours most heartily and gratefully, JAMES ASHCROFT NOBLE.

Beside the Bonnie Brier Bush sold on its own merits, apart from advertisements and reviews. The public somehow got to know of it, and soon almost every one was reading it. There is no great mystery about its success. Charles Reade's recipe for a good novel as given to David Christie Murray ran thus: 'Make 'em laugh, make 'em cry, make 'em wait.' Ian Maclaren made his readers laugh and cry, and when the matter is considered this will appear no small feat.

He was avowedly a sentimentalist in literature,

and it is from this point of view that his work in fairness must be considered. M. Texte, in his admirable and sympathetic study of Rousseau, has treated the whole question of sentimentalism in literature with masterly skill and insight. His analysis applies to all sentimentalists, from the least to the greatest. He begins with the flower and crown of sentimental novels, the incomparable *Clarissa Harlowe.* He tells us how when we first read that epoch-making book, curiosity is stirred after a few pages. A vague atmosphere of love floats like a half-evaporated perfume from the dimming pages. The names take on colour, the shadows start into being, the old memories live and move before your eyes. Hours pass, and still you read on, your emotions stirred, and as it were rocked by the rhythm of the long-vanished existence. At one part it all becomes deeply pathetic. Then there is keen agony; a cry of despair rises from the depths of the past. 'What is this story to me and to you?' you ask—brushing away a tear as you say so. If realism is the art of giving the impression of actual life, Richardson is the greatest of realists.

But though Richardson's achievement remains unsurpassed, Rousseau made great and definite contributions to the literature of sentiment. In the first place, he provided a framework for the picture of life. The novel of Richardson's time was a drama without stage scenery. Rousseau felt this. Bernardin de Saint Pierre tells us that he found fault with Richardson's work as a whole, because he did not attach the memory of his readers to any spot the scenery of which we should have liked to recognise. It is impossible, he says, to think of Achilles without at the same time seeing the plains of Troy. We follow Æneas along the coasts of Latium. Virgil is not only the painter of love and war: he is also the painter of his native land. This characteristic of genius is lacking in Richardson. Rousseau places the history of sorrows and raptures in a memorable frame. Mr. Barrie and Ian Maclaren do the same. There are certain figures whom we shall always see upon the brae in Thrums; the farm-houses in Drumtochty are peopled by friends. Nature herself is brought in as one of the characters, and plays a great part in the drama. Their passionate attachment to the Glen is one of the chief charms of Ian Maclaren's characters. He knows the misery of the dispossessed in Scotland, of those who have been driven from

> The place that we cling to, puir simple auld fules,
> Of oor births and oor bridals, oor mirths and oor dules,
> Where the wee bits o' bairnies lie cauld in the mools.

There are no more beautiful passages in his idylls than those which describe the sun shining on the river below the mill, the caller air blowing down the glen, the narrow road through pinks and moss roses to the dear old door, the place where the birch bends over the burn and the primroses grow under its shadows, the corner of the kirkyard where a hardy rose-tree has opened the last flower of the year.

Under the guidance of Rousseau, the sentimentalists have turned to humble life, and have glorified love. Lowell has said that the clearing away of the woods scants the streams, and in the same way civilisation has dried up some feeders that help to swell the current of individual and personal force. In Drumtochty there were few events. The ploughing match, the school examination, the winter lecture where an inhabitant of the glen moved a vote of thanks, and the Sabbath day, ranked as the most important of outward things. These are admirably described in the idylls. Ian Maclaren had that taste for details and that faculty for exactly observing little facts which make such passages vital. And if the outward is little, the inward is great. The stories are full of love, and the author gives a deep lyric accent to his praise of the affection between son and mother, between sister and brother, between friend and friend. Dr. Maclure sums it all up: 'Wark comes first, an' the fechtin' awa' wi' oor cauld land, an' wringin' eneuch out o't tae pay for rent and livin' pits smeddum (spirit) into a man. Syne comes love tae maist o's an' teaches some selfish, shallow cratur tae play the man for a wumman's sake; an' laist comes sorrow, that gars the loudest o's tae haud his peace.' But all the stories illustrate Lacordaire's great saying that love has but one word to utter, and while it is ever saying it, it never repeats it. To Ian Maclaren, as to all true sentimentalists (I am using the word in its nobler sense) love is an irresistible need of the soul. With all its long procession of troubles, anxieties, and sorrows, love is the highest and deepest manifestation of immortal being.

A parallel of profound interest is to be found in the place assigned to religion by the older sentimentalists and the new. The position of Ian Maclaren seems to be the same as that of Rousseau. Rousseau always professed to be religious. He thought that there was a certain want of moral depth and grandeur wherever religion was left out, and he would probably have said that this was necessary, for without religion the loftiest reaches of conduct were a form of insanity. At the close of his life Rousseau rejoiced that he had remained faithful to the prejudices of his childhood, and that he had continued a Christian *up to the point of membership of the Universal Church.* The words precisely describe the religion that is glorified in Ian Maclaren's books. He is not unjust to Evangelicalism, and one of his noblest characters is Burnbrae, a Free Church elder. But he lingers with most love and understanding on the Moderates—Drumsheugh, Dr. Davidson, Dr. Maclure, and Jamie Soutar. Maclure, who has the best means of knowing, declares that if there be a judgment and books be opened, there will be one for Drumtochty, and the bravest page in it will be Drumsheugh's. There is very little sympathy with modernity; the ministers who talk about two Isaiahs are laughed at, but there is just as little sympathy for extreme Evangelicalism. Plymouthism is treated as hypocrisy; high Calvinism as almost too monstrous to be mentioned; while the particular forms in which the religion of revivals expresses itself are described with evident dislike. In this Ian Maclaren differed from his friend George Macdonald, whose books are full of dogma, and have suffered in consequence. But he is with Rousseau who was wont to insist that the Christianity which appeals only to the moral conscience is alone conformable to the Spirit of Christ. Conduct, character—these were the great results and tests of true religion.

It is a fair question, 'Have we true pictures in these idylls? Is it thus and thus that people act or ever acted in a Scotch parish?' It must be remembered that idylls do not pretend to give a full chronicle of life. They try to seize the moments at which the hidden beauty of the soul leaps into vision. They do not take in the whole circumference of truth, and they do not profess to take it in. But they include a far wider area than is ever compassed by cynicism. And surely it is a great and precious gift to be able to detect the divine in the carnal, and to recognise angels in the disguise in which we always entertain them. It is much to be able to see and to show the perennial nobleness and heroism of the homeliest human nature. No doubt, if these only are described, the stories may and must cloy. But there was in Ian Maclaren the saving sense of humour. He had very keen eyes, and he let us see at times that few things escaped them. He could have written a realistic chronicle at which his critics would have started; he could if he pleased, and we believe he did in many cases give us *nec deus, nec lupus, sed homo*; but it was his avowed aim and end to bring out the idyllic element in life, and he thus helped to slake the eternal thirst of our nature for those waters of the ideal that glimmer before us and still before us.

Did Ian Maclaren's idylls wholly escape the dangers of sentimentalism? This is a question which cannot be answered in the affirmative. No doubt a disproportionate space is given to descriptions of deathbeds. The feelings are deliberately and cruelly harrowed by an accumulation of pathetic incidents and words. Watson himself was well aware of this. All he had to say in reply was: 'We ministers rarely see the brighter side of life. We are tolerated at weddings I admit; we are more at home at funerals. People do not ask a minister to share family festivities. He most often hears painful disclosures, and meets death from day to day. This is apt to have a very sobering effect on his mind.' It will not be supposed that I am trying to fix Ian Maclaren's place in literature, or to compare him in point of power with the great names I have mentioned. But I have aimed at showing that something is common to the whole school of sentimentalists. The worth of Ian Maclaren's contribution will be determined by time, and when all abatement is made, there is that in his work which may perhaps endure. Anyhow, no one can possibly attach less importance to his books than the author did himself. On the side of his ministerial work he was very sensitive. Criticisms from members of his own church or congregation hit him very hard; for unless the charges were outrageously exaggerated, his great modesty made him doubtful whether he had not been found wanting. Any opposition from those of his own fellowship plunged him into the deepest depression. Nothing upheld him like kindly words from his people. But speaking after a close intimacy, I can say that I never saw him either depressed or elated by any criticisms of his books save on one occasion when it was suggested that he had not taken sufficient pains. He never looked at his books after they were published; he never allowed them to be spoken of in his family circle. In private conversation even with those concerned in their production he seemed to shun the subject, and often had to be forced on to a discussion of business details. In the inevitable reaction which followed his great popularity, some critics heartily abused his stories. This abuse did not wound him. If his books were praised without restraint, and if his name was ranked with that of Scott, he chuckled and reached out a hand for his waste-paper basket; if, on the other hand, someone had criticised him unmercifully, he usually agreed quite genuinely with the sentiments of the writer, and put his review in his scrap-book. I never saw him show the faintest resentment at any purely literary criticism. The fact is that he looked upon literature as a mere diversion from the actual work of his life, and did not consent either to stand or to fall by it. He used to speak with a kind of humorous perplexity about the fact that Ian Maclaren was better known than John Watson. Even in the first blaze of his popularity, his head was never turned. 'Were I a young man,' he would say, 'I might be lifted, but this literary fame has come to me in middle life, and I know how to estimate it.' He was amazed by the success of the *Bonnie Brier Bush*. 'A cheerful blaze,' he once remarked, and added quietly, 'while it lasts.'

His first book *Beside the Bonnie Brier Bush*, published in 1894, was succeeded by *The Days of*

Auld Lang Syne, partly reprinted from *Blackwood* and other magazines in 1895. The two books are in reality one, and should go together. By this time his great popularity had crowded his life with engagements of every kind, and he was not able to do his literary work in quietness, as he had done it at first. All his other volumes were written under pressure, and show signs of it. But his third volume, *Kate Carnegie and those Ministers*, though not successful as a novel, contains much of his very best work. On this point I may quote a letter from the New York dramatic critic, Mr. William Winter:—

January 31st, 1897.

I shall always prize the book that you have sent to me, and I shall always remember you with affection. When reading *Kate Carnegie*, I have been especially impressed with its insight into Scots character, both by delineation and suggestion, with its many flashes of humour, its felicity of description, its extraordinary freshness of spirit, and the grace with which it produces artistic effects, by perfectly simple means. I was especially pleased with the character of Doctor Saunderson, and for me the story struck twelve on page 201, at the old man's night of prayer for the happiness of his young friend. The feeling is pathetic beyond words. I shall read now *The Days of Auld Lang Syne*. Major Pond has very kindly assured me of your safe arrival home, and he has sent back the books in which you did me the honour to write, and has given me a portrait of you in a pretty little gilt frame, which now adorns my study. You have left a delightful memory in America, and your visit will be attended with long results of good; I wish you every blessing.

Kate Carnegie, published in 1897, was followed by *Afterwards and other Stories*. The title story is intensely pathetic, and provoked much criticism. Elizabeth Stuart Phelps wrote of it with unstinted admiration. He himself was inclined to prize it above most of his writings. There followed *Young Barbarians*, a book for boys, published in 1901. It was cordially received, and had a great circulation. Latterly he became almost morbidly anxious to comply with every invitation addressed to him, and no fewer than four of his books, two of them books of fiction, appeared after his death. These were *St. Jude's*, a book of Glasgow stories, and *Graham of Claverhouse*, his first regular novel and his last. To *Claverhouse* Watson gave much hard work. He was familiar with the history of the period, and it is admitted that his construction shows great skill. It is a serious and important work, though he himself was conscious that there was not enough dialogue in it, and that the plot was not skilfully handled. It was an indication, however, of what he might have done in new fields if his life had been spared. I shall have occasion to touch separately on the theological books he published under his own name. In addition to these he wrote many articles and stories in newspapers and magazines which have not been collected.

The effect of the publication of *The Bonnie Brier Bush* on the manner of his life was very great. He became almost suddenly one of the best-known men in this country, and in America. His table was crowded every day by requests for his services—requests to which he responded with prodigal expenditure of energy.

In 1896 Watson received the degree of Doctor of Divinity from the University of St. Andrews. Very shortly after the offer had been received, Professor Taylor wrote on behalf of his Alma Mater, the University of Edinburgh, asking him whether he was pledged to receive the degree from St. Andrews, or whether he was still open to receive it from his own University. Watson felt bound to accept the degree first offered to him, but was much gratified to know that his Alma Mater desired to count him among her Doctors of Divinity.

FROM PROFESSOR TAYLOR

February 18*th*, 1896.

Rev. and dear Sir,—It was reported to-day at a meeting of our D.D. Committee, that the University of St. Andrews had resolved to offer the degree of D.D. for your acceptance.

Our Committee have been agreed on your name for some little time back, but do not report to the Senators till the 29th.

In the circumstances I am instructed by the Committee to ascertain whether you are already pledged to receive the degree from St. Andrews, or whether you are still open to receive it from this University, in which latter case the Committee would nominate you to the Senators on the 29th.

The Committee had quite counted on having you on their list, and had no idea that St. Andrews was likely to be beforehand. In any case it may gratify you to know that your old University desired to count you among her Doctors of Divinity. Kindly oblige by an early reply to say how you stand, and believe me, sincerely yours,

M. C. Taylor,
Dean Faculty Divinity.

His first great journey was to America, where in 1896 he undertook a great lecturing tour. This was an event so important in his life that a special chapter must be given to it.

CHAPTER X

FIRST TOUR IN AMERICA

THE popularity of *Beside the Bonnie Brier Bush* and *The Days of Auld Lang Syne* made a great difference in Watson's position. He became well known to the British and the American public. His services as a speaker were demanded from all quarters. In 1896 he arranged with the well-known American lecture-manager, the late Major J. B. Pond, to make a tour in America. Mrs. Watson accompanied him, and the three months that followed were perhaps the busiest and most exciting of all his life.

Lecturing has been dignified in America by such men as Emerson. Looking forward to his work on the platform, Emerson wrote to Carlyle: 'I am always haunted with brave dreams of what might be accomplished in the lecture-room—so free and so unpretending a platform—a Delos not yet made fast. I imagine an eloquence of infinite variety, rich as conversation can be, with anecdote, joke, tragedy, epics and pindarics, argument and confession.' Emerson's own literary work is largely determined by the needs of the lecture. The lecture had to fill an hour and to be vivid, varied, picturesque and stimulating, or the audience would begin to tire before the end. It is told of Horace Greeley that once, travelling with Henry Ward Beecher, he passed a country town and said: 'I had once a successful lecture there.'

'What do you call a successful lecture?'

'Why, more people stayed in than went out.'

Major Pond, a shrewd and practised observer, has given his impressions of Watson as he appeared at the beginning of his journey. 'Dr. Watson is a tall, straight, square-shouldered, deep-chested man of middle age, with a large, compact, round, and well-balanced head, thinly thatched with brown and greyish hair, well-moulded refined features that bear the impress of kindly shrewdness, intellectual sagacity, and spiritual clearness, tempered, too, with a mingled sense of keen humour and grave dignity. The eyes are open, fine, and clear in expression, and thoughtful and observant to a controlling degree.' Mr. Pond also comments on the alertness and force of Watson's movements. In his full vigour he often reminded me of Mr. Chamberlain in the keenness of his glance, his quickness, and his decisive energy. Mr. Pond's opinion of his oratorical powers is given thus: 'His voice is excellent, because its tones express the feeling to be conveyed. It is skilfully used, with fine inflections and tonal shadings that give emphasis and delicacy to his delivery. His mobile mouth easily lends itself to vocal changes. He is not an orator in the usual sense of the word, but he is a speaker who readily holds an audience to the last moment.'

Before commencing his work with Major Pond Watson delivered at Yale University the Lyman Beecher course of lectures on Preaching. These discourses were afterwards published in a volume called *The Cure of Souls*. They contain much autobiographical matter slightly disguised. Watson delivered his lectures to the Yale students extempore, and delighted them with his humour, while he moved them by his seriousness. Yale University, from which he received the degree of Doctor of Divinity, is one of the first Universities in America, and Watson was greatly impressed by its stately surroundings and by the ability and the courtesy of its professors.

I have before me Major Pond's programme of Watson's lectures. It includes ninety-six engagements between October 1 and December 16, 1896. The welcome of America was so generous, frank, and universal that to find a parallel men had to go back to the days of Charles Dickens. Pond, a man of unrivalled experience, said that he saw more happy faces while accompanying him than any other man was privileged to see in the same length of time. During every one of his ninety-six lectures Watson had as large audiences of men and women as could be crowded into the largest public halls in the principal cities of the United States and Canada. For the most part, he gave readings from his own books, but whether he gave readings or lectures the result was the same.

At times the strain almost broke Mrs. Watson lown, but she faced the ordeal bravely. As for Watson, he never seemed to flag. Hardships, delays, and difficulties were encountered with the utmost good nature. Between the lecturer and his manager a strong affection grew up. Both had the constant exhilaration of unvaried success. It would be vain to attempt any detailed record of their experiences. Suffice it to say that everywhere Scotsmen greeted them with unrestrained enthusiasm. But others were equally cordial. From the public men of America, men like Mr. Cleveland, Mr. Carnegie, and Mr. Roosevelt—from the ministers of all denominations—from the leading men and women of letters, Watson had the most flattering tokens of goodwill and admiration. The Presidential election was going on, and the contest between M'Kinley and Bryan was very keen, but this had no effect on the popularity of the lectures. Pond, however, thought it well to fill in the early portion of the tour in Canada, and he noticed the air of pride which Watson and his wife showed as soon as they knew they were in the Queen's dominions. They had a great reception in Canada. At Ottawa the lecture was delivered for a clergyman of the Anglican Church in the Knox Presbyterian Church. Sir Wilfrid Laurier, the Premier of Canada, who is a Roman Catholic, presided. The incident pleased Watson. 'Isn't this a wonderful country? Think of it; I, a Scotch minister, have given readings for a clergyman of the Church of England, in a John Knox Presbyterian Church, introduced by a Roman Catholic!' Watson had great pleasure in the blithe spirit of the West. He liked to think that in the great new country the boy nature predominates among the men to the end of their lives.

At Oberlin, where Watson was the guest of the College Dean, the election returns had brought the news of a M'Kinley triumph, and the students' enthusiasm knew no bounds. They surrounded the house where Dr. Watson was staying, built a number of bonfires, and remained there most of the night, shouting 'What's the matter with M'Kinley? *He's all right!*' The day after the election when they reached Cleveland, which is only seven miles from M'Kinley's home, they found the whole population hoarse. The streets were covered with papers, old boxes and barrel-hoop irons, ashes, and embers of bonfires, and hardly a soul was to be seen at ten o'clock in the morning. They were used up. In registering, Watson asked the clerk of the hotel, 'What's the matter with M'Kinley?' and he got it good and strong: '*He's all right!*' Everybody in the room and in the vicinity shouted.

At Pittsburg Watson was met by Andrew Carnegie, one of the warmest admirers of *The Bonnie Brier Bush*, one of his staunchest friends to the last. He had two audiences of some three thousand people.

At Philadelphia, at Washington, at Baltimore where he was the guest of President Gilman of Johns Hopkins University, and especially at Boston where he was the guest of Mrs. James T. Fields, Watson had overflowing audiences. The culmination of his success, however, was the dinner given to him by the Lotos Club at New York before his departure. On that occasion Watson gave an address which is worth reprinting as a deliberate expression of his attitude to America.

Mr. President, and Gentlemen of the Lotos Club:—Your President has referred to Bohemia, and has indicated that he thinks there will be struck up an alliance between Scotland and Bohemia—on first sight, one of the most unlikely alliances that ever could be consummated. The President no doubt has many things in his eye, and when we remember the careless garb of a Bohemian and the kilt of Scotland; when we remember a Bohemian's tendency to live, if he can, in a good-natured way upon his neighbours, and the tendency of my respected ancestors to take any cattle that they could see; and when also we remember that a Bohemian's sins are all atoned for by his love of letters, and that all the hardness and uncouthness of Scotland may well deserve to be passed over because no country has ever loved knowledge or scholarship more than Scotland—I declare the President is predicting a most harmonious marriage.

Your kindness, gentlemen, is only crowning the great kindness which I have received during the past months—a kindness which I never expected, and a kindness which I am fully conscious I have never merited. Were I a lad of twenty-five, I declare it would be dangerous, for after the audiences that have been good enough to listen to me, and the favour I have received, also at the hands of the distinguished men of letters, I declare, if I were twenty-five I might be confused about my position. But, gentlemen, when one receives as much kindness as one has in America, it doesn't—if you will excuse in this most cultured club an expression not quite within the range of literature—it doesn't swell one's head. But, gentlemen, it does something better; it swells one's heart.

Any man who has only entered the republic of letters within a few years, and who is fully conscious of his imperfections and has never counted on attaining to any great standard of art, through his slowness in beginning and through the exigencies of his position, can yet obtain the favourable ear of the public simply because he deals with humanity. Humanity will add what is not possible to men richly endowed with the spirit of letters alone; it will add to such an accomplishment a grace that no recent recruit, no amateur writer, ever can.

I am convinced, Mr. President, that if those men whom we look up to and who sit in high places, whose witchery of style and magnificent genius we all respect, could withdraw themselves from the study of certain mottoes which they believe are fantastic, and certain sides of humanity confined only to literary coteries and to great cities, the triumph they have won in the world of letters would be as nothing to the triumph they would win if, with all their genius, they laid their hand upon the heart of the common people.

During these months it is impossible that one should travel to and fro without having formed impressions; and it is pleasant to go back with such entirely friendly and kindly impressions of the nation whose best thought and feeling are represented in this room. One thing that profoundly impressed me—I am speaking in perfect seriousness—was the courtesy of your people. Without any question—and I am not saying this for the saying's sake—your people are the most courteous people one could meet, whether he be travelling on the road or engaged in ordinary intercourse. Courtesy may be tried by various standards, and possibly the highest form of courtesy is respect to women. I have never seen anywhere, and certainly not among continental nations, who rather boast of their courtesy in this direction—I have never seen such genuine, unaffected, and practical courtesy paid to the weaker and gentler sex as I have seen in America.

Courtesy also can be tried by general agreeableness. During my tour—and owing to the arduous exercise of my friend, Major Pond, I have never stayed long in one place—I have travelled far and wide and haven't always been able to ride in parlour cars. I have, consequently, seen a great deal of people; but with the exception of one single person, and she was an immigrant, and, I have no doubt, a delightful woman, although somewhat indifferent as to her personal appearance, with the exception of that single individual, I have met no woman and no man in the cars with whom I would not be willing to sit in the same compartment or the same seat of the car during a day's journey. That seems to me a remarkable thing, but it may seem to you nothing. To us, from a European standpoint, it means a great deal. It means the comfort of your people; it means the self-respect of your people; it means many things on which I congratulate you as a nation.

And, sir, what has interested me deeply is that while you are contending with the difficulties which fall to the lot, not only of a new and growing people, but of a nation into which is flowing the very refuse of Europe, there is throughout your people a great love of letters and of art. I have seen again and again in the houses of men who are, as they say in Europe, self-made, great evidence that their love is not set merely on the things that a man holds in his hand, but on the means of culture through which we see into the unseen and the beautiful. Some of the most lovely pictures which can possibly be obtained now are contained in the houses of those men. They do not have their pictures, gentlemen, merely as pieces of furniture, which they have bought for so much money, but the men who have them, as I can bear testimony, are men who can appreciate the beauty of those pictures and who are in no mean degree art critics. On the other side I have been assured that if a bookseller has a rare book, one of those lovely books that we all like to have, with a creamy and beautiful binding like that of the past, and marked, perhaps, with a king's or a pope's arms, it is not in England that he finds a purchaser, but in America. And, Mr. President, I would congratulate you on the fact that to your high spirit and great enterprise you are also adding a love of the past, and especially that love of letters and art which is surely the height of perfection.

I would only add, Mr. President, one other thing, and it is this, that while the good-will between the old country and yours can be maintained, and is going to be maintained, by honourable international agreement, we are encouraged to cherish the hope that the two nations will be bound more and more closely together, until at last the day comes when from Washington to London may go forth a voice on the great international question of righteousness that no nation will dare to pass by. While that can only be secured, and is being secured, by the agreement of eminent statesmen, yet, surely, gentlemen, the coming and going of individuals treated kindly and hospitably after a most friendly fashion on this side, and I trust also treated after the same fashion on the other side, will weave together many bonds that will not only unite men of letters and men of grammars, but will also unite our two great nations with silken cords that can never be broken.

During this journey Watson for the most part rested on Sundays, but on December 13th he preached his last public utterance in America in Plymouth Church. Thousands thronged the neighbouring thoroughfares, and the majority were unable to obtain admission. Watson thus took leave of his agent:—

TO MAJOR POND

Dec. 16, 1896.

DEAR MAJOR POND,—The day has come when we leave America and return home, and as I look back on our campaign I am much impressed by the ability with which you conducted the operations from beginning to end, and your unfailing courage, good temper, and kindness.

You will forgive me if at times I was depressed or irritable. It is a Celt's infirmity; but I have never failed to note your care for our comfort and your sacrifices on our behalf.

Accept with this note a little case for your expeditions,

and as often as you use it—out with some greater star—give a thought to Drumtochty and its story-teller.

Accept for Mrs. Pond and yourself this sincere assurance of our regard, and believe me ever,—Yours faithfully,

JOHN WATSON.

November 22nd, 1896.

DEAR C.,—Your kind and welcome note came without delay, not because I am famous, but because I am notorious. Such kindness no man can ever have received from a foreign public, and I have never deserved it. It does not swell my head, but I confess it swells my heart. And when my dear and faithful friends at home are pleased my heart grows fuller.

We are wonderfully well and enjoying ourselves immensely, but we count the days till we stand on the deck of the *Majestic*. Oh to see the home again and you all. Our love to you in Princes Park.—Yours faithfully,

JOHN WATSON.

The Major offered him the large sum of 24,000 dollars for twelve more weeks of lecturing. Watson firmly declined. He had promised his people to return, and his work at Liverpool was awaiting him. But it is worth noting that neither he nor Pond ever doubted his ability to go through another twelve weeks of the strain.

Among the many tokens of appreciation he received, none was more valued than this from the medical men of Boston:—

November 26th, 1896.

DEAR IAN MACLAREN,—It was the desire of many members of the medical profession in this city (Boston) that a more pretentious compliment (we could not proffer a warmer one) should be extended to you during your stay in Boston in the shape of a reception and dinner.

Having learned from Mrs. F., however, that your time here is fully occupied, and that your strength is taxed to a corresponding degree, we beg that you will accept these roses and the accompanying letter as a slight token of the warm place you occupy in our hearts, and as our high appreciation of your beautiful tribute to our profession in the 'Doctor of the Old School.'—Most cordially, your obedient servants, GEORGE GAY AND CLARENCE BLAKE.

Immediately before leaving America Watson was presented with an address from the Brotherhood of Christian Unity, in which he was thanked for doing 'a work of unspeakable value in awakening and uniting the deepest sympathies of our common human nature. To this great blessing you have added another by formulating a Creed of Christian life which embodies the spirit and essence of Christ's teachings. The change of emphasis from doctrine to life expresses a demand of the age and will give a new spirit and form to Christian civilisation. We accept your Life Creed not as a substitute for the historic creeds, but as an interpretation of them.' The Creed referred to in the address was as follows:—

A LIFE CREED

I believe in the Fatherhood of God. I believe in the words of Jesus. I believe in a clean heart. I believe in the service of love. I believe in the unworldly life. I believe in the beatitudes. I promise to trust God and follow Christ; to forgive my enemies, and to seek after the righteousness of God.

Watson's whole heart went out to America. I question whether any visitor from the old country ever took more kindly to the great nation of the West. There was something in the atmosphere of America that was eminently congenial to him. He made some of his best friends among Americans; he looked with unbounded hope to the future of the country; he would have been more than content to spend his days there as a private individual, though he thought himself too old to take public office and begin a new career. He had two more visits to pay to America, and it was in America that he died.

To the problems of civilisation and Christianity in the West he gave close and continued study. He considered that there was an American type of character—a native-born American representative of a great, a coming, a fruitful, and a successful race. The most wonderful thing about the American nation seemed to him its almost miraculous power of assimilation. If amongst those stirring and bustling people an Irishman, a Scandinavian, a Polish Jew or an Italian was drafted in, there would be the beginning of a change in him, and in one half of those cases the child would be an American, while in the case of the other half the grandchild would be an actual American. This stock drew in, changed, and made its own that enormous mass of population that from year to year was flung upon its shores. The American influence was in general reforming and deodorising. People went over to America often very low in the social scale, and by and by they were fairly good citizens, while their children were excellent citizens. There was the power of the salt of the sea in the nation which would take into it the refuse of a city, and purify it, and leave the sea as fresh as ever. Then again the Americans were a patriotic people. The Republic was twice baptized in the blood of its best citizens. He thought that the victory of M'Kinley over Bryan was decided by a genuine feeling of patriotism that rose throughout the American nation. While the election seemed to be fought on bi-metallism there was another question behind it, and that was: Could a State maintain its honourable position that proposed to pay its debts with 57 cents for a dollar? When the country realised that the victory of Mr. Bryan's party would mean the affirmation of a principle that would end in the repudiation of duty, there was no doubt about the result of the election. Over the whole country men forsook their party, and men who had no party gave themselves immense trouble in order to vindicate the honour of the nation, and in that they proved their patriotism.

Another opinion he held was that an educated American was the most courteous of men. There was a mixture of cordiality and simplicity among the best of Americans which was to be found nowhere else. The American woman added to the severe good taste of an Englishwoman a certain grace, and redeemed the cleverness of the Parisian from the suspicion of trickery. 'Blood and climate have united to produce a felicitous result, where the gravity and dignity of the Anglo-Saxon have been relieved by a certain brightness of spirit and lightness of touch which would be out of place, and might be even offensive in rain and fog.'

The courtesy of American editors, their warm appreciation of what they accepted, and their politeness in assigning reasons for refusal, their quite marked graciousness of manner, were an example to the whole world. Among the younger University men in Yale and Harvard he found an easy and agreeable bearing with just the proper flavour of deference to superiors. Above all, Americans stood nobly the real test of good manners which is a man's bearing to women. On this he never ceased to dwell. 'From end to end of America a woman is respected, protected, served, honoured. If she enters an elevator every man uncovers; in a street car she is never allowed to stand if a man can give her a seat; on the railways conductors, porters, and every other kind of official hasten to wait on her; any man daring to annoy a woman would come to grief.' This might seem to be exaggerated, and yet it was well for a strong and restless people to be possessed with noble ideas of women, and from the poorest to the highest man to be engaged and sworn unto her service. The woman cult in the States is in itself a civilisation and next door to a religion.

Of the lavish and considerate hospitality of America he had naturally much to say. What counted dearest in it all was the genuine kindness behind it. 'The Americans are a kind people, and they are not ashamed to allow it to be seen.' Few things irritated Watson more than the manner in which English visitors sometimes requited American generosity.

When an Englishman who has been treated like a royal personage, and never allowed to live a day in an hotel, finds it in his heart to write disparagingly of his hosts, it is better that what he writes should not be published. And if a learned and eminent person should be most warmly received in congenial circles, and should so disregard the usages of society that he was declared to have carried himself 'like a Saxon swineherd before the Norman Conquest,' and to have secured for himself the undisputed possession of one house, his host and hostess having finally despaired and fled, then it might have been better for that distinguished man and for his native land if he had remained at home. It is right, however, to add that such primæval manners were original rather than national, and did not endear him to every heart even in England. One must sadly admit the fact that

Englishmen are not greatly admired or ardently loved by the American nation, but the reason is not always realised. It is not the amazing folly of our Government in the War of Independence, nor the unfortunate conflict of 1812, nor even the avowed sympathy of English society with the South in the Civil War, although all those mistakes have left a heritage of bitterness. What irritates Americans quite as much as any of our family quarrels, so it seems to one visitor, is the attitude of the individual Englishman. He is supposed—with some measure of truth certainly—to be unsympathetic and critical, or fearfully condescending and patronising—in fact, to sniff his way through the States. Very likely the poor man is simply dazed by the noise and whirl of life in that electrical atmosphere, or is laying himself out to please. It does not, of course, show much tact to advise an American woman who was meditating a visit to Scotland to read Sir Walter Scott—whom a good American knows from *Waverley* to *Count Robert of Paris*—but it was not really meant for an insult, and when an Englishwoman congratulated an American on speaking without a twang she intended to pay a compliment, and it was unnecessarily cruel to congratulate her in return on not dropping her 'h's.' Our hand (and our humour) is heavy, and a people ought not to be judged by insular *gaucherie*; it may conceal a true heart. What is sorely needed is more going to and fro between the countries—English going West as well as Americans coming East—and more friendships between individuals and more understanding one of the other. It ought to be laid to heart by every visitor to the States that he is travelling among a bright, emotional, kind-hearted, sensitive people, and it might be useful for his clever hosts to remember that their guest belongs to the same stock, where it is quite honest and grateful, but proud and shy, and where it has no nerves.

The vastness of America was another impression which constantly deepened. Between the islander in his trim little home and the American in his immense domain there was necessarily a very considerable difference. A strain of bigness ran through the American and all his ways, which was on some sides very invigorating, but perhaps not always unattended by the defects of a refreshing quality.

Watson saw that in America life was wide and buoyant and full of vicissitudes. A man might have nothing to-day and be rich to-morrow; he might be rich one day and poor the next. The tides ran in and out with immense velocity, and the scene was ever changing. Again, in a large unclaimed country, men got a spirit of enterprise so fearless and ambitious that it amazed an old country man. Enterprise comes with room—daring, ambition, willingness to run risks, and quickness of mind. Where the individual has his chance on his own merits, life is like the *Arabian Nights* in sudden and astonishing transformations. A hand labourer may become president of a railroad, a clerk may become a millionaire, a small farmer become a President.

The unfinishedness of America struck him, and often with delight. The vivid contrasts, the luxuriant abundance, the unrestrained originality, the untouched resources, the easy independence of the New World were in happy contrast to the ancient order. 'One has a piquant sense of freshness in a country where nature breaks in upon civilisation, and the simple ways of the past assert themselves beside the last results of modern invention.'

He was not blind to signs of danger in the West. The darkest of these he judged to be the restriction of population, and of this he wrote fully and frankly. He thought also that there was a certain extravagance in America, though he was willing to plead that he might be subtly influenced by his thrifty Scots blood.

We can only stand aside and wonder at our kinsman who gets his money so easily, who holds it so lightly, who spends it so lavishly, a man of a very princely habit, and far removed above thought of saving. And yet it may be allowed us to shake our heads and have some misgivings as to whether this prodigality is for the good of individual character and the upbuilding of a people. Is the ostentatious waste of food in hotels wholesome or justifiable, where the menu is bewildering in variety, and the portions supplied beyond all necessity, and more is taken away than is used? Does it conduce to stability and self-restraint to be quite indifferent about to-morrow, and to reserve nothing of to-day's earnings? Have not the farmers traded recklessly on the virgin resources of the land? Have not the forests been improvidently cut down? Is there not everywhere a certain want of prudence and management which cannot in the long-run minister to moral strength or even to material wealth? If it be true, as is contended, that every great empire has been built up on thrift, this means that the homeliest of virtues does not end in the accumulation of money, but results in the creation of manhood. And the best friends of America therefore desire that amid all her prosperity, she should not fall away into wasting and luxury, but ever retain and cultivate that habit of simple and severe living which was shown by her Puritan forefathers.

Another danger he saw in the marked abstinence from politics, general and municipal, of the leisured and cultured classes in the State. They would bestir themselves and take part in any great crisis, but in ordinary circumstances they looked out on the public life through the loop-holes of retreat. They refused to touch public service with their finger-tips, and so left it too largely to place-hunters, wire-pullers, and professional politicians, with results that might not be corrupt as some candid critics alleged, but were at least less than ideal. 'The patriotic spirit in America, and far too much in other places also, seems to exercise itself over great crises, foreign or domestic, and to be indifferent to the conduct of ordinary affairs. The worst feature in American politics is the "boss," who is the power behind the throne, and of whom no one says any good thing.'

Watson had much to say about the humours of the campaign, but I have room for one story only. At the very start Major Pond made his one mistake. He has given his version of the affair in his book, *Eccentricities of Genius*, and I may supplement it from Watson's own tale. The friends were going to Newhaven, and when the train began to slow the Major sprang to his feet.

'Guess,' said he, 'we'd better hurry, or else we'll be carried on to New York'; so Watson, his wife, and the Major left the cars in haste, and the train, the last train of that day, went on its way.

'Where is our carriage?' demanded the Major, standing outside the station with the 'stars' behind him. 'What carriage? The carriage ordered to be here for Major Pond and his "star." That car-man is a back number. He's not on time and the contract's broke. Get me another carriage,' he said to the railway man.

'Can't get one now, Major. Too late. All off for the night.'

'Do you give me to understand, young man,' and the Major spoke with awful impressiveness in the darkness lit by a single lamp, 'that the University city of Newhaven cannot supply a covered conveyance with two horses for an American gentleman in public life and a distinguished visitor? You are not worthy of your privileges as a citizen of this cultured community.'

'Newhaven, Major, was that what you said? Why, this ain't Newhaven.'

'Not Newhaven?' and the words fell syllable by syllable from the Major's lips. 'May I inquire the name of this settlement?'

'Call it Maryville, Major,' and it was plain the

railway man would have boasted had he not been afraid. 'Can't get to Newhaven to-night.'

'Maryville!' and the Major fixed the presumptuous porter with a gaze so fearsome that the man slunk into the darkness with a muttered apology for the existence of the place, and the Major still looked at the spot where the man had been consumed. After a full minute of profound silence, during which the 'stars' were silent and motionless, the Major wheeled round and led the procession through the booking-office and along the platform to the extremity. When he could go no further he stood again for a space communing with himself, and then he turned, and this is what he said:

'Maryville! No! It never happened before, and if it happened twice the public career of J. B. Pond would be closed. Maryville!'

He led the way to a very respectable hotel.

'Can this hotel,' inquired the Major, still speaking with an accent of chastened humility, 'supply two foreigners who have lost their way with accommodation for the night?' As for himself, the suggestion was he would sleep on the street. He departed, refusing to be comforted, turning at the door, and saying 'Maryville.'

Next morning he reported that he had slept little, but had gathered his past 'stars' round his bedside and imagined what they would have done if he had landed them in such circumstances at Maryville. It all ended well.

'No,' said the Major, 'I am not sorry that this has happened once, for it has let me know what kind of people I have got to deal with. Brought them, two helpless and confiding strangers, to Maryville at 11.15 on a dark night, and put them up there for the night without a toothbrush or a hairpin, and what did they say? Not one bad word either from the one or the other. Spoke to me like a parson in a case of personal bereavement. Comforted J. B. Pond in his first professional mistake, and they had been only a fortnight in the United States. What did they do? Pretended it was a picnic and said they were enjoying themselves, and appeared next morning as prettily dressed as if they had had two Saratoga trunks. Wanted to look after J. B. Pond and see that he had taken his natural sleep. This is Christianity,' the Major concluded with enthusiasm, declaring afterwards that he knew from that moment the tour was going to be a pronounced success.

In this connection I may tell a story a little out of its proper place. Among Pond's numerous clients was Matthew Arnold. Arnold was no great lecturer. He puzzled the Major very much. He gave a hundred lectures in America, and nobody ever heard any of them, not even those sitting in the front row. The Major did his best to induce Arnold to take lessons in elocution, but to little purpose. Arnold went through his task cheerfully, but said nothing to his agent when he received his fees. This the Major somewhat resented, and as a practical man he looked upon the whole performance as ridiculous. He would have valued a kind word from Arnold in the trying circumstances. But on a later visit to America, Ian Maclaren was the guest of the lady who had been Arnold's hostess. She told him that when Arnold came into her house after a dispiriting night some one had expressed sympathy with him in having to put up with the company of so vulgar a person as Major Pond. Arnold drew himself up. 'Major Pond,' he said, 'and I have not been brought up in the same way, and our tastes are somewhat different, but I have always found him a very kind man and strictly honourable.'

CHAPTER XI

WORK IN LIVERPOOL

WATSON returned to Liverpool, and was welcomed by his congregation on Christmas Eve 1896. He took up his pastoral duties with renewed energy. He told his people that three months could not blot out the memory of all that he had received from them. It was his prayer that he might be their faithful and loving minister in days and years to come.

The prayer was answered, but the course of Watson's life was materially affected. His reputation was now international. Crowds of Americans visited his church every Sunday: he was constantly pressed to deliver lectures and sermons all over the country. He was also 'much exposed to editors,' and all demands made upon him were answered to the best of his power. The work done at Sefton Park was never diminished. He was not often absent from his pulpit on Sundays, and his week-night services were faithfully kept up. Nor were his pastoral visits diminished. He continued faithfully to seek out the members of his flock. He had always the greatest sympathy with domestic servants, and as members of his congregation they each received a visit. Very often Watson would be seated in the kitchen and the mistress of the house would never know that the famous preacher was giving consolation and advice to her maid. A hostess once said, 'I had never any idea my waitress was in trouble until I heard quite by accident Dr. Watson inquiring after her mother, who, I learned, was seriously ill.' But in addition to all this work he had henceforth at least two sermons or lectures in other towns during the week, and often double the number. He had long railway journeys and exhausting social engagements. It was a puzzle to his friends that he should devote so much of his time and energy to this way of living, but there is no doubt that he liked it. He enjoyed the change of scene; he was glad to make new friends and to have friendly human intercourse with them. The applause and good-will of enthusiastic audiences cheered him, and wherever he went he drew crowds, and he knew that he had opportunities of helping ministers and giving an impulse to congregations. He made himself at home very easily wherever he went, and strangers very often became friends. Thus his life, with a few interruptions, went on for more than ten years. For Watson it was a life full of sunshine, though clouded at times by the effects of overstrain.

That it overstrained him was often very evident, but he recuperated quickly. It was certainly injurious to his literary work. Much of this had now to be done in trains and in such brief intervals of leisure as he could command. The main portion of his leisure was strictly dedicated to his work for the pulpit.

Watson found on his return from America that he was the object of a heresy hunt. It was never a serious affair, but I refer to it because it gives an opportunity for referring to his theological books. Of these the first appeared about the same time as the *Bonnie Brier Bush*, and under his own name. It was entitled *The Mind of the Master*, and was followed by *The Life of the Master*, *The Doctrines of Grace*, and several smaller volumes of a practical and devotional kind. These represented the main elements of Watson's preaching, and the conclusions to which he had fought his way after searching inquiry. The mere titles of the books are enough to show the direction in which his mind turned. Christ was to him the centre of theology and preaching. He held that the older Presbyterian theology had done small justice to the humanity of our Lord, and that it had ceased to be useful in so far as it was not inspired by the Spirit of Christ. But he held firmly to the Catholic doctrine of the deity of Christ, to the Incarnation, and to the Atoning Sacrifice.

Some of his friendliest critics held that there were certain contradictions in *The Mind of the Master*. They were not backward in paying tribute to its literary power and beauty, and to its profound and constant sense of the incomparableness of Jesus. But they complained that Watson disparaged the Apostles, as when he wrote, 'St. Paul has touched excellently in various letters on the work of the Holy Spirit, and his words have fed many; but all the words that ever came from that inspired man are not to be compared with the promise of the Comforter given in the upper room.' They also compared phrases like 'It must be remembered that Jesus had moods, and that He sometimes lost heart.' They thought that theologians and the Church were unduly disparaged. It was the general opinion, however, that the book was to be welcomed for the emphasis it laid on the authority of our Lord's teaching, and for its brilliant and suggestive exposition of the Gospels. The few ministers who took action complained that Watson leaned to Unitarianism. He himself did not attach great importance to the matter, though he was slightly perturbed. He held his peace till the prosecution, if it may be so called, had ceased, and then he made an explanation and modified a few sentences. He said that there were two grounds where he found himself in agreement with his critics: 'One is the style, which once or twice has been unchastened, and from which certain expressions, which to certain minds suggested irreverence, will be removed. And the other is the apparent denial that the sacrifice of Jesus, besides being an ethical power, had also a vicarious virtue, which were to ignore the deeper reference of certain of the Master's most solemn utterances. He were indeed a foolish and heady writer who did not learn something from critics who have been candid in their disapproval, but also generous in their appreciation.' On the distinction which he drew between the Gospels and the Epistles Watson stood firm.

Before any one can claim an absolute spiritual identity between the utterances of Jesus and His Apostles, he must hold not only that they were penmen, but that they were simply pens in the hand of a Divine Power. And this conclusion no reasonable person could accept. Besides it is fair to ask this question : Even on any theory of inspiration, however rigid or extreme, could the Holy Ghost convey the same revelation as regards depth and clearness through a man, however faithful and holy, as through the Son of God? This is not a question of the player, if one may use this figure, but of the instrument: and if truth has to pass through a medium, then there must be some difference between the very mind of Jesus and the mind of Jesus as possessed and assimilated by St. Paul. This argument really goes back to the doctrine one holds of Jesus' person, and presupposes His deity. It appears to me, although others who as firmly hold the same doctrine do not agree with me, that His deity invests His own words with a solitary authority.

Perhaps in the last issue the question must be settled by a reference to fact. There may be some who can find limitations in the words of Jesus. I do not envy such men. I hope that I may never be found in their number. When it comes to pass that we localise Jesus, it will not be possible to believe Him Son of God. Many must find limitations in St. Paul, with all his greatness—limitations of style and thought, inseparable from his nature and education. We miss in the Epistles the majesty of utterance, the note of universality, the elevation above every local condition, the revelation of God as of one looking on the face of the Father. The Epistles are surely the holy place, but the Gospels are the holiest of all, where is seen the very glory of God.

It may be added that the case came up at the meeting of the Presbyterian Synod in Sunderland as a petition from eleven ministers and twenty-four elders asking for an investigation of Dr. Watson's writings, but making no definite assertion of heresy. The Synod almost unanimously refused to receive the request, and so the matter ended. Shortly after Dr. Watson was called to St. John's Presbyterian Church, Kensington, London. At first he thought that the change might benefit himself and his congregation, but he was soon made to feel that his place was in Liverpool. 'As I began to realise the strength of the bonds which united us and the possibility that my work here in church and city may not yet be done—that the desire for change may be partly selfish, and be really a longing for relief, that it might be hard to secure one who would unite you all together as we have lived—it seemed to me at last that it could not be God's will that I should leave, and that in going my heart should be half-broken.' After that he discouraged all invitations to other spheres, resolving that he would remain in Liverpool so long as he continued in the active pastorate.

I give some letters written to Mrs. Stephen Williamson at this time:—

TO MRS. STEPHEN WILLIAMSON

January 15th, 1898.

Dear Mrs. W.,—We go to Cannes and shall there be guests with the Carnegies, who are to have a yacht in readiness. Then we ramble to Mentone, San Remo, and then home from our furthest point within ten weeks.

If I could get an interview with Mr. Gladstone I should be lifted. It would be a treasure to remember, and might—(if in good taste)—be bread to the penniless.

TO THE SAME

August 27th, 1898.

I hereby certify that I have examined Mr. Maclaren, and find that he is suffering from slight tendency to obesity, that he is apt to go sleepy about 11 p.m., and that the drowsiness has not always departed at 7 a.m., and that his appetite is about normal. I take a favourable view of the case, and believe that by a course of mild mountain ascents Mr. Maclaren's health may be restored.

John Watson, M.D., F.R.C.P.

TO THE SAME

November 9th, 1898.

Dear Mrs. Williamson,—You will receive in a day or two an early copy of *Rabbi Sanderson*, which you allowed me to dedicate to you.

It is a 'bit' from *Kate Carnegie*, and I hope you like the old scholar.

Have three new stories—bags made in Scotland.—Yours affectionately,

John Watson.

TO THE SAME

December 8th, 1898.

Dear Mrs. Williamson,—It gave me regret, 'of course' (as they always say in Scotland), that I could not be one of your suite, walking with Mrs. Tom, chief lady in waiting at the function, but I had meetings all day. The Laird would tell you how we were occupied, wandering from meeting to meeting like bees from flower to flower, listening to one another with greedy delight. But, as you know, 'of course,' both of us would be ready any time to hear you.

Glad you like my *Collector*; Wallace (*Glasgow Herald*), in an article in the *Bookman*, speaks highly of it too, and forms his careful and discriminating view with a sentence so encouraging regarding my 'mastery' of the 'short story' that I dare not quote it.—Yours to command,

John James M'Jinks.

TO THE SAME

June 6th, 1899.

Dear Mrs. Williamson,—Allow me to say that I have been thinking of you with more than ordinary friendship during three days.

Your mother was one whom even a stranger began to

love at once, for her spirit and goodness, and not least as a beautiful type of *Scots* womanhood. Round her gathered the interest of her husband's name, but to you Mrs. Guthrie would be associated with the sacred ties and memories of home.

Where the old home is closed it seems as if the past had faded and disappeared, and the future presses upon one's soul. Let us thank God for the good hope.—With kindest regards, your affectionate friend, JOHN WATSON.

Very few letters survive from the correspondence between Dr. Watson and Professor Drummond. When Watson was in America Drummond was suffering from his last illness. There follow one letter written to Drummond just before he died, and two letters to Drummond's mother:—

TO PROFESSOR HENRY DRUMMOND

February 3rd, 1897.

DEAR HENRY,—Since coming home I have been minded to write you, but have had no time. A letter from Lady Aberdeen received this morning, in which she alludes to you, has given me decision.

We had a very pleasant tour in the United States, and received no end of kindness. My connection with you helped me, and George had gone before and blasted the way.

I saw the Eastern and Middle West States, and had a run through Canada. Some day I hope to see the far West. Wherever I went the people seemed bright, shrewd, and pushing, and to a stranger most courteous. Their feelings to our country I judge to be most cordial, but then they are much influenced by fits of patriotic feeling, and by the tricks of politicians.

How has it been with you? Are you making some progress to recovery? I told all who asked that you were going to get better bit by bit, and you must pay your instalments as I pledged my word.

If there is any one with you who can drop me a line, I should be grateful.

If I can get a day in end of March, I'll come with my report of America. Meanwhile we unite in love to you, and I am, your faithful friend, JOHN WATSON.

TO MRS. DRUMMOND

March 14th, 1897.

MY DEAR MRS. DRUMMOND,—Yesterday I received intelligence of the place and hour of my friend's funeral, and it gives me poignant grief that it is out of my power to be present.

On Monday evening I have for some time been engaged to lecture at Birmingham, and the time renders it impossible to get relief.

I shall be with you in spirit, as the earthly remains of your noble son, and my friend of boyhood, are carried along the road I know so well, but of all men to me it seems easiest to think of him as alive for evermore.

With profound respect, and our heartfelt sorrow, believe me, yours very faithfully, JOHN WATSON.

TO THE SAME

June 8th, 1897

MY DEAR MRS. DRUMMOND,—You cannot imagine how much touched I was to-day when the links came, and how soft my heart is as I look at them on my desk.

I shall value them deeply for Henry's sake, and altho' I do not wear gold, and have lately laid aside a mourning ring in memory of my father and mother, yet from time to time I will use the gift that belonged to my friend.

I am pleased that you liked the article. It was not a eulogium, it was plain guarded truth, it was Henry as I knew him from my boyhood.

I hope you are being comforted, and that God is nearer than ever. Now may I ask a favour for Henry's sake, that you never again call me Dr. or Mr. but John, as once you did in years past. There are few of early days to say the word: will you grant me this? We unite together in warm regard for you and yours, and I remain, yours affectionately,

JOHN WATSON.

CHAPTER XII

SECOND VISIT TO AMERICA

DR. WATSON was induced by Major Pond to make a second American lecture tour which began on February 19, 1899, and terminated on May 10th. Lectures were delivered in New York, Philadelphia, Cincinnati, Louisville, and Chicago, but for the most part new ground was occupied. Watson travelled through California lecturing at San Francisco, Monterey, San José, Fresno, Los Angeles, and other cities. He closed his tour at Minneapolis. He had the old welcome everywhere, and in general very large crowds. During his journey out the *Teutonic* passed through a hurricane:—

It was an awful, a majestic spectacle, such as one is never likely to see again, and certainly does not desire to see. The wind blew from three different quarters in turn, and the waves were about forty-five feet high. At their base and in the trough they were black; midway upwards they were a very dark green; towards the crest the dark green brightened into emerald, and the waves were crowned with clouds of white foam, through which once and again the sunlight broke. As a wave of this size and beauty approached the vessel one felt that it was certain to cover it from stem to stern. If it had, such a wave would have broken in the whaleback deck at the bow, have swept away the boats, possibly might have carried away the officers' quarters forward, and even have destroyed the bridge. As it was, the vessel lifted on the approach of the wave, and rose like a seabird on the billows till at last her bow passed through the crest of the wave, while the streams of emerald poured along the side of the vessel, and the white spray was driven by the wind over the bridge and above the funnels. Now and again the crest of a wave would strike upon the beam, flooding the deck with water and making the ship quiver from end to end.

Such was the excellent management of the captain that during the whole voyage the vessel did not receive the slightest damage, and no person on board—neither seaman nor passenger—was hurt. Of course there were incidents in such a voyage, and it was not wonderful that when a bottle of water emptied itself upon the face of a sleeping passenger in the middle of the night, and he heard at the same time the crash of a huge wave upon the side of the steamer, he should feel that it was time to make an effort for his life. It is interesting to know what a man does in these circumstances, and this particular passenger rushed up the companion, equipped besides his night things with a life-saving apparatus, which he found in his cabin, and a pair of boots. What he was to do with the boots, and where they could be of any particular service in that emergency, he had not stopped to consider; 'but it was not more foolish than the action of another passenger in a like emergency, whose provision besides a life-belt, and that was everything else that he had, was a tall hat.' As the passengers came up the river they saw with great regret the *Germanic* sunk at her dock through an accident, with only her funnels above the water. In New York it was a blizzard, and the streets were piled high with banks of snow.

I do not propose to give any detailed account of this journey. Happily some of his own letters are available. They are addressed to his Sefton Park congregation:—

New York, February 21st, 1899.

DEAR FRIENDS,—Friends were waiting at New York to receive us, and we are again established in our quiet, commodious room in the old-fashioned Everett House, which to our mind is most preferable to the up-town hotels with their small rooms and endless bustle and show and fashion. Here, at least, one can have peace even in the midst of busy New York, and in this hotel many Englishmen have stayed in turn, from Mr. Matthew Arnold in the past to Mr. Anthony Hope yesterday. Many friends called upon us to congratulate us upon our safety, and to bid us welcome after the Atlantic, and on Saturday we left for Newhaven, the seat of the University of Yale. Prof. Fisher, our former host at Yale, was standing on the platform when we arrived, and gave us the kindest of receptions. He is a typical don, so scholarly, so witty, so gentle, and it is a privilege to live in his house, where one breathes humanity in the old Latin sense, and is brought into contact at every turn of the conversation with the wisdom both of the present and past. Beneath his roof one meets all kinds of scholars, and every one seems at his best, so that one has the benefit of a University in the form of social intercourse. Yale reminds one of an English University, because its buildings are scattered here and there, and some of them are now nearly two hundred years old, and because the scholars at Yale have the old-fashioned love of accurate and delicate culture, and are altogether cleansed from showiness and Philistinism. Upon Sunday morning we went to the University Chapel, where I preached before the President and Professors, and where I preached, which is a different thing, to fifteen hundred students of the Universities. One looked upon a mass of humanity in the bright and intelligent faces, and was inspired with the thought of the possibilities in those lads who would be the clergymen and lawyers and statesmen and great merchants of the United States. If they are interested the 'boys' have no hesitation in letting the preacher know, and have endless ways of conveying their weariness. For my subject I took 'Jesus' Eulogy on John the Baptist,' and made a plea for selflessness as the condition of good work and high character. In the evening I spoke to about five hundred students in the beautiful hall of the University Christian Association. This time I took for my subject 'Faith and Works,' and afterwards met a number of men who were exceedingly kind, and, as is characteristic of American University men, very gracious and courteous. During my stay with Dean Fisher I had the opportunity of conversation with several distinguished Biblical scholars whose names and whose books are known on both sides of the Atlantic, and to a general practitioner like myself this intercourse with experts was most instructive and stimulating.

Yesterday we returned to New York, where we are spending a few days doing nothing except seeing friends and receiving callers, and generally resting and enjoying ourselves. To-morrow evening I shall have the pleasure of dining with Mr. Rudyard Kipling, and on Thursday evening with a number of the leading clergy of our own Communion, and others. In the end of the week we go to Philadelphia, to a large Presbyterian meeting, and afterwards to Boston. These visits we make to knit up old ties and to visit our former friends, and when they are over we shall start for the West. While in New York we hope to see our old friends of Sefton Park, the Abbotts and the Gernons, as well as some young men belonging to the home Church.—Believe me, your faithful minister, JOHN WATSON.

Washington, D.C., March 9th, 1899.

DEAR FRIENDS,—Since my last letter I have revisited that most English of all American cities, Philadelphia, and have seen many friends I made on my former visit. I lectured once in the Academy of Music to an inspiring audience, and I preached in a suburban church once; but the main purpose of my visit was to meet with my brethren of our Church in the city of 'brotherly love.' I spoke on a theological subject at their conference, but really gave them the substance of my sermon on the 'Grace of God,' preached at home; so you see that what suits Sefton Park suits Theological Clubs. The club agreed also with the home Church that I was a most orthodox man. I regret, indeed, to say, that a recent heresy case in the Presbyterian Church of England was looked on here as a farce, and afforded much amusement. I was guest of the Presbyterian Union at a banquet to which three hundred ladies and gentlemen sat down. This is a society of laymen, which exists for social intercourse, and I gave, after dinner, some account of the religious situation in England. It appears that there is also an extreme ritualistic wing in the American Episcopal

Church, and one rector assured me that some of its members were practically Romans in all except their obedience to the Pope. There is, however, in the American Church what no longer exists in the Church of England, a strong and numerous Broad Church party. This party has its home at Harvard, and has owed much to Phillips Brooks and Professor Allen, of Cambridge, and gives a position of intellectual dignity to its Church.

We have seen Boston, and have again been the guests of Mrs. Fields, whose husband was the justly famous publisher, and himself a man of letters. This home was the haunt of the Boston set—Emerson, Longfellow, Lowell, and the dear 'Autocrat,' and many are the stories one heard of them. Our own chief writers had also pleasant relations with this house, and one heard much at first hand of Dickens and Thackeray and Matthew Arnold. Every third book in the library had some delightful association—a first edition of Milton — a *Don Juan* on which Byron had written, that from this copy future editions were to be printed, and the author hoped that the printers would not mis-spell, or mis-print, or miss-anything else; a book (rare) which Charles Lamb was able to buy, because it had six pages wanting, which he had supplied in his own neat handwriting; and a hundred other treasures. In Boston I had the pleasure of showing the 'Face of the Master,' which is Sefton Park work, since it is the joint production of the minister and the clerk of the deacons' court. There was a large audience, and the slides were much admired.

Washington impresses more than ever as a city which is already imposing, and which is going to be magnificent. Its plan is that of a wheel, where the Capitol is the centre and the long avenues are the spokes. The Capitol and the Congressional Library are noble buildings, and it is most heartening to find that no sum of money is too great to spend on colleges and libraries and every form of education.

This will be the redemption of materialism and millionairism.

To-day we had the honour of an interview with the President, with whom were the secretaries of the Navy and War; he expressed his deep sense of the friendliness of Great Britain during recent times, and at a dinner which Mr. Gage, the Secretary of the Treasury, was so good as to give us last evening, at which we met several members of the Cabinet, our host proposed the 'two flags.'

At the Philadelphia banquet after the 'Star-spangled Banner' the company sang 'God save the Queen.' Much pleasant reference was also made to a message sent by her Majesty in answer to the offer made by the U.S. Government to send home the body of Lord Herschell in a warship.

On Monday, having seen our Eastern friends, and visited again places we liked, Mrs. Watson and I start for the West, and, by the time you receive this letter, about half our time of absence will be over.

With constant remembrance of you all, and especially the invalids,—Your affectionate minister, JOHN WATSON.

Denver, March 29th, 1899.

DEAR FRIENDS,—Yesterday we had a new, and it might have been a sad experience. As we were steaming along in the train at fifty miles an hour, our car gave a sudden jerk, then another and another, then sprang forward, tossing us about in our seats, then backwards, and then we stood still. A lady was thrown into my arms, and then on to the floor; Mrs. Watson sat unmoved. As I looked up I saw the negro porter of our car standing in the doorway, white with terror, and I then realised that there had been an accident.

When I looked out from the platform of the car (we were at the tail) I saw that the whole of the train was wrecked, save one car and our own.

The engine was standing, but not on the rails; 150 feet of the track had been ploughed up, the sleepers broken into little bits and the rails flung about in all directions, one being in a field, one in a ditch at the foot of the slight incline. The huge Post-Office car was standing half on the track and half on the bank, and leaning over at a dangerous angle, while the body was almost separated from its iron framework; the baggage car was lying on its side on the bank and its frame sprawling over the track; a passenger car lay body and frame on its side in the ditch below, another kept the track although not the rails, and threatened to topple over, while our brave Pullman stood firm.

I went forward at once into that other shaky car and found our Pullman conductor (a capital fellow), who told me that he was afraid the train conductor and baggage man were pinned down by the luggage in the baggage car, and in that case might be killed. The brakesman came along, one hand like a jelly, but very plucky. The first thing to do was to flag the train, that is, to stop the next train running into us; then to give assistance to the prisoners. In every car there is a little cupboard containing an axe and a saw, with a glass window to be broken in case of need. It was broken with considerable celerity, and we went forward to the car which was lying in the ditch. Already the engineer and the fireman who were unhurt, as well as the P.O. clerks who had only been knocked about in their car, had released the train conductor and luggage man who had escaped injury as by a miracle. They were saved simply by the fact that there was so much luggage in the car it had jammed and could not rock about. One man in the passenger car lying in the ditch had been thrown half through the window, and then had broken the rest of the window with a piece of luggage, and had crawled out into the ditch. The window at the end of the car was broken by means of the axe, and through the opening the passengers were assisted to get out. Much to our amazement and relief there were no dead in the car, and while several had painful-looking wounds there was perhaps only one seriously injured—an elderly man who had been much knocked about and had received a serious shock. We brought him to our car, where a bed was made up for him and we gave him restoratives. There was a young doctor in the other car, which had not been injured, and he dressed the wounds of the other passengers, so that our car became for the time a little hospital. When we found that this most dangerous-looking accident had resulted in no loss of life, a circumstance which greatly astonished the railway people, we took a couple of photographs of the wreck, which I hope may turn out well and will remind us in after years of our escape from great danger, and it might have been sudden death. A few hours afterwards we were taken on by special train to a town called St. Joseph. We travelled in the superintendent's observation car which has a glass compartment in the end. We had thus an opportunity of seeing the rails, and were not greatly impressed either with the straightness of the rails or the solidity of the bed. Looking back from our own car upon the track over which we had passed just before the accident, we could see rails which were not in their proper places, but seemed to be bent, and various of the sleepers which were turned up in the accident were more than half rotten. It appears to me as an unprofessional person, that the American cars are much in advance of our English railway carriages, being not only much more convenient, but also much stronger, and that we owed our safety to the weight and solidity of our Pullman car, but it also seems to me that the track of the American railways is not so carefully or thoroughly made as the English is, and I believe this is generally allowed in America. The great railways are, however, renewing their tracks, and I should think in the case of the Pennsylvania and the New York Central nothing is left to be desired.

We were interviewed as a matter of course in the next town after the accident, and I was careful to impress upon the reporter that none of our party had received the slightest injury beyond the shaking and the alarm. I pledged him that this account should be given wherever the news happened to be sent, but we have already received a number of telegrams inquiring about our safety.

On Wednesday I had the honour of lecturing in Lincoln, the capital of Nebraska, and the seat of the State University. We were guests of the Chancellor, and met the Governor of the State and his wife, as well as the heads of the departments in the University. From Nebraska we started on a long and most interesting journey across the prairie lands of Nebraska and Colorado. Perhaps our nerves had been a little shaken by our experience of the day before, but we certainly did not enjoy crossing the river Platte on a narrow and evidently insecure wooden bridge. The river is very broad though not very deep, and was swollen by the winter's snow, and large masses of ice were floating down. The train passed across at the slowest speed, and three times halted, while from our car we looked down straight—for the bridge had no sides—upon the ice grinding against the wooden supports of the bridge. It was with a sense of relief we reached the solid land again, for, though we had learned that trains might suddenly go off the rails on the land, we had also learned that an accident of that kind might not be so serious as it looked; but, if a bridge had collapsed, then it is not likely that any person could have escaped. The season here is very late and cold, with snow upon the ground and ice, while the streams seem to be swollen with spring floods. All day we were crossing what was once the prairie, but is now either farm land or stock farms. The houses are very far apart and look very lonely, but now and again we came upon the beginning of a town—some fifty houses around a railway station—and it was pleasant to notice that the largest building in these infant towns was already a public school. Nebraska has a magnificent system of education, and as the settlers are intelligent, industrious, hardy people, one feels certain that a fine race will be reared on the plains where the Indians and buffaloes not very long ago roamed at their will. One of our party had scouted all over these plains in the year '65 with a hundred cavalry, and more than once could point out small rivers by which they had encamped. He had met many of the famous Indian chiefs, and could tell many strange stories of the Indian's cunning and cruelty. He was very enthusiastic, however, about the healthiness and pleasure of life on the prairies, where they slept in the open air and rose at daybreak refreshed and exhilarated for the march of another day. As we journeyed along we saw several dog towns, where the curious little communities of prairie dogs live; and although the snow kept them indoors for the most part, one or two paid their respects to us as we passed. Sometimes we came upon a herd of horses called bronchos, which we were told by our friends were the best horses a man could ride for scouting work, and we also saw herds of cattle, but the buffaloes are, of course, long extinct except in parts. We also saw three cayotes, which are the prairie wolves, trotting along only a short distance from the railway track. They are cunning and vicious brutes, which will not attack a strong animal or a man, but who fasten on any crippled ox or any horse which has got lame, and which is left alone. One station was named Arapahoe after the tribe of Indians of that name. We are now in Denver, a city of about a hundred and fifty thousand inhabitants, and from the capital one can see the vast range of the Rocky Mountains which are covered with snow. We are about five thousand feet high, and to-morrow at Colorado Springs shall be about six thousand. We then go through the Rocky Mountains by the Royal Gorge, unless it be blocked with snow. From Salt Lake City we shall go direct to San Francisco, and we hope that we then shall pass direct from winter to spring. On the day that we landed in New York, after the blizzard until this present has been bitterly cold, with frequent falls of snow. This letter will be posted on Good Friday, and I wish you all an Easter greeting, which will come to you late, but I hope will come when the snow has gone and the buds have begun to open, the symbol of the Resurrection.—Your affectionate minister,

JOHN WATSON.

Salt Lake City,
April 7th to 11th, 1899.

DEAR FRIENDS,—Since I wrote my last letter we have made a great journey from the East with its blizzards, frosts, raw cold, and depressing sky, to the far West with its summer sunshine, greenness, and flowers.

We started from Denver on the Rio Grande, notwithstanding that several trains had stuck in the snow, and that the engine of another had jumped the track, killing the engineer; but the railway people were very kind and made every arrangement for our comfort. The first day we only went as far as Colorado Springs, where many smitten by chest disease recover health in its dry, bracing air. It seemed the healthiest place for an invalid we had seen in America. There is a prosperous and delightfully situated college at the Springs, and we were the guests of President Slocum. We also visited the romantic seat of General Palmer, who had built a house for himself in one of the deep valleys in the mountains. The Lodge is at the entrance of the valley, and the approach winds for a mile or so through woods and over streams and at the base of huge cliffs. The house stands where the valley opens in various directions, and is the most picturesque I have seen for many a year. A mountain stream, whose pleasant sound could be heard in the drawing-room, ran at the foot of the knoll on which the house is built. Before the house rises a pillar about a hundred and fifty feet high, solitary, austere, commanding, one of those curious sandstone formations which are the curiosity of the district, taking all shapes from a lion to a toadstool. The house is of wood. The woodwork within was very fine, and as one looked out from a room where the carved oak furniture was relieved by the trophies of the chase, upon crag and pine and waterfall, with the pungent odour of the woodfire to stimulate the brain, the imagination of a countryman was satisfied.

We left the Springs on a beautiful morning, the second we have had since we landed, and in a few hours had entered the Royal Gorge, which makes a way for the trains through the heart of the Rocky Mountains. We sat on the platform of the last car. We preferred this to riding on the engine on account of the beauty of the afterview. A stream had cut its passage deep in the mountain, and the railroad followed the windings of the river, some of them very sharp and sudden indeed. Above us on either side were the precipitous cliffs, and beside us the river. At one place there is no room for the track, and it is carried above the stream on a platform suspended from the cliffs. We saw at one curve the engine which had left the track lying upside down in the bed of the river, but the body of the engineer had been extricated and removed. About eight o'clock in the evening we had reached the height of our ascent, and the snow was falling heavily. The conductor was afraid we might be caught in the Gorge through which we would pass at midnight, and we went to bed with chastened hope. When I awoke we were going through banks of snow ten feet high which washed our windows as we rushed along, but we were going at fifty miles an hour down the pass to Salt Lake City. In the morning we had entered the plain in which the city of the Mormons stands. Once this was a waste of barren land, and dry as dust. Brigham Young, the leader of the Mormon pilgrims, looked at this inhospitable land with the eye of faith, and saw what it might be made. He struck his staff upon the ground and declared this to be Mount Zion.

Under the patient, intelligent labour of this extraordinary people, the wilderness has been made to rejoice like the rose, and has been studded with nice little houses surrounded by gardens and fields. The feature of the Salt Lake City is the Temple of the Mormon faith, into which no Gentile is allowed to enter; within this place the rites of marriage, which with the Mormons is eternal, as well as extensive, and the baptism for the dead are performed. In the latter rite Mormons secure the salvation of their ancestors who died before the revelation given the latter-day saints. In the same grounds is the Tabernacle—an unsightly building, with a roof like an inverted boat, which holds upwards of ten thousand people, and is so perfectly constructed for acoustic purposes that a whisper can be heard easily at the farthest distance, and also the sound of anything falling. The organ is a fine instrument, and was played for our benefit with much taste; the choir had won the first prize at one of the great competitions, I think at Chicago. It consists of about one hundred and fifty voices, and can be raised to five hundred on occasion, all carefully trained. Near the tabernacle stands the Assembly Hall, which was full in the evening when I lectured. The judge of the city presided, and several of the Mormon dignitaries were present. In the forenoon I had an interview with two heads of the community, and received much courtesy as well as information at their hands. One of their bishops showed us over the city, and was a most agreeable man. Mr. Moody was preaching in Salt Lake City when we were there, and the Mormon papers were most favourable; their only criticism was that he did not state the 'Plan of Salvation' with sufficient clearness. From this you will understand how evangelical the Mormons are, and how suspicious they are of doubtful doctrine.

We are accustomed to smile at Mormonism at home, but an American has reason for concern. The Mormons hold the State of Utah, and they have overflowed into two other States. A Mormon Senator has been sent to the Congress, who is an avowed polygamist, and the churches are much concerned. The position is made the more difficult by the fact that, apart from their 'peculiar institution,' the Mormons are a hard-working, law-abiding, and moral set of people. They are, in fact, a survival of the early process of civilisation, and are now a return in their family arrangements to semi-barbarism, which in course of time will die out.

And now for California.—Your affectionate minister,

JOHN WATSON.

Redlands, California, April 14th, 1899.

MY DEAR FRIENDS,—If you had only travelled with us for

two hours this morning through orange groves and within sight all the time of the Sierra Mountains, through an atmosphere which was both warm and cool as well as deliciously clear, and then could sit with us, as we wish you all could, especially one or two dear old friends, and the invalids, in our room at the 'Casa Loma,' Redlands, California, then you would agree with us that it was worth enduring the wilderness journey through the snow and the alkalies to reach this land of Goshen.

But let us take things in order, from the land of Mormons onward. After the desert, and the passage through the hills which guard the Mormon land on its western side, we awoke to find ourselves crossing the river at Sacramento, the capital of California, and were surrounded by the rich green of the winter wheat. In a little time we came to a bay of the Pacific, across which our train was taken on a steamer, and opposite us in a cleft of the hill lay a most picturesque village, with white walls and red roofs, reminding one of Italy or Spain. Very likely it was as unromantic as any other American village if you had penetrated its heart—and certainly its fame was not associated with any saint, but with Heenan the prize-fighter, who came over to England to maintain the honour of America against Tom Sayers, and who was called the 'Benicia Boy.' At Oakland, the town opposite San Francisco, on the other side of the most ample harbour in the world, we left the train and crossed the bay in a steamer, watching eagerly for a glimpse of the Queen of the Pacific Coast and the Golden Gate, but the atmosphere was foggy. We were met at Oakland by one of the heads of the Southern Pacific, which controls the railways of California, and on whose system we have been travelling ever since. He has been most kind to us, and at every place his agents have seen to our comfort. Fifty years ago

San Francisco was a village, forty years ago it was a rowdy town where men were shot in the streets, and lynch law alone administered justice, now it is a city of 350,000 inhabitants, well built and excellently ruled, with the finest set of street cars in any city of the States. The private residences in the higher part of the city are very fine, and have a beautiful view of the bay. The Mayor of San Francisco is a man of note, even in this country where every second man you meet seems to be 'the most remarkable man in creation.' He is young, very rich, well bred, of fine tastes, an Irish Catholic, and devoted to the interests of the city of which he had been twice Mayor, and he is endeavouring to infuse a spirit of civic patriotism into the city life. At a banquet, where your minister was the chief guest, he made an admirable speech, and the next day he came to the Palace Hotel—a magnificent house—where we were staying, and took us out for a drive through the city park, and round the outskirts of the city in a four-in-hand. The park is large, well laid out, and ends at a headland where a hotel commands a fine view of the mouth of the harbour, and stands off the western point of this continent. Opposite is Seal Rock, where, as we sat at luncheon, we could see the seals disporting themselves on the rocks by the score. Afterwards we drove by the seashore and saw the fortifications, and on returning to the city passed through that strange quarter of San Francisco where the Chinese live after their fashion, and afford a Western an opportunity of appreciating to some degree the life of the Celestial. One night I spent an hour in Chinatown, visiting the temples and opium dens, returning to our hotel with a sense of profound relief.

Last Saturday we had an altogether delightful day at Palo-Alto, the seat of the famous Stanford University, which stands in its own grounds, surrounded by vineyards, and meadows and gardens, all its own; for in one place or another this fortunate seat of learning owns some 80,000 acres of land as an endowment. The University is an extensive wine producer, and has also a very fine stud of trotting and race-horses, the bequest of Governor Stanford, from both of which sources the University derives a large income. The buildings are in the Spanish Mission Architecture, and when they are relieved by creeping plants, will be very satisfactory. The Professors live in charming houses surrounded by trees and roses, and here we began to appreciate the luxuriance of California. From Palo-Alto we went to Monterey, on the coast, where we spent two days in the loveliest hotel I have ever seen. It stands in a pleasure-ground of a large size, rich in trees and flowers, and has within its estate a drive of eighteen miles by the shore, with many striking views of the Pacific, and through woods with grassy glades. We saw here one of the old Spanish Missions, which in past days did so much for the Indians of that land, but which were long ago despoiled of their property.

From Monterey we have come to Southern California, and for this week have been living in an earthly Paradise, driving through air laden with orange blossom, along roads surrounded by orange groves hanging with fruit, and sitting in gardens amid banks of roses; one garden had three hundred varieties, and another had a thousand kinds of different plants. Anything more pleasant than the climate at places like Stockton, Los Angeles, Pasadena, and Redlands, or anything more beautiful than the homes with their tasteful architecture, luxuriant gardens, graceful indigenous palms and perfect turf, one cannot imagine. What strikes one more than anything else is that all this overflowing fertility is artificial, the achievement of human ingenuity, together with plenty of water. Ten years ago the district of Redlands, for instance, was absolutely barren waste, and now is a succession of orange groves, fringed by palms and rose bushes, and made musical by the little rivulets of running water. We visited the finest place in the district —a garden of some three hundred acres, with woods—which was a grassless, treeless, unsightly pile some seven years ago. Now you drive or walk through brakes of roses, Banksia, Gold of Ophir, American Beauty, of carnation and stocks, verbenas, geraniums, marguerites, broken by palms, camphor-trees, azaleas, till you are bewildered by the variety and richness. Our host believed that in the garden he could grow almost every plant between the tropical and arctic regions. I write this letter in another garden, where the sun is struggling to get at me through the palms, and yet it comes to me that the spring in England is still more beautiful, and my heart says, 'Oh to be in England in April.' On Tuesday we shall have reached my farthest point outwards, San Diego, and then we shall start on the return journey, *viâ* the Canadian Pacific, Winnipeg, St. Paul, and New York.

This letter was pleasantly interrupted by a budget of letters from home, and news of the Church and family, and now I close it on Sunday morning. I am sitting by a stream of pure swift-running water, some twenty feet wide and four deep, which passes through my host's grounds, and which never runs dry because it is a part of the irrigation system. On the other side is a grove of pepper-trees, where some of the party are lying in hammocks, and beyond are palms. Along the side of the stream is a bank of geraniums, and a little further a rose-tree is trailing its flowers in the water. My host, a fair-haired young Californian, is crossing a rustic bridge with his wife, a pretty Bostonian, he in blue, she in white, to visit the stables. In a few minutes we shall be in a phaeton, behind a pair of swift-trotting Californians, and our host will drive us to the nearest kirk of our faith, where I shall sit with Mrs. Watson, and somewhere in the prayers make petition for the friends who are far away, and pray that it will be well with you on Sacrament Sunday,—Your affectionate minister, JOHN WATSON.

Coronado Beach, California,
April 20th, 1898.

DEAR FRIENDS,—We are now on the home stretch, which is to be round about and deviating, but which, starting at San Diego, within twelve miles of Mexico, will land us at Winnipeg, in North-West Canada, where I expect to conclude this, my last letter to the magazine.

From Diego we journeyed back to San Francisco, and have made a delightful two days' excursion to Santa Cruz, which is a very pretty watering-place on the coast, where you sleep with the boom of the Pacific billows in your ears as they break on the beach below your room.

As we have had to abandon the Yosemite Valley excursion on account of the lateness of the season and the fatigue we should have, we drove from Santa Cruz to see the 'Big Trees,' which fall only a few feet below those in that famous valley. One was 300 feet high, and contained 200,000 feet of timber; another had a compartment at the base, in which General Lamont and a party of explorers lived with (moderate) comfort. We had then a most romantic drive down a valley which in its views and wood scenery reminded one of Switzerland. Our horses were excellent, the road had the most interesting curves and hung over ravines at the foot of which the stream was crawling, and one of our number drove at a very fair rate—so that none of us could weary for two minutes.

We are now journeying through the rich plain between San Francisco and Sacramento, the capital of the State, where we rest for a few hours, *en route* to Portland, Oregon.

Sacramento was *en fête*, and I never saw so many stars and stripes at the same time. With the national flag, of which every one just now is proud, mingled flags of all colours, but on each the symbol of our faith and the motto, 'In this sign thou shalt conquer.' These were the banners of the Knight Templars, an old and influential organisation of Masons who were holding their gathering from a wide district here. Companies of elderly gentlemen of venerable and imposing appearance paraded the streets with bands of music and banners, and the knights were dressed in gorgeous array, and wore swords with gold scabbards. It was with difficulty we could get food, and we crept along back streets with the feeling of intruders, if not spies, on all this glory. We slunk on board the cars for our two days' journey to Portland with a sense of relief, and awoke next day in perhaps the finest scenery we have yet seen, crossing that range of mountains which close in California from the North, and of which Mount Shasta is the crown. All day long we ran along the foot of wooded ravines, and by the side of brawling torrents, or climbed the side of high hills by a series of ascents till we reached the crest, from which we could look down on the valley far beneath. We were sitting at breakfast and enjoying the view, when the car began to bound and rebound after the fashion we had learned to recognise, and we knew we were in for another accident. The dishes were crashing in all directions, passengers were holding on to anything that they could grip, and the coloured waiters had bolted like rabbits. Our car remained on the rails, and so did every other except the baggage car in the front of us, which had jumped the track and had been dragged along by the train, half on the track, half off. As we were crossing a bridge, this might have been a most disastrous accident. As it was, an engine—we had two, and sometimes three—went on to the next station and brought down a wreckage gang, who set the ponderous car on the track again in the cleverest way, and in little more than three hours we were off again. We spent the time wandering about the woods, and envying two passengers who produced fishing-rods, and returned with at least one trout to the train.

By this time we were again in the dining-car at luncheon, when once more the train came to a halt with a sudden jerk, breaking more glass and giving us a slight shake. We began to speculate quite calmly which car had left the rails, and we were only faintly interested to learn that one of the engines had broken loose and gone off on its own account. It was reclaimed, and we started afresh, and no more accidents hindered our enjoyment of the magnificent scenery, although we only got a glimpse of Mount Shasta, one of the highest of American mountains. Next morning we arrived at Portland, the chief city in the State of Oregon. After a public luncheon, where a bright speech was made by one of the leading lawyers, Mrs. Watson and I were driven to the Park above the city to see the distant view of the hills, but the day was misty, and we had to believe in the grandeur we did not see. Next morning we left for Tacoma, on Puget Sound, where we were the guests of the resident partner of our Liverpool house, Balfour, Williamson & Co., and it made us proud, as Liverpool folk, to learn not only the greatness of this firm, but also to hear from public men one testimony to their honour and their philanthropy.

We made a very pleasant journey from Tacoma to Seattle, another seaport, on a swift little steamer, and got a glimpse of Puget Sound, one of the most beautiful pieces of water in the world, not unworthy of being compared to the West of Scotland. Seattle has a lovely situation upon a hill sloping down to the Sound, and spreads over forty miles square, with a lake of seventeen miles long behind. The gradients are extremely steep, but there is an excellent system of street cars by which you can go up hill and down rapidly and comfortably as in San Francisco and in every American city, however hilly. As we sat in one of these admirably appointed cars, we could not help thinking of those heavy lumbering cars wherein we used to sit, and of the poor horses which dragged us up hill in Liverpool. Last visit to America, I was much alarmed by the energy and enterprise of the Americans, and prophesied the danger of their competition in iron and work, but at last held my peace, because I was given to understand that as a mere layman in such matters I had been deceived by our boastful cousins. One's sad forebodings have been more than justified now, when the Americans are landing engines, rails, pipes, and, I think, iron in England. It is not possible to travel here and note the resources of the country, the restless energy of the people, their inventive ingenuity and their commercial dash, without fear for our share in the commerce of the future, especially if we are ever to be held back in the race of competition by an obsolete system of denominational education, our superstition about free trade, and our ignorant trades-unions, which insist on the incapable workman being paid the same rate as the capable, which oppose all labour-saving machinery and deny to the clever artisan the reward of his labour. At Seattle we visited the home of a former member of Sefton Park congregation, situated on a height overlooking Puget Sound. We were glad to find our friends so prosperous, and were also pleased that they were as keenly interested as ever in the old Church.

As the *Kingstown* was wrecked and the steamer in her place was too slow to make the time, we had to abandon the sail up Puget's Sound and our visit to Victoria: we went direct to Vancouver, passing some lumber camps on the way, the first we had seen, and passed with a thrill of patriotic emotion the station where the Stars and Stripes floats at one end, and the Union Jack at the other. We were again in our own land, and there is none in all the world where justice is so impartially administered and political life is so pure as the Empire of Queen Victoria,—may God bless her!

We were met at Vancouver Station by Mr. Wilson Kilgour (son of our beloved elder) and his wife, who showed us the beauties of this new and very picturesque town, which has risen at the terminus of the Canadian Pacific, and promises to have a great future. As we saw the *Empress of China* lying in the harbour, which could hold the navies of the world, we were reminded that through this place our American Empire is knit to our Empire of the East, and the girdle of our dominions made complete.

Next day we started on our long journey over the Pacific, the longest railway in the world—9000 miles—as it is one of the most skilfully made and the best managed. One of its chief officials showed us much courtesy and gave us valuable information, and when we left in our very handsome travelling room, it was furnished with flowers and photographs of the route. Our drawing-room, in maple and strawberry-coloured silk, which at night is a bedroom with a little dressing-room, made the prettiest home for three days we have ever had, and at our rear—we are on the last car—there is a platform with glass sides where we see the retrospect. It is, however, quite impossible for me to describe what we have seen in the last thirty hours.

As we passed through the Selkirks and the Rockies, so marvellous are the works of nature in this region for grandeur and beauty that we both agreed that nothing we had seen in Switzerland could for one moment be compared with what awaits the traveller between Vancouver and Calgary, on the Canadian Pacific. Sometimes we ran beside the deep swift Frazer River, swarming with salmon; sometimes in deep gorges over a torrent and with high cliffs on either side; sometimes close to a glacier as large as all the famous glaciers of Switzerland put together; sometimes we climbed an ascent at the gradient of 1 in 4; sometimes we went up on a loop of four parallel ascents; sometimes we skirted the base of mountains rising 8000 feet above us, draped in snow and breastplated with icebergs. As the sun set last evening we looked back on Mount Stephen, covered with snow, and having on its bosom a glacier 800 feet in thickness, hanging over an immense cliff-glen, and glistening, while the snow had the faintest shade of pink. Gradually clouds began to gather and envelop this august sovereign, and the valley beneath grew dark. Our audience was over, and we went to rest with holy joy, and with this magnificent and inspiring picture before our minds we went to our room, and with this I shall close these letters. To-day we are travelling over the prairies both monotonous and lifeless, save for an occasional herd of cattle or horses, a little colony of prairie dogs, and at wide intervals a settlement, where the platform is enlivened by a group of Cree or Sioux Indians, or the red coat of one of the North-West Police, one of the smartest bodies of cavalry in the world. To-morrow we hope to be in Winnipeg, and thence shall proceed by St. Paul and Chicago to Boston, where we shall spend a few days with friends, and we hope to be home on May 24th by the good ship *Teutonic*, having seen God's wonders by sea and land, and received many mercies at His hands.—Your affectionate minister, JOHN WATSON.

CHAPTER XIII

WESTMINSTER COLLEGE

In the meantime Dr. Watson had begun to take an active part in the general work of the Presbyterian Church of England, especially as Convener of the College Committee. The College of the Church had worked in Bloomsbury for fifty years, and had sent out no fewer than 336 students. An excellent training had been given in spite of inadequate means. But for some time there had been a feeling that the College should be planted at Cambridge, and two members of the Church offered a site and a gift of £20,000 to facilitate the change. These ladies were Mrs. Gibson and Mrs. Lewis, both of them eminent Biblical scholars. Watson strongly desired that the Presbyterians should have their College at Cambridge. He held that if the Presbyterians went to Cambridge they would possess the ancient heritage that was theirs in the name of God and the Puritan faith. Others were gripping the highest centres of thought and education in the country. At Cambridge they would be at the centre, and he was not afraid that their men would pass from the Puritan faith to the Anglican faith. There was strong difference of opinion in the Church, but both sides came together in the end, and decided on the migration to Cambridge. There was still a very large sum of money to be raised, and the main responsibility for collecting it fell upon Watson. His remarkable powers of persuasion and his dauntless energy accomplished the great task of raising in a comparatively small Church the necessary sum. He went through the land pleading the cause of a learned ministry, and wherever he went he received generous gifts. In order to have the College opened free of debt it was necessary to raise £10,000 in a brief space of time, and £16,000 were received in five weeks. The gifts were of every amount from a shilling to £1000. They came from all kinds of people, including working men and little children; they were accompanied by evidence of the most intelligent interest in the work of the College and the warmest expressions of goodwill, and everything was given with cheerfulness and enthusiasm. The College was opened in October 1899. At the morning service Dr. Watson presented the keys to Dr. Moinet, the Moderator of the Synod, and he in his turn placed them in the hands of Dr. Dykes, the Principal, to have and to hold with all due authority. Congratulatory addresses were delivered by Professor Ryle, now the Bishop of Winchester, Principal Fairbairn, and Principal Rainy. Dr. Ryle assured Dr. Dykes and his colleagues of a welcome free from any taint of suspicion or jealousy, and referred to the Reformation and its work done here in England once for all, and not to be undone. Dr. Fairbairn warned the Presbyterians at Cambridge against regarding themselves as a Scotch colony. Westminster College to do its principal work must be the Westminster, not of Scotland, but of England. Principal Rainy laid stress on the importance that Presbyterian Churches have everywhere attached to an educated ministry, and believed that the removal of the College to Cambridge was a wise step. In the afternoon Dr. Watson presided over a very large representative and sympathetic assembly. Among the speakers were Professor Jebb; the Vice-Chancellor, Dr. Chawner; Dr. Butler, the Master of Trinity; Dr. Moule, now Bishop of Durham, Professor Macalister, Mr. Stephen Williamson, and many others. This was one of the greatest days in Watson's life, and next to his work in Sefton Park Church he reckoned the work he had done for Cambridge. He was specially thanked for the noble efforts he had made on behalf of his Church, efforts which had been crowned with success which even the most sanguine could hardly have ventured to anticipate, and which augured well for the future of Westminster College.

Through the kindness of Principal Dykes, a friend whom Watson regarded with the utmost affection and admiration, I am able to print some of the letters which Watson addressed to him in the course of his eager campaign.

TO PRINCIPAL OSWALD DYKES

September 3rd, 1899.

My dear Principal,—The better day the better deed. Mrs. W. was in church to-day, staying with one of her sons, and I looked in this afternoon. He had just been reading the appeal for the College, and immediately offered a thousand pounds, in addition to his former handsome donation, to back up our effort. Of this sum he reserved the right to use £500 in doing some special thing, as the completion or adornment of the building.

This is very encouraging. I propose to go from church to church in Liverpool begging. With a long pull, a strong pull and a pull together, we may do it.—Yours hopefully,

John Watson.

PS.—I am good for another hundred pounds.—J. W.

TO THE SAME

September 6th, 1899.

Dear Dr. Dykes,—I am much obliged for your kind letter of yesterday, and your approval of all I am doing. One incentive to work, is that you may be encouraged in your sacrifices, and your hands held up in the high places of the field.

Now another piece of good news. Lady Gray has sent £500 to be entered 'In Memoriam.'

I'll write weekly to the *Presbyterian* to keep the pot boiling. If the Church got enthusiastic we should romp in.

A Cadger.

TO THE SAME

September 8th, 1899.

Dear Dr. Dykes,—Mr. Samuel Smith has promised £250 on condition the debt was cleared, and in addition of course to his previous subscription of £450.

Mr. Smith writes to me this morning, enclosing a cheque of £50 to make his £450 into £500 all paid, and he also promises another £500 if all the debt be cleared off, which will make his contribution in all £1000. This is, I think, most generous on his part, as you may remember that he was opposed to the removal of the College to Cambridge, and holds somewhat strong views about the utility of Universities and Colleges. He would have liked to have been present at the opening, but he is going to America in a few days. He is now very cordial about the College, and I think that he would like to keep in touch with it, and that he might prove a very good friend in the future. He has the utmost confidence, as he well may have, in you, and there are times when the good man thinks that the Convener is not himself so bad as he may appear.

I am going to blow a blast in the *Presbyterian* of next week, and perhaps in the *British Weekly*, which is the quarter where I was heard last time.

Do you think that you could write to Sir Donald Currie, who is in your sphere of influence, and any of the Regent Square men who are likely to give? It might be an argument with the advocates of the Church Extension Fund, that the sooner they get our little applecart out of the way, the better for their coach and four. By the way I forgot to mention that another friend of the College who has given liberally has promised £250 more, but his name is not to be mentioned at present. The money cannot be paid till the Synod of 1900, but it is as good as gold. We are moving on, and the thing must be done. I am going to a public meeting at Cardiff on the 26th, and a meeting is being arranged at Carlisle, and another at Birmingham. I am also going to Leeds and Hull, as I think I told you, and I am beginning to make arrangements in Liverpool. One minister having given me a chance, others have not yet replied, but I shall waken up the place on Monday at the Presbytery meeting. So far as I can see, it means night and day work, and terrible cadging until the 17th. I know it is not right to ask this, but really when it comes to begging, one's conscience gets as hard as leather, and I was wondering if it would be possible for you to take a church in London before that date. Croydon and Streatham, and perhaps Wimbledon, ought to be looked into. I am going to try to fix up a flying visit myself. Of course if you feel this impossible, you will say so, and you will believe that I am most anxious to save you labour in every respect, knowing that this cadging ought to be left to a man with the kind of intellect and manners which Providence is pleased to bestow upon a commercial traveller. JOHN WATSON.

TO THE SAME

September 9th, 1899.

MY DEAR PRINCIPAL,—It is just immense: we are going to do it, yet not *we*, wherefore *Laus Deo*. You will by this time have received my letter with notice of Mr. Smith's generous intentions. This effort in all now comes as far as I can make out to £5265. I hope your list will reach me in time for next week's papers. I propose to publish this in the *British Weekly* and *Presbyterian*, and exhort the Church to rise as one man to finish the job. Am going to

Cardiff, Birmingham, Leeds and Carlisle, and Hull.—Your faithful partner, JOHN WATSON.

Dykes, Watson & Co.;
Commission Agents and Solicitors.

TO THE SAME

September 16th, 1899.

DEAR DR. DYKES,—The conversion of Mr. M. shows that there is a work of grace in the man, and that nothing is impossible. Last night I spoke at Mr. Hutton's church at Birkenhead, but there was a great storm of wind and rain, the meeting was small and heavy. Some congregations are difficult to rouse, but one has to fight away. The result was not very good, but they promised to make it better, and to let me have the result in the beginning of the week. I have just been organising one or two meetings where I cannot go myself, and am arranging if possible a meeting at Croydon, which I shall take along with Wimbledon and Norwood next week. The telegraph boy lives in the garden, and the click of the Remington is never still in the house, while assistants and secretaries write on the stairs, or any place where there is room. Were it not that I am paying my own charges in College matters I should be afraid to send in my bill, for between office and travelling expenses it would sink the fund.

What, however, is my work compared with yours? And I do trust that you will have a good holiday, which you so much need, and be in great form for the opening. After that event I propose myself to go to Monte Carlo, but my wife thinks that it would be safer for me with such a large amount of College Funds within my reach, to go with her to St. Leonards, and to stay at a house in that district where whist is the only game.—With constant remembrance, yours faithfully, JOHN WATSON.

TO THE SAME

September 25th, 1899.

MY DEAR PRINCIPAL,—Your letter of the 23rd has just come, and found me for a wonder in my own home, to which I returned on Saturday at three o'clock after a pretty stiff week's work. The week was, however, very successful on the whole, so that on Saturday night we were very close to £8000.

What about my sermons, do you say? They are composed in the train, in strange studies, early in the morning, between twelve and one at night, or during the chairman's remarks at public meetings, from which I always abstract my mind, as they are mainly taken up with references to the *Brier Bush*, and not to Westminster College, which is the only thing with which I am now concerned.

By the way, no cards of invitation to service, luncheon, reception, or anything else have come here, and so I gather that you will accept this cadging about the country as my share of public appearances. Should I be wrong in this idea perhaps you would let me know, and Mrs. Watson would make an effort to be present. A number of our office-bearers are threatening to descend on Cambridge that day, staying in London for the night. What about tickets at least for the opening service and reception? Our people have done well by the College and I hope will do well in the future, and even altho' I were not there myself I should like some of them to be there. Mrs. Watson and I will come and attend everything whether we are invited or not, these being our manners and habits of life. I hope this letter may reach you. Letters addressed to my home are sent after me to where I am exploring for gold, upon swift dromedaries or dog-sledges or any conveyance suitable to the district.—Yours faithfully, JOHN WATSON.

TO THE SAME

September 29th, 1899.

My dear Principal,—Many thanks for your letter of the 28th. It is very good of you to write so often and with your many duties, and if I do not write to you in return, by my own hand, it is because I have so many letters to write that my hand sometimes shakes, and is then even more difficult to read than usual.

Many thanks for not asking me to come up to the committee meeting, as this kindness leaves me free for the cadging. Let me follow up my wire by saying that one of Anderson Scott's people has subscribed £1000, and as I was up to the £9000 this morning we have finished the business. I propose, however, to complete my programme, and raise every penny I can, altho' I shall not practise any deception. One never knows what may be needed in a building account till every account be in, and the money paid, and of course there is always a certain risk about subscriptions until the cash is in the bank. I want to make certain that the whole building be finished and paid for down to the last garden shrub and kitchen pan, so that there be no charge hanging over the annual account. When we are at it our little Church must finish the job well, and show that if we be one of the least we are one of the bravest tribes of Israel. The meetings have everywhere been most loyal and enthusiastic. The spirit of the Church is fairly up, and is rising every week.

With regard to the opening service, it seems all right. I am personally alarmed that I have to speak three times at the luncheon, and I cannot discover from my paper where you are to speak at all. You ought either to propose the University of Cambridge, or as I fancy may be intended, altho' not mentioned, Westminster will be proposed by some one and associated with your name.

I shall do my best to see that, however hard your work may be, it shall not be made harder by financial worries about College Funds. I go to Carlisle to-night to send the fiery cross up and down the borders. The lads there are already clamouring for letters to read aloud from their pulpits, and everywhere declaring they must have a share in Westminster College. I do not believe any Principal ever began his work in a new College with more popular interest and with more hearty prayers for him and for his College.—Yours beggarly, JOHN WATSON.

TO THE SAME

October 4th, 1899.

MY DEAR PRINCIPAL,—Our correspondence is surely the happiest in the world next to a love one, because we are mainly engaged now in intimating fresh gifts to the College.

Since I wrote to you I have been at Carlisle, where there was not much money, but a large meeting and good hearts, and at Birmingham where there was more money and also a vast deal of heart. Birmingham is quite sound, but requires a little encouraging, and I have an idea that next year if it could be arranged that a few of you big men should go down to the Midlands, not to beg, which I believe is the only thing I am really fit for, but to bid the people be of good cheer, it would do a vast deal of good. However, that 's another story.

The money still comes in, and I hear of another £500 paid at the office by an unobtrusive person, who prefers to call himself G. B., which is very encouraging. Other donations are coming in, and there is generally a sound of much rain. You will notice by to-morrow's *Presbyterian* the line which I am taking, which is that there will be many expenses before we have done with the College, and that we must get in the last penny. My opinion is that the spirit of the Church is now so strong that we shall finish this subscription gloriously. You will enter the College supported by the enthusiasm and prayers of the whole Church.—Believe me, yours beggarly, DUGALD MACTAVISH.

TO THE SAME

October 25th, 1899.

MY DEAR PRINCIPAL,—Once more let me congratulate you on the great success of last Tuesday. Nothing could have been better arranged, and we are all extremely indebted to yourself and your assistants in this matter. There are one or two matters on which I should like your mind as they concern the future history of the College. First of all there is the annual income, and this must be increased. I shall make this week a strong appeal that every church should now give loyally to the support of the College, and that our larger churches should increase their giving. We must not do anything even in appearance to isolate the College from the Church, for that would be contrary to our principles, and it would also be very ungrateful to the people of all kinds who have so loyally supported us, and whose sympathy is so genuine. We must, however, have a subscription list, and a body of men who will make the fuller endowment of the College their heart's desire. Permit me also to add that I shall not be satisfied until the Principal of Westminster College has a larger salary.

As you will notice I did not remain for that committee meeting, for I was tired and worn out, but I should like to have a talk with you about the House Committee. It appears to me that it ought to be, as it was before, a sub-committee of the College Committee, and to be responsible to that committee especially as it will have to deal with many financial details.

Another thing that occurs to me is, that with the enormous responsibility laid upon you in representing our College in Cambridge, and making this new departure with its great issues, you must not be troubled with any detail. It would make the gods laugh if the Principal of Westminster College had to deal with books and bed-makers; it would also be a disgrace to those of us who had anything to do with the business affairs of the College.—Yours faithfully,

JOHN WATSON.

I give a few more letters written to Dr. Dykes about this time:—

TO PRINCIPAL OSWALD DYKES

October 27th, 1899.

MY DEAR PRINCIPAL,—As I am writing and may not be troubling you again with a letter before November, I would like to say that my mind is still more than ever fixed not to accept the Moderatorship, even if my name should be brought forward through the undeserved kindness of my brethren and the recent efforts which I had the privilege of making for our College. No man ought to undertake a duty for which he is not fitted, and certainly nature never intended me to undertake such high functions. I can cadge for money or deliver a lecture, or take the chair at a business board, or preach the Gospel in a simple fashion, but I cannot sit in the throne of a Church. On this matter my mind is made up, and as it is not right the Moderatorship should ever be refused, I venture to ask you as the leader of our Church to prevent my name being brought before, or at least being discussed by the nomination board.

Another matter I would like to mention at this early date in order to have your mind upon it when the time comes for action. As my work in the removal of the College to Cambridge, and its establishment there, has been finished, and as I think there will be no grounds for anxiety on account of the yearly income, I propose to do what has been in my mind all along, after my seven years of office, to resign the Convenership of the College Committee.

My reasons for this step are briefly these: that such offices should not be held too long by one man, because he is apt to grow ineffective. That a new man feels bound to do some new work, and that my successor would have an excellent opportunity in endowing the fourth chair. That I think I have given enough time during these years to be my share of public work in the Church, and ought to do more for my own people from whom Church work has taken me a great deal of late. I am not any more suitable for a Convener than for a Moderator, and I shall be very glad when I leave these high places and go down again into the ranks of the working ministry from which you took me in 1892, and to which I shall return with much relief.—I am and shall ever be your loyal supporter, JOHN WATSON.

TO THE SAME

October 31st, 1899.

MY DEAR PRINCIPAL,—To-day I do not dictate, rather supplicate. First a word of thanks for your kind letter, and its commentary on various matters. Second: Do let me slip out from the Cabinet, and be a Queen's messenger or some such person. The goodness of my brethren has been the best reward, and one far more to my mind than office. No one in my place could be offended for no one has been better treated, and every one knows how unfit I am for the business of Church Courts. May I offer this, for in everything I wish to please you, that I will continue Convener for a year, if there be no word of the Moderatorship.—Yours unofficially, J. W.

TO THE SAME

November 10*th,* 1899.

My dear Principal,—I am greatly obliged, and I am also much humbled by the trouble which you have had to take about my case. This week I saw the two Fathers of the Church, and they both gave me very kindly and sound advice. Perhaps it may be only putting off the honourable day, but in the light of what was said I intend to decline the nomination for 1900, and to do so on the grounds that I am going to rest.—Yours faithfully, John Watson.

TO THE SAME

November 29*th,* 1899.

My dear Principal,—You have had so much trouble about the Moderatorship, that it is only right to thank you and to let you know that I have decided to leave myself in the hands of the Church, but like other people whose minds vacillate in regard to questions of expediency, I am now as miserable in accepting as I would have been if I had declined.

I consulted my friend Nicoll, who told me three things in order. First, that he didn't consider it any particular honour. Secondly, that as I had been offered it, I must accept it; and lastly, that he didn't know a more unsuitable man. I consulted my Elders, who declared with two exceptions that people would be disappointed if I didn't take it, the minority holding that it was a matter for my own concern. I did not write to my Scots friends, because they would have written with one accord after the manner of Scots Kirkmen, to say that they were interested to hear that we had a Moderator, and to ask where our Synod met. Already I am receiving letters exhorting me to buy the Moderator's handbook, which the writer says is shortly to be published by Mr. H., and will, he says, have one chapter on how to clear your throat, and another on how to twirl your eyebrows. This book the writer assures me is to be brought out in the Badminton series, and as my correspondent is one of the leading members of my Church, and a future Moderator, he ought to know.

Seriously I cannot lift up my head nor my heart till May 1901 if I be spared so long. Allow me to thank you for the honour which you have done me in proposing my name, and to express my hope that during my year of office I may do nothing to bring discredit upon my Church.—Yours faithfully, JOHN WATSON.

CHAPTER XIV

THE BOER WAR

On October 9, 1899, the British Government received an ultimatum from the Boer Government in South Africa demanding that 'the troops on the borders of the Republic should be instantly withdrawn, that all reinforcements which had arrived within the last year should leave South Africa, and that those who are now upon the sea should be sent back without being landed.' Failing a satisfactory answer within forty-eight hours, 'the Transvaal Government will with great regret be compelled to regard the action of Her Majesty's Government as a formal declaration of war, for the consequences of which it will not be held responsible.' Her Majesty's Government next day instructed Sir Alfred Milner to inform the Government of the South African Republic that the conditions demanded by the Government of the South African Republic are such as Her Majesty's Government deem it impossible to discuss. There followed the great Boer War.

Watson at once sided with the Government, and set himself to stimulate by every means the patriotic spirit. He was by no means a blind partisan. He could do justice to the character of the Boers, and also to their claims, but he held that the war was justified, and he believed that war had its uses in the providence of God. Besides doing all he could in Liverpool to encourage men to go out, he preached from time to time on the subject. He thus incurred the attacks of those who believed the war to be unrighteous, and it is well known that a considerable number of the English Nonconformists were on this side. He was invited to preach on a special occasion in Wesley's Chapel, London, on March 2, 1900, and Mr. Chamberlain had agreed to preside at a public luncheon after the sermon. Strong objections were taken by many Wesleyan Methodists to Mr. Chamberlain's presence, and the luncheon was abandoned, much to the disappointment of Watson and many others. But Watson had preached to his own people a sermon in December from the text 'When Thy judgments are in the earth, the inhabitants of the world will learn righteousness.' He protested against the spirit which is ever carping at a man's own country, and ever prophesying the worst, and declared it was not wonderful that people should lose patience with public leaders who were chiefly concerned about the interests of some foreign country, and never really caught fire except in pointing out the faults of their own.

'Whatever may be our view regarding the original necessity for this war, and the spirit of diplomacy which led to its outbreak, we were agreed in the final crisis that war could not be escaped without dishonour and the denial of duty; and we were also quite convinced that it would be crowned with a speedy triumph.' But the grievous humiliation of our people in a land which had been for England the grave of high reputations and gallant lives had its purpose. If we had carried everything before us we should have been intolerable 'both to God and man, and the song of the drunkard would have gone up to heaven. . . . If a few weeks ago we were drunk with militarism, we have been thoroughly sobered, and are in a position to consider our ways, and to learn the meaning of the Divine judgment.' He pointed out that the arrogance of the nation sorely needed to be checked. 'We have not in Europe to-day—with perhaps one doubtful exception—a single friend. Yes! and what is more galling, there is not one of those ignorant, sinful nations, as we reckon them, which does not think that we are wrong, greedy, unscrupulous, and oppressive.' Also greed of wealth had brought us into our present state, and had led to the death of so many brave men. 'What is certain is that the immediate occasion of this disastrous war was the desire of a pastoral people to retain the control of their own country, and the determination of a handful of mine-owning millionaires to seize it for their own ends. They were not themselves brave enough to fight, and now they are not generous enough to give, being as mean now as they were cowardly before, but they were cunning enough to induce a gang of criminal adventurers to make that raid for which we are all now paying, in sorrow, or in blood, and in the end to set by the ears our great empire and this little nation of country-folk.' He characterised the Boers as 'Jews of the Old Testament time, removed only from the period of Judges by their kindness to their enemies after the fighting is over. But still there are two things which cannot be denied, they are strong men, both in body and heart, able to endure and ready to fight, and according to their light and training they fear God. When I read that the Boer commandos were sent off to the war with religious service I did not laugh. It is better that men should go forth to their death filled with prayers, than with strong drink, better they should go from a place of worship, than be gathered from public-houses. When I read that companies were engaged in prayer during battle, and that our shells killed them praying, I did not triumph, for I knew that such a people would be hard to beat.' He concluded on an inspiriting note:—

The war has come and the war must be fought to the end, and I make no doubt, notwithstanding all our reverses in the beginning, that we shall gain the victory; and I make as little doubt, notwithstanding many fears, that our victory will be for the good of South Africa. We have sinned in departing from the living God and caring overmuch for this present world, and therefore we are being punished as Israel was punished. Yet Israel was God's instrument in fulfilling His purpose of moral education throughout the world, and England, if one can make anything of history, has been God's instrument in spreading civilisation and administering justice among savage or oppressed peoples. If the only end this war would serve were to give fresh fields for greed and gambling, then the best thing that could happen to our country would be defeat, but if the end shall be the establishment of liberty and order, and equal rights to all men, whether Dutch or English, black or white, in South Africa, then we shall have in our generation another evidence that God is over all, bringing light out of darkness, and making the sin of man to praise Him.

It may be seen from this that Watson was by no means an indiscriminating partisan, that he saw the weak points on the English side and the strength of the Boers. But when he spoke to the Wesleyan Methodists in March he delivered a message of comfort to England. 'Are any man's eyes so blind that he cannot see the mission of England? Have not we been surrounded by the seas and our national character formed for purposes that we can recognise? What nation has ever planted so many colonies, explored so many unknown lands, made such practical contributions to civilisation, set such an illustrious example of liberty ?' He praised the nobler spirit which God had given England during the progress of the war. 'I do not say we are a wise people—there are foolish people in a large nation ; I do not say there have not been peevish complaints, shrill, high-pitched, shrieking voices ; I do not say there have not been ungenerous criticisms ; but I do say that all that has been but the spume on the surface of the water, and that throughout our homes—and a minister knows the homes of a people, and the tone of the homes is more than the cries of agitators—through the homes of our people there never has been a nobler spirit, more unboasting courage, more unfaltering confidence in God. Has our army,' he asked, 'ever stood higher in bravery, in patience, in confidence, than to-day ? from that old man that went out stricken in his own heart, and at the age of seventy led the armies of England to victory, down to the laddie who would be in the front line of fire, and when one arm was disabled shifted the bugle to the other hand and blew till he fell.' He triumphed in the adhesion of the Colonies. 'A covenant has been made between England and her Colonies, and the covenant has been sealed with blood, and to-day England and the colonies are one. They reviled us, those nations of Europe, with exceptions, they reviled us ; but it does not matter what the outside world says if your own family is true.'

TO PRINCIPAL OSWALD DYKES

January 3rd, 1900.

My dear Principal,—The result of the War Sermon has been a stream of correspondence, whose writers regard me either as a prophet or an ass. As the division of opinion seems nearly equal, I fancy that I am in 'de middle of de road.'—Yours afflicted but determined,

The MacWatson of MacWhat.

TO W. ROBERTSON NICOLL

17 *Croxteth Road, Feb.* 22, 1900.

Dear Nicoll,—I send two of the articles promised with dates of publication, March 25, April 25, or nearest days.

Have just received anonymous post-card, *i.e.* this morning's *B. W.*, urging that I and my sons should go to the front, as the country could afford to lose us, which has greatly tickled the family.

How are the people created who write and post these things, and are they beyond grace?—Till Wednesday evening, yours respectfully, John Watson.

With the officers who were unfortunate in the South African War, Watson had a warm sympathy, and especially with Sir Redvers Buller. He wrote a paper, 'News of a Famous Victory,' describing how the tidings of the relief of Ladysmith were received in London:—

Each man took the news in his own fashion, one laughing and slapping his legs, another crying and speaking to himself, a third rushing out to cheer, and I, why I, being an unemotional Scot, remembered that if I fooled away any more time, reading news of victories, I might lose my train, so I rushed back to the hansom.

'Is't all correct?' the driver leant down from his perch, determined not to let himself go till he was perfectly certain that, not only the straight tip had been given, but that at last the event had come off.

'All right,' I said; 'Buller's army have driven back the Boers, and the advance guard has entered Ladysmith.'

Whereupon he whipped off his hat, and standing up in his place, a stout, red-faced Englishman in sporting dress, he gave a cheer all on his own account, and then when I got in he opened the trap, and shouted down, 'Old Buller's done it; he had a bloomin' tough job, but he's a game sportsman, and I said he'd do it. And old Buller's done it!' Again he celebrated the event with a cheer, and we started for Charing Cross.

It was a record of actual experience, and he reprinted it in his little volume, *His Majesty Baby and some Common People.* It drew the following letter from General Buller:—

FROM SIR REDVERS BULLER

Dec. 20, 1902.

Sir Redvers Buller presents his compliments to Dr. Watson and thanks him for the copy of *His Maiesty Baby*, which he has duly received.

Sir Redvers highly appreciates the gift as a present from an author whom he admires. He is naturally pleased and complimented by the article, but above all he is grateful for the kindly sympathy to which he attributes the origin of the gift.

TO W. ROBERTSON NICOLL

17 *Croxteth Road, 7th November* 1900.

Dear Nicoll,—You may be interested to know that I have been doing my best for that boy you introduced to me, and that I heard yesterday that he is likely to get a place in one of our best shipping offices. It is not certain, but the omens are favourable, and the case is in the hands of one of my elders, who is not easily beaten, and who you will be pleased to know is taken with the lad.

I have finished Morley's *Cromwell*; it is an excellent piece of writing and on the whole sane in its judgment, but as history, not to be compared with Firth or Gardiner. Although this is a valuable remark and contains news which might not otherwise reach your ears, I make no charge, I am that kind of man.—Yours wearily, John Watson.

TO A CLERGYMAN'S WIFE

November 29th, 1900.

I am obliged for your courteous letter of the 21st, which I could not answer sooner as I have been from home. You are quite right about the apparent inconsistency between the hope expressed in *The Potter's Wheel*, regarding the ultimate home-coming of children longed and prayed for, and the painful facts of character referred to in *The Doctrines of Grace*, and which seem likely in some cases to blight that hope, but is it not this antimony throughout Holy Scripture, where you have the will of God working for our salvation, and passages that seem to imply that that will must be fulfilled, and again other passages of warning and foreboding? The Bible often seems to be in two minds, and we also not only may be but ought to be in two minds, hoping with all our might, and yet laying to heart the awful permanence of character.

One of his warmest friends, Sir Thomas Grainger Stewart, an eminent Edinburgh physician, was at this time lying on what proved to be his deathbed. Watson writes him a letter of cheer:—

TO SIR THOMAS GRAINGER STEWART

January 10*th,* 1900.

DEAR SIR THOMAS,—It does not follow, although perhaps it ought, that because I write this letter there is something in it worth reading. Nothing is happening here except Influenza, which keeps me very busy, but is not a cheerful subject for a sick room. This plague divides our interest with the war, about which we feel very anxious, and about which we are holding patriotic meetings. We had the most influential meeting in the Town Hall that I have seen for many years, when some of us spoke for the fund to arm our Yeomanry. Several of my neighbours' sons, and some of them in my own church, who are riding men are going out at their own expense, horse and man together, and I think it is a noble thing that young men should be giving up luxurious homes and risking their lives for the Empire. This is one good thing amid much which is doubtful and painful. I have been preaching in my own church that every young man should now be drilled, and I am thankful to say that my eldest son and several of his friends went down and passed the medical examination next day, and if he had not been already a volunteer, I think he would have offered himself for the army.

In the meantime, or rather to fill up the time, I am to act as Moderator of the Presbyterian Church of England. As my term of office begins at the end of April and I have much to learn, I am already calculating a dignified walk on the street, and clearing my throat in a sonorous way, and waving an eyeglass while I speak, and have been trying, with poor success however, to put off old friends who wish to shake hands at New Year's time, with a couple of fingers and a noise in my throat. For a whole year I shall not be an ordinary man, saying what I think and going where I please, but shall be pouring forth pompous platitudes with fearsome gravity, and travelling from bazaar to bazaar, and from one foundation stone to another, besides addressing religious bodies as an ambassador from a friendly power. It will be, if I dare compare small things with great, as if I were physician to Her Majesty the Queen, and had you been in your usual health I should have come North to learn some tricks of speech and manner from you, especially how to go backwards without sitting down abruptly on the floor, or descending like a battering-ram on some great lady.

The weather to-day is much brighter with us, and much more may I hope it is with you, and this ought to do you good and help you to regain strength. We have passed the turn of the year, and Spring is not so very far off, for I cling to the old-fashioned idea that Spring begins on the 1st of February.—Yours ever faithfully, JOHN WATSON.

Alias IAN MACLAREN.
,, Pastor Hairy-bed (of Galatia).
,, Terence O'Watson (Cork).
,, The Moderator Elect.

The end came soon, and the letters to Lady Grainger Stewart explain themselves.

TO LADY GRAINGER STEWART

December 22*nd*, 1900.

DEAR LADY STEWART,—It is a very busy time, and my hand is weary at this season. You will excuse a vicarious type, for I wish to assure you that when we think of our friends at this time we remember you and yours in the earthly home with affectionate regard, and we do not forget those who are in the Father's House, and who remember us. May you have at this time that peace which the world cannot give, and which it cannot take away, and that joy which Christ had even looking forward to the Cross, and may the love of God be your dwelling-place.—Your faithful friend,

JOHN WATSON.

TO THE SAME

February 15*th,* 1900.

DEAR LADY STEWART,—You will by this time have read my humble tribute to the memory of your beloved husband, and my valued friend. It is inevitable that you should think it less than it should be, but that is the disability of any pen in the public press. What I wrote was from my heart, and you see it has an honourable place in the paper. Kindly accept the assurance of my sympathy in your loss of so distinguished and so dear a husband. If there ever be anything in which I can serve you or yours you will command me for the sake of the days of the past, and you will ever believe me to be,—Your affectionate and faithful friend,

JOHN WATSON.

CHAPTER XV

MODERATOR

THE great services which Watson had rendered to his Church, and the prominent position he had taken in the country, made it natural that he should receive the highest honour his brethren could confer. Accordingly, he was appointed Moderator of the Presbyterian Synod of England in April 1900. He had been used to joke on the ways of ecclesiastics, and from some points of view it was comical that he should occupy a great ecclesiastical office. But his banterings on this subject must not be allowed for a moment to disguise the truth. I do not believe that any honour Watson ever received was more valued than the Moderatorship, and this for a very simple reason. He was thoroughly loyal to the Presbyterian Church of England, and he valued with his whole heart the esteem and confidence of his brethren. He had hesitated previously about occupying the chair, especially when he was suspected of heresy, but when he saw that the tribute was unanimous and cordial, he received it with unfeigned delight and gratitude.

The Moderator of a Presbyterian Church presides over the meetings of the Supreme Court, and is expected during his year of office to serve his Church by preaching on special occasions over the country. Perhaps no Moderator ever flung himself into this service with more joy and more generous expenditure of heart and effort than Watson did. In truth, he was never the same man after his Moderator's year had expired. He had drawn too heavily on his great resources. From all over England incessant demands came to him, and he responded to them up to his power, and beyond it. During the whole year he had only two evenings for his family—Christmas and New Year's Day. It was then that he showed certain signs that his powerful constitution had been injured. One of these was insomnia. But it was a happy year, assuring him as it did of his place in the heart of his Church. His name was by this time so well known, that wherever he went he could at any time command a crowded audience. 'This,' he wrote to one of his sons, 'shows not that your father is a great preacher, but that he is well known, which is a rather different thing.' But his sermons, his addresses, and his kindly fellowship in the manses of his brethren, stimulated the whole life of the Church.

Among the most important duties of a Moderator is his address to the Synod. Dr. Watson was most heartily welcomed to the chair, and it was pointed out that while the evangelical party in former times looked with suspicion on the literary efforts of their ministers as tending to draw them away from their proper work, he had used his great literary reputation and position to serve more effectively the Church to which he belonged. Watson took as his subject the theme which lay nearest his heart—Faith and Humanism. Humanism he defined as the love of the beautiful both in literature and in art, together with that culture of one's mind and that unrestrained joy in living and that fulfilment of one's nature, which lent an undying youth to the classics of Greece and Rome, which was the charm of the European renaissance, and which to-day is casting its ancient and pagan glamour over the brightest minds of the generation. Faith was that knowledge of God and that discipline of the soul, together with that service of man which from the beginning have affected the more spiritual minds of the race and created saints, whose literature is contained in the writings of prophets, apostles, theologians, mystics, whose children have been the missionary, the martyr, the evangelist, the philanthropist, whose renaissance has been those revivals of religion which have renewed the face of society. He deprecated the Puritan suspicion of letters. He affirmed that the masters of literature had been the friends of

Christ. He pleaded that a tender regard should be shown to the many thoughtful and devout persons who had been affected by the atmosphere of the day, and had ceased to believe in the essence of the Christian creed. He asked whether it would not have been better that the government of the Church in critical periods of thought and action should have been, not in the hands of the extreme right, by which he practically meant the evangelical party, but rather under the control of the moderate left, by which he meant those who held the faith of Christ with a cultured moderation. He allowed that the debate between more faith and less culture and more culture and less faith had to be settled by the facts of history, and he owned that it was Luther rather than Erasmus who had spread Christianity. 'It was not the cultured school of moderate clergy, but the evangelicals who, with the exception of Boston and Witherspoon, had not one writer among them; who were rough in style, out of touch with men of letters and bigoted in doctrine, that were the saving salt of the Church and of vital religion in the age when both were threatened with decay.' What had to be striven for was a reconciliation. 'When one goes to the root of the matter, the central doctrine of the Christian faith can never be acceptable to humanism, save where some great humanist is also a greater Christian, for it is necessary to lay it to mind to-day, and to insist upon it with all our strength, both of intellect and of emotion, that the very heart of Christianity is the deity of our Lord Jesus Christ.' Christianity goes deeper than humanism ever can, for it is a salvation and not merely another system of morals. 'With the Incarnation we have the revelation of God, the Divine Fatherhood, an atoning sacrifice for sin, the victory over the things which are seen and the assurance of a blessed immortality. The race is no longer hopeless, human history is no longer a dreary tragedy, the grave is no longer the close of life.'

Professor Stalker, who was present at the Synod where he was Moderator, writes:—

> There also I had the privilege of seeing him in one of the crowning moments of his life, especially one day, when he must have spoken for over two hours; first, in giving in as convener, the College Committee's report; secondly, in reporting on his own campaign for the extinction of the debt on the new buildings at Cambridge; and, thirdly, in responding to a vote of thanks from the Synod for his efforts in that cause. Never have I seen any man—not even Principal Rainy in the Free Assembly—with a body of men, for the time at least, more completely in the hollow of his hand; and never have I seen a man on any occasion display such a profusion and variety of powers.

As Moderator Watson had to present to the King on his Coronation the address from the Presbyterian Church of England. He was excessively nervous on this occasion, but showed no trace of this in reading the document, while his delight in the opportunity—for the King had no more loyal subject—was very great. In this year the union between the Free Church of Scotland and the United Presbyterian Church was consummated at Edinburgh, and Dr. Watson conveyed the congratulations of the English Presbyterians in a speech at a great meeting where over 7000 were present. He was not in the fullest sympathy with the union, partly because he thought the Highlanders did not receive full justice, but mainly because he earnestly desired a reunion of the whole Presbyterianism of Scotland. In his speech he pleaded that both Churches should work each from its own side of the wall towards a complete reconciliation. His own view was that the Church of Scotland should have spiritual independence conceded by Parliament; that the endowments should be sacredly reserved for religious purposes; and that there should be a kind of disestablishment which would not interfere with the State recognition of the United Church as the Church of Scotland.

TO A FORMER ASSISTANT IN SCOTLAND

January 12th, 1901.

I am obliged for your last letter and all its kind words, but I fear very much that it will be long before I can visit you in what is called an official capacity. My strength is being heavily taxed by this Moderatorship, which is far heavier than I ever anticipated, and my congregational work is being rather neglected.

I have resolved if I be spared to remain at home, excepting in fulfilment of one or two engagements made long ago, for two years, attending to my church and my duties in Liverpool, and occupying my private time in a very important work, which I promised to do three years ago, and have hardly yet touched, which will take my spare time for some years. You are now, however, in a Church so great and rich in theologians, orators, lords, and distinguished people of every kind, that the visit of an English Presbyterian, even of a former chief, could only be of the smallest importance. It is indeed good of you in your high places to think of us at all, and I have a shrewd idea that your invitation was meant as an act of kindly encouragement to a struggling foreign missionary.

TO W. ROBERTSON NICOLL

17 *Croxteth Road,*
Liverpool, 19*th February* 1901.

Dear Nicoll,—As I am writing, I hasten to add that I do not propose as a rule to write daily, but will occasionally pass a Sunday. I received quite a number of letters about *Church Folks*, very pleasant and friendly, but in many cases wanting some qualification put in about the minister's busy life. Do you think it would be any use to take notice of those criticisms in a future edition? My impression is that you could not have a keener discussion in the *B.W.* than on the question of whether the Ministry really uses its time well, and whether it is up-to-date in its knowledge. Forsyth is with us just now as a missioner, and preached a very earnest sermon last night. He has a very impressive gift of repetition which I believe is most useful especially in appeal. The great want of preachers to-day is unction, tenderness in dealing with the human soul, affectionate appeal, and insistence upon the Eternal commonplaces of religion.

With this lofty oracle I beg to subscribe myself, your obedient servant, EPAPHRODITUS HIGGINBOTHAM

(Auroraville, U.S.A.).

CHAPTER XVI

LATER YEARS

DR. WATSON was much exhausted after the completion of his work as Moderator. He sought to relieve himself of some responsibilities, and he took occasional holidays. But it was not in his nature to rest. The concluding years of his pastorate at Sefton Park were full of public and pastoral labour, though their routine was not broken by any unusual incident. He went on preaching and lecturing through the country, and he was busy with his pen. Fortunately I have letters of his own which record the main events. In this letter to Dr. Dykes he explains his plans:—

TO PRINCIPAL OSWALD DYKES

March 7th, 1901.

MY DEAR PRINCIPAL,—It is, I am sorry to say, impossible for me to continue longer in the important office of College Convener, and I will briefly state my reasons. First, it appears to me that I have held this office beyond the time expedient for a Convener, and that a change would bring in new ideas, new energies, and new ambitions. Second, the special work with which I have been identified, namely the removal of the College to Cambridge, and the clearing off the building debt, has been finished, and at the moment when a man's special work has been concluded the break ought to come and he ought not to begin another work, which he would have to leave unfinished, namely the increase of the College income, and other matters. Third, this is a very important work, and therefore may well invite the services of one of our best men, who would not be inclined merely to take up the College after all the important work had been done, and be merely a routine official, as some Conveners are, imagining no great thing, but simply giving in mechanical reports. A mere harbour captain, instead of the captain who brings the vessel from port to port. Fourth, such a man would have an enterprise entirely his own and separate from mine, in which his credit would be involved and an honourable name could be made, and in asking for funds he would appeal possibly to new clients, and certainly with a new voice. Fifth, during the last year I have felt very much overstrained, and am very tired both in mind and body. My health has been suffering, and altho' I work hard, I do so with much less physical strength than that given to most of my brethren, whose robustness I envy. I hate talking about one's health, but I may mention that no insurance company would take my life as it now is, altho' I was once a sound man. One thing I certainly gave to our Church, and that was my health, for I was once considered a first-rate life. Besides, and perhaps this is more important, my mind has of late been flagging very much, and through the desultory life I have been leading, I am behind in reading, and have had too little leisure for thought and spiritual culture. My preaching, therefore, has been failing, and the life of my congregation suffering. If Sefton Park Church is not to decay, and if I am to maintain its pulpit and its spirit, I must for some years retire from public Church work. Sixth, my plan is to give up all public work outside Liverpool, without any exception, for at least two years, except now and again a lecture to some literary institution, which is a little variety, and which I enjoy, and in Liverpool I propose to confine myself to the most important objects and meetings. I quite hold that every man ought to give his share of public service to the Church, but I think I have done mine, and will gladly allow others to have their opportunity.

Pardon me stating my reasons at such length, and accept this wearisome letter, which has grown into a sermon, as a proof of my respect for you and the care which I have given to your letter.—Yours faithfully,

JOHN WATSON.

To a friend abroad he sends some home gossip.

October 18th, 1901.

As I am obliged to go slowly this winter, lest a worse thing befall me, I have an occasional half-hour of leisure, and as you are wandering to and fro, and might like to have some home gossip, I send you this budget of varied intelligence, altho' as my hand does not remain steady for so long a letter, I must send it in type, for which no doubt you will be grateful remembering how difficult my writing is to read, even at the best.

If I remember rightly, you left in the best of weather, and that weather continued until the end of September, which altogether was a lovely month, and made one wish it had been included in his holidays. This afternoon, Mrs. Watson and I go to Delamere Forest where the Countess of Derby is to open the Consumption Hospital.

We promised to go, and I am down on the card for the vote of thanks, and so we must go, but as it is raining heavily and the weather has fairly broken, we would rather stay at home. For the much needed rain has come now, and we have had gales and torrents within the last week or two.

F. preached on September 15th, two most learned and able sermons for which we were all grateful. Altho' F. is one of the most learned theologians in England, yet you could not have had a more genial guest in the house, and after he had discussed Theology and given us a mass of information, it was his pleasure to call on the Japanese mice, which have recently been added to our family, and to see those exceedingly funny animals doing their waltzes.

Perhaps the chief event in Liverpool since you left has been the visit of Lord Roberts, who distributed medals to the volunteers, and others who had won them in the war, and had a great reception. Jack was out with our Scots Regiment helping to line the streets, and a very wet day they had of it standing in their kilts with the rain blowing about them. We all wish that this weary war were over, and I make no doubt you are praying for the same end, for you have entered into the depths of its sorrow. I trust that you have been comforted in your great sorrow, and I can assure you, altho' people may not always be referring to it, you are in the thoughts of many, and have still our deepest sympathy.

Last Sunday I preached in Marylebone Church, London, to a very large congregation, but always feel happiest at home, and firmly believe that there is no congregation so intelligent, so broad-minded, and so kindly as Sefton Park. I am now in the twenty-second year of my ministry in Liverpool, and sometimes grow a little tired, but when I think of the kindness I have received and the prosperity God has been pleased to give us, I take courage again. Did any one suppose twenty years ago that Sefton Park Church would have had such a history? We have good cause both for humility and for gratitude.

If you have time amid all your journeys and your sight-seeing we shall be glad to know how it fares with you, that you are well, and enjoying yourselves in the States. Have you seen the Indian summer on the Hudson, and the glory of the St. Lawrence, and the magnificence of Washington, and are you going to cross the Rocky Mountains? By this time, however, you must be tired of a letter that is growing into a sermon, and so with our united affectionate regard to you both,—Your faithful minister, JOHN WATSON.

Watson had published during his Moderatorship what is perhaps his ablest theological book, that on *The Doctrines of Grace*. In this he made a resolute attempt to translate the main doctrines of theology into current speech. The most orthodox of his critics were disarmed. He was deeply gratified by an appreciation from Dr. Horton, who described the book as 'a signal illustration of Grace in the widest sense of the term—Grace of style and Grace of thought; the Grace of a man, and the Grace of God.' He also worked at his *Life of the Master*, which was published, with special coloured illustrations, in *M'Clure's Magazine*. This book, which is highly elaborated, had a considerable sale both in its more expensive and in its cheaper form. He was working also at his school sketches published under the title *Young Barbarians*.

As the winter of 1901 passed on he became very weary, but was reluctant to take a holiday.

TO W. ROBERTSON NICOLL

17 *Croxteth Road*,
Liverpool, 28*th November* 1901.

Dear Nicoll,—Your kind and welcome note came last evening, and the words of commendation encouraged me, first because your commendation is to me, as well as to the public, very weighty, and second, because being in low spirits a pat on the back moves up my ears and tail.

With Black's book came down Neatby's book,[1] and I now send a review. The book interested me so much, as well as the whole subject, that I have written at some length, but I hope the article may not be uninteresting. You have done a valuable service in securing that book. Do not suppose, however, I cannot write short notices of books when I am so minded, or the book requires no more.

You ask me whether I am going to Egypt, and my first reply is that as the newspapers have said everywhere that I am going I must be going. I may also add, depending on the newspapers, that I am to be 'accompanied by Mrs. Watson,' that I am to visit the military stations and to compare notes with the chaplains, that on returning home I am first to write a report on the chaplains' work, for whom I don't know. Second, to write a book on Egypt; and third—but this grows wearisome.

As a matter of fact, I was asked to go with one of the most delightful men in Liverpool, and as a guest for six weeks in Egypt, and my wife and my friends thought I ought to go,

[1] *A History of the Plymouth Brethren.*

and I, being always anxious to get rid of work if I can, and do as little as possible, besides not being well, was strongly inclined to go also. But—it sounds like a Pharisee, and nobody will believe it—I did not think myself justified in taking six weeks out of the winter's work. In fact, the prime cut of the joint. So I am not going, but under medical directions am playing golf as much as possible, and when you come down once more to see us, which will be at our golden wedding, I will challenge you to a match.

I am quite unnerved, and can only sign myself,—Yours penitently, JEREMIAH MACWHEEP.

PS.—Review sent to you as I am writing.—J. W.

TO PRINCIPAL OSWALD DYKES

November 26th, 1901.

MY DEAR PRINCIPAL,—Very many thanks for your friendly letter, and I am none the less grateful that I am not going to Egypt. I was invited to go with a small party of men for six weeks, and my wife and elders thought I ought to go, but I declined for the simple reason, tho' it sounds like a Pharisee to say so, that I did not think it right to be absent six weeks from my work and family at the meeting of the years. But I am going very slowly this winter, and playing golf a good deal.

So far as I can see I am not likely to startle the committees or Church Courts by my presence for some time. The last thing I did at a Church Court was to protest against the pleading in connection with the translation of my colleague to Scotland. Would you believe it, but as you know Church Courts better than I do, I fancy you can believe anything in the way of pompous unreality, that in face of the fact that Mr. —— had told his people that he was going, after indeed having preached as a candidate for the place, and the Presbytery in Scotland had actually affixed the date of his induction, and he had accepted that date, and made his arrangements accordingly, three days before our Presbytery met five commissioners from F. argued at considerable length, that we should consent to his translation, and warned us of the injury that would be done to F. if we refused? We afterwards asked prayer for guidance, when the whole matter had been settled as far as any human affair can be settled till it happens. I made a strong protest, and afterwards received assurance of hearty approval from laymen of intelligence who were present and who simply detest those exhibitions, but the reverend fathers present, I rather think, disapproved of such revolutionary ideas, and the leader of the Scottish deputation, a typical ecclesiastic in voice and build, declared with emphasis in a letter to me afterwards, a very indignant letter I may add, that they were not sure of Mr. ——'s coming, and if they had been would never have come south. As Mr. —— said to me, 'what the man means he may know, but I don't, for I had agreed to the date of the induction.' And Mr. —— also expressed his hope to me that the people in F. would not perpetrate the stupidity of a deputation.

Why do I weary you with this? Because I have some hope that you may add to all your services of the past this other, namely, the simplification of our forms, so that this immense unreality in connection with Calls may be brought to an end, and the scandal among laymen may be removed. In Scotland the people may enjoy these farces, in England they do not understand them.—Believe me, your humble country brother, JEREMIAH MACWHEEP

(Village Pastor).

It was impossible to hold out very long, and he went to Egypt.

TO MR. COLVILLE

Luxor, December 15, 1901.

My dear Colleague,—It is afternoon with us, and through the window we see the palms and hear the trickling of the water in the garden of this beautiful hotel, where, after the most delightful journey up the Nile, we arrived this morning.

Everything has gone well with us since we started, the sea was like a lake. At Port Said, one of the chief men of Egypt laid himself out to do us kindness, and told us more than many of us could ever learn about Ismail, Gordon, Arabi, Kitchener, Mahdi, and the Canal, and accompanied us to Cairo, showing us Tel-el-Kebir on the way. Our passage up the Nile was perfect, and now we have settled till the 26th in the midst of beauty and sunshine. I slept last night from eleven to seven, which is very unusual; it rather rested me, and I think of keeping the habit up.

We visited the Temple of Denderah yesterday and had a ride through the rich country where poverty is unknown. If England had done nothing else our Nile has at least redeemed and blest Egypt, where the people have peace and contentment. I trust everything goes well at Sefton Park. Please give the people every good wish on Christmas Day, and say that I am already feeling better.

John Watson.

TO FREDERICK W. WATSON

Luxor, December 16*th*, 1901.

Dear F.,—One of the most delightful things in the world must be to ascend the Nile in a steamer which goes slowly and calls at many places,

The river is very broad and runs at a great rate, is of a light brown colour and has usually high banks, along which the people on foot and on donkeys are ever moving. Village follows village, each with its palm-trees, native vessels going up opendecked with huge cargoes under one large sail, for the north wind is now blowing up the Nile, or dropping down with the current. Sometimes we pass a swell-decked passenger steamer, hired by a millionaire for the winter, with his lordship sitting on the deck, and a host of gaily-dressed sailors in attendance sprinkled about. As soon as the steamer whistles we know that the boat is in the way, and it is one interest to watch how skilfully the native boatmen work her. Sometimes with their enormous sail they are caught in a squall where the hills approach the river, but not often, and then the Dahabeah may go over, but no lives are lost, as the Nile inhabitants swim from infancy like ducks, and dive as perfectly.

At the stern of our steamer a boat is towed, and standing aft I once saw a pretty little scene. The Nile banks have many birds, and one, a charming creature in black and white, a water wagtail, I guess, having some friends up the river, and seeing that we carried passengers, lighted on the boat, and by and by went down as it were into the cabins. It then mounted the prow, where it stood flirting its tail and examining the steamer in front of it. Why not go by the steamer like other tourists, and so it examined the ropes by which the steamer held the boat, and then it selected one which seemed the safest, and began to come along, so daintily, balancing itself by its long graceful tail, now again fluttering with its wings and pretending that it was afraid of falling, and every minute I expected to see it land on our boat, when something alarmed it, perhaps our Arab steerage passengers may have moved on the deck below, but it gave an apologetic glance at me, murmured something about a friend on the bank, and darted off with many a graceful motion on the water and through the air, and I saw no more of my Nile Wag-Tail, a brief pleasant acquaintance.

To-day we made a long excursion to the tombs of the Kings, twelve miles in the donkey saddle; but you must not judge the animals we had to-day by the feeble creatures we have at home. My donkey was white, handsome, and very strong, and cantered with the invalid as if your father had weighed five stone instead of nearly eight.

Alas, everybody has had letters except poor me, some at Cairo, some here. Ill-luck always follows me in letters, but I am keeping my poverty dark, for on a former occasion when I travelled with some men, they used to read portions of their letters to me, which I resented deeply.—Your affectionate father, J. W.

TO THE SAME

'SS. Amasis,' December 20th, 1901.

DEAR F.,—Cards you have had and messages, but I think no letters, altho' I had a very charming one from you. For which many thanks.

Luxor, altho' most interesting through its magnificent antiquities, temples, and tombs, and altho' the hotel is excellent, grew unendurable through the dogs. Every Arab has one—a long, hungry, ill-tempered brute, who sometimes lies in front of his master's mud-hut and does his best to catch you as you pass, which is his day occupation. After nightfall he mounts the roof of the house, and makes ready for night duty. For a short time he contents himself with a few disconnected barks, by way of tuning up, and then about eleven the concert fairly starts.

One is leader, and he opens with a long plaintive howl—a solo on a high note, and after two seconds the whole chorus, or let us say orchestra, joins in, each in his own key, or with his own instrument, and we have a piece of Wagnerian music which lasts twenty minutes, after which there is a pause broken only by applause from the cocks of the district, and a bravo from some jackal. As I am not a hardened attender of the Philharmonic though a lover and performer of religious music, one or two pieces satisfied me for the night, but the concert lasted from eleven to five, neither the chief soloists nor the chorus showing any signs of fatigue. Your father allowed himself to wish that every dog in the district, and there appears to be one thousand one hundred and nine exactly in Luxor, had been sent to—a dog's home in Cairo.

So having visited the Grand Temple in Karnak in addition to those mentioned in preceding letters, and having had a camel-ride and a sail on the river, we went on board this fine steamer, and on her will go up to the first cataract and see the great dam being made on the Nile, and return on her to Cairo, being on the river ten days. The heat is very great and to some extent reduces our pleasure. If you complain of cold in England you would complain of much of the fiery heat which keeps one perspiring night and day. Our steamer has just stuck on a sandbank, which gives variety to the journey. Love to the menagerie.—Your affectionate Father.

On his return he delivered a course of lectures on 'The Scot in the Eighteenth Century' at the Royal Institution. The lectures were very well attended. He received the following note from Sir James Crichton Browne:—

February 27th, 1902.

Dear Mr. Watson,—The Royal Institution is much beholden to you for your recent lectures, which were well up to its highest literary standard. They charmed all who heard them. We shall probably make another appeal to you for assistance one of these days. Were you to give a Friday evening discourse the theatre would be crowded.—With sincere esteem, yours most faithfully,

James Crichton Browne.

TO W. ROBERTSON NICOLL

18*th November* 1902.

Dear Nicoll,—A few nights ago I was dining with some men who meet to discuss everything in Heaven and on earth and in the waters underneath the earth, and amongst other theories raised, one man, not devoid of intelligence, gave it as his opinion that one of the objects the Government had in the present Education Bill, or at least one of the results they knew would come from it, would be the destruction of Denominational schools. Personally I had difficulty in believing that Balfour was so utter a Machiavelli, and I wish to cling to that optimistic view.

My faith in human nature is, however, much shaken by the fact that the editor of the *Expositor*, who is supposed to be its friend and protector, has insisted upon a man whose mind is doddering, devastating the pages of the *Expositor* with a subject which has been adequately treated by eminent scholars, and about which the proposed writer knows very little more than a village Pastor. He is sorry to think that the days of the *Expositor*, a useful, though didactic magazine, are so near an end, and humiliated as he has been chosen to give the *coup de grace*.

There is still time for repentance and a way of escape.—Yours sadly but hopefully,

JEREMIAH DUNDERHEAD,
M.A. (MINNEHAHA),
D.D. (AKROPOLIS),
PRESIDENT Y.X.Z.W.A.,
EX-CHAIRMAN P.Q.T.S.

TO THE SAME

The University, Glasgow, Dec. 1, '02.

DEAR NICOLL,—Wire just come to me at Glasgow, where I have been preaching before the University. Am so engaged that I cannot get five minutes for article. Three requests from London! I feel Dr. Parker's death as a personal loss: although I had only known him for a year or two I had learned to love him: his heart was as good as genius.—In haste, yours faithfully, JOHN WATSON.

PS.—Preached yesterday in Bute Hall, University, to largest congregation ever in building. Many not getting in about 2500, on 'The Snare of Ease.'—J. W.

TO THE SAME

17 *Croxteth Road,*
Liverpool, 8th January 1903.

DEAR NICOLL,—It would have given me satisfaction to have written a notice of Mr. Smith's book, but I cannot do that or anything else at present for the following reason. On Monday morning, after some pretty hard work on Sunday and the preceding week, I had a nasty attack of illness, centreing mainly in my head, and have just crawled into my study in a very shaky and confused condition. My doctor says I must take care, and I have cancelled every engagement outside my church to the end of July, and I shall write nothing, and indeed, as a matter of fact, can write nothing which is not absolutely obligatory. May I add again with the voice of an old man near the end of life that if, after what has happened to me from taking a Moderatorship, you ever do the same, then your blood be upon your own head?—Yours feebly and confusedly,

JEREMIAH MACDOTTLE.

For 1903 we have several letters to his friend, the Rev. Dr. Aked, now of New York, who was abroad in ill-health.

June 13th, 1903.

MY DEAR AKED,—You are a greater preacher, but I am an older man, and so I take the liberty of dropping the Mr. on condition you will drop the Dr., and it makes the matter easier to me, because I want to begin by quarrelling with you. Whether the new cure of which I hear such wonderful things includes an iron and quinine tonic I do not know, but a quarrel is just the thing to pick you up. My grounds are two, and the first is, that you should have put yourself to the trouble of writing an answer when I did not expect such a thing, and when you ought not to be writing letters of any kind. This ground of quarrel, however, I do not propose to labour, because I was much touched with the kindness of your letter, and also by the somewhat disparaging account you give of yourself. I had hoped that you were in a better state, for what we hear in Liverpool is cheering, and I earnestly trust that when you wrote the cloud was only a passing one, and that you are really to be another of those many splendid cures which the new treatment is accomplishing. My memory recalls at this moment three eminent ministers of the Scots Kirk who suffered from bad lung disease in their early days, and when I knew them, men past middle age, were said in popular speech to have only one lung, and who all died, the last quite recently, at ages varying from a little over seventy to just touching ninety, and who rendered immense service in their day. One of them indeed, quite a distinguished person, lived so long that he became quite a terror to a congregation from which he drew a retiring allowance, because he not only had a colleague, but that colleague grew old, and a third man was needed; and it seemed likely as if there was going to be a geological formation of colleagues, one upon the other, and all resting on the old red sandstone of this gentleman, aged ninety, and who from the age of about twenty-five had only possessed one lung. Another of these pre-scientific cures certainly slipped away about the age of seventy, through hard work on a tour in the East, and heart disease through excessive stoutness. He was a great speaker, but he did so well with one lung that if he had had two his congregation might have sat in their own homes and heard him distinctly. And we have a minister in our own English Church who broke down badly in the early fifties with lung disease and went to Australia, which was the cure then. He celebrated his jubilee three years ago, and is convener of a committee on the Jews, and never knows an hour of bad health. Such instances I have hastily collected from my memory, and all that was in the days before Copernicus; the things I see now pass belief. Why, two years ago I visited a young lady who was lying in bed, utterly helpless, and I bade her good-bye, when they persisted in taking her down to Heswall—I thought they had better have allowed her to die in her own room—and the preposterous young woman is not only alive, but has grown absurdly stout, and can't even get up a cough to show what she used to be.

But I hear you saying to Mrs. Aked, 'Poor Watson, he is falling into his anecdotage,' and so I will hasten on to scold you soundly, which is my second ground of quarrel for speaking of your work being undone. This from a Prophet of the Lord, and from an Elijah sent to Liverpool, is wickedness, and I trust immediately afterwards the Angel who attends to you brought you food, and that straightway you were delivered from the snare of the evil one. You have lifted up your voice and testified for righteousness all those years, and will you dare to say that your work is not in its essence eternal? You have braced men up to fight the World, the Flesh, and the Devil, you have brought many thousands, who would likely have gone to no other preacher within the sound of the Evangel; you have built up the Kingdom of God as Blake would say, built up Jerusalem 'in England's green and pleasant land.' It is the way you Baptists (I mean John, not the denomination) have of depreciating yourselves, and I prescribe that you read the Eulogium passed by our Master upon John Baptist, when he sent the despairing message to Jesus. It is the greatest ever spoken of any man, and I like to think of that big brave man, thinking in Herod's dungeon that his life had been a failure, and Jesus lost in admiration, declaring in face of the people, that of all the stock of Israel there had been none like John. The world looking at Herod in his banqueting chamber and John in his dungeon, would judge there was no doubt which of the two had failed. And there was no doubt. The Judge of all men was already giving the decision, for 'The world passeth away and the lust thereof, but he that doeth the will of God abideth for ever.' John the Baptist's work undone! I do well to be angry, yea even unto swearing.

'Taking to preaching now.' Suppose I am exaggerating.

If the thing be true I am saying I defy you to reject it, so let me hear no more about undoing, but rather thank God that for those thirteen years you have been able to do so much which remaineth, and so I bury the hatchet and declare peace. But upon two conditions, that you do not add the weight of a straw to your daily duty of making your cure by even the shortest note, but ask Mrs. Aked of her kindness to send me a scrape of a pen or a post-card—mark you, a post-card only—telling me how it fares with you, and that you never again speak of your work being lost.

This country is seething with excitement over Mr. Chamberlain in his new rôle of the Prophet of Protection, and the situation is unexampled, for no one knows how far the Government is with him, or what he himself hopes to do. It is a dangerous situation also, for the prosperity of the country, since anything that affects our trade, touches us vitally, but I can see one good, and that is that every person not cursed with intellectual frivolity will be obliged to face the economic question and to think it out for himself, and it seems to me that the curse of politics of late years has been that people were refusing to think, and that the political machine was managing everything, which would eat out the national life.

In literary circles the excitement is the last Carlyle publication by Froude's executors, and the general view is that it is absolutely shameful. Those poor Carlyles. They had genius beyond measure, and the defects of their qualities were that they did fret and quarrel, but they also loved one another, and now when they are gone, it is a crime to open the grave. The best books in fiction of late have been *Lady Rose's Daughter*, by Mrs. Humphry Ward, better written, I think, than any of her other books, though not of course raising such burning questions, and *The Pit*, an American novel, dealing with Chicago speculations by a very powerful writer of Zola's school who has since died, but I dare say you have seen both of them. By the way, if a parcel of magazines arrive soon of varying qualities, you can either read them or fling them away as it suits your mood.

With very kind regards and constant remembrance,—Yours faithfully, JOHN WATSON.

TO MRS. AKED

June 19th, 1903.

DEAR MRS. AKED,—Will you tell Dr. Aked that there is to be a passive resistance meeting here, and that it is to be addressed by N——? My information indeed is from N——, who wrote asking whether I would take him in for the night, and if I objected to outlaws. I told him he would be doubly welcome here, because I not only objected to the income-tax, but like every other Highland Celt, objected to all taxes. The movement seems to be spreading in England, and tho' my own judgment does not go with it, I am as much opposed as any one to a bill which imposes religious tests upon a branch of the Civil Service, and treats Nonconformists most unfairly. I hope to live to see those unjust provisions removed from the educational laws of the country, and to that end shall always speak and vote, altho' I have not seen my way to be a passive resister.

This controversy is, however, being overshadowed by the economic debate which is beginning to rage through the country, and which also concerns the welfare of the people.

I trust Dr. Aked is making some improvement, and that in spite of bodily weakness, he is in good heart. He is much missed in Liverpool, and is warmly remembered by many.

Believe me with many kind regards,—Yours faithfully,

JOHN WATSON.

TO THE SAME

July 2nd, 1903.

DEAR MRS. AKED,—It was most gracious of you to send me a personal letter, and I thank you for its friendly contents, but chiefly for giving me such good hope of your husband's ultimate recovery. His restoration to the fighting ranks will be a reinforcement of righteousness, and will straighten the line like the sound of a bugle call.

Dr. Aked may be interested to know that according to my measure I lifted up my voice last Sunday night against compensation for publicans in any shape or form that was to come from the nation, but I expressed the desire of many for compensation from publicans for all the misery they had wrought in England, for the wounds which they had inflicted on 'the daughter of my people.' Yesterday Mr. Arthur Chamberlain, who is coming forward as a champion of temperance, addressed a meeting in the Concert Room of St. George's Hall, and made one of the most powerful and convincing speeches in defence of the recent action of the magistrates and reduction of licences that I have ever heard. His words have the clean cut of a scimitar; they not only divide the bone of a hostile argument, but what is more difficult, and the finest test of a Damascus blade, they slice in two the gossamer lacework of many fallacies.

Dr. N—— was our guest when he spoke in favour of passive resistance to a large and enthusiastic audience. As on this matter I am not a stalwart, believing that we can best gain our ends by the ordinary methods of democracy, reasoning and voting, I was not present, but did my best to fit the champion out for his crusade and to refit him when he came home. I have not yet despaired of democracy, and hope to see the day when there shall be a national system of education in the land, with no tests and free from the control of all priests. Believing that tests and Priests have been a heavy weight upon the progress of the race, and from this pious belief I do not exclude the Jewish Priesthood (so curiously admired by good people), who were as great a curse on the whole to their nation as on the whole the prophets were a blessing.

Some few days ago I sent off a few magazines light and heavy, but I think all interesting, and mainly perhaps heavy, including the best edited magazine of public criticism I know, the *North American Review*, which combines our solidity with what the Americans pleasantly call 'snap.'

Trusting that Dr. Aked continues to improve, and with very kind regards to you both,—Believe me, yours faithfully,

JOHN WATSON.

TO DR. AKED

October 15*th*, 1903.

MY DEAR AKED,—The bazaar yesterday opened as it appeared to me with great spirit. There was a large attendance. Mr. G. was very cordial, and it would have done you good to have seen the enthusiasm of the people at every reference to your name. It gave me great pleasure to be present, and I had my few shambling remarks typed in order that I might send them to you, not because you are likely to be impressed by the pedestrian style, but because it will let you know that I have tried in my dry Scots way to express the sympathy of my heart with you and yours.

Every one at Pembroke was most kind, and they had a

beautiful bouquet for Mrs. Watson, which I carried home to her in vicarious glory, for the day was so dreadful and she was rheumatic, and so she is bitterly regretting that she missed the personal pleasure of receiving the bouquet. We were both much touched by this thought of us, for by a special arrangement of the Creator a man is so constituted, that he is better pleased to have kindness shown to his wife than to himself, and the wife is of the same make only more so. The tears always come to my heart when a Scots woman speaks with pride of 'my man,' for see you, out of all the world she has chosen him, and he has chosen her, and he is 'her man.' It was my doubtful fortune once to give the marriage address at a fashionable wedding, and I struck the note of 'my man,' and charged the bridegroom so to carry himself in the lists of life, that the bride would be able to make a boast of 'her man.' And as I am a living sinner, I declare to you, there were mighty dames in lace and jewellery who had to fall back on their scraps of handkerchiefs, and men present who had somewhat ostentatiously to readjust their eye-glasses. For, to quote Kipling (quite incorrectly):

For the Colonel's wife and the Corporal's wife,
Are just women beneath the skin.

Will you thank Mrs. Aked for her most kind letter, and the good news in it, and believe me with friendly remembrance,—Yours faithfully, JOHN WATSON.

June 17*th*, 1903.

DEAR MAJOR N.,—Your letter came when I was from home, and I now write to express my deep gratitude to you as our Commanding Officer for the kind congratulations which you have sent in your own name and that of the battalion on the occasion of our silver wedding.

We have had a very happy life, and one part of our happiness has been that we have shared our interests in common, and amongst them none has been more genuine than our devotion to the battalion.

It has been a subject of great satisfaction to me to see so fine a national regiment, and any slight service I have been able to render has been amply rewarded.—I remain, yours faithfully,

John Watson.

CHAPTER XVII

CONVERSATION

ALL who knew John Watson, however slightly, agree that he was at his best in conversation. As one of his most intimate friends has said, he poured out his intellectual wealth in a stream of talk which was far more marvellous than either his speaking or his writing. His talk was largely made up of Scottish stories, and they were told elaborately and at length. In fact, they were character sketches rather than stories. He would select an individual representative of a type and build up by one detail after another a living portrait. Principal Fairbairn has best described his manner in conversation :—

He was always a favourite in my house, although he was difficult to entertain—one indeed became breathless in the attempt to keep up with him, for his speech was vivid and his tongue was quick. Hence I was prone to be, in his society, subdued into an unwonted yet characteristic silence. I can indeed well recall, during a comparatively recent visit to his house at Liverpool, how I ventured on a tale which was very familiar to me. He and his family laughed heartily when they heard it; and then a son turned to me and said: 'Wait, sir, till you come back, and your story will be so dressed up that you will not know it as your own.' My wife used to say that Watson's setting of his tales was better than the stories themselves, and here she spoke the truth. A friend of his, who is also a friend of mine, almost as welcome in our house as he ever was, is also famed for the stories he tells; yet it was always easier to entertain the two apart than the two together. The two apart could be compared; together they each annihilated the other.

It has been held by good judges that anecdotes ruin conversation, and in this there is a certain amount of truth. Watson could not be called ordinarily a good listener. He seemed always anxious to have the next word, and his prodigality of reminiscence and invention outdid most competitors. When any one really wished to state his case and to have his help, he was most punctilious and careful in his attention. On committees and in all the transactions of business he was the same. But in an ordinary company, or with an intimate friend, or in his own home circle, it was he who did the most of the talking. He had, however, a talent for silence, and in his own house usually spoke very little except at table. Often, too, in a walk he would be absorbed in thinking.

Humorous as he was, he had a dread of the gift. He believed as firmly as Walter Bagehot that a sense of humour is a hindrance to practical success in life. To have an eye for the recurring comedy of existence might be a joy to the individual and sustain him among the labours and stupidities in the day's work, and might also be a joy to his friends. But in the daily calling it was a peril. If one with a real palate for comedy happened to be a clergyman, then he ran the greatest risk in his association with good people.

He will be afraid to attend a religious meeting lest some worthy speaker, having raised his audience to the highest pitch of pious expectation, should topple over into an anticlimax, as when one of the best of men enlarging upon the ubiquity of the Jew, and the consequent advisability of making him a Christian, gave the following illustration: 'I was recently at a funeral,' he said with much unction, 'and as I stood before the coffin I noticed that a man on the right of me was a Jew, and on the left of me was a Jew, and before me stood a Jew. But,' he concluded cheerfully, 'thank heaven it was a Christian corpse.' Funerals will always be to the minister cursed with humour a double trial, because comedy lies so near tragedy, and the fountain of tears springs so near the fountain of laughter. It gets upon this poor victim's nerves when a neighbour whom he has seen from the window coming along the street, round-faced and chirpy, enters the room with a long-drawn expression of dolorous woe as if in the hall he had whipped on a tragic mask, shakes hands with the undertaker instead of the chief mourner and sits down beside the minister, remarking with a sigh which stirs the atmosphere, 'Very sudden and much missed; here to-day and there to-morrow.' One unhappy clergyman still blushes with shame as he recalls an incident of his early days when in a northern city he was sent to take a funeral service in the kitchen of a working man's house. They sat round him, eight Scots artisans, each in his

Sunday black, with his pipe projecting from his waistcoat pocket, and his hat below his chair, looking with awful immoveable countenance into the eternity. It seemed irreverent to speak to any of the graven images, but the poor minister required to know something about the man who had died, and so he ventured to ask the monument next him in a whisper what the deceased had been. Whereupon the figure answered with a loud, clear voice, 'I dinna ken mysel', for I juist cam here wi' a freend,' and then addressing a still more awful figure opposite, and in an even more aggressive voice, 'Jeames, what was the corpse to a trade?'

He used to quote Mr. Gladstone as a politician who had gained greatly by his lack of humour.

Had Mr. Gladstone, for instance, possessed the faintest sense of the ridiculous amid the multitude of his rich and brilliant talents, he had not been able to address a crowd from the window of his railway carriage, to receive the gift of a shepherd's tartan plaid or an elaborate walking-stick, or if my memory does not fail me, a case of marmalade, until his impatient fellow-travellers insisted that the train should go on, and it departed to the accompaniment of the statesman's elegant peroration. But it was just because Mr. Gladstone could do such things, and was always in the most deadly earnest about everything, from the Bulgarian atrocities to the making of jam, that the British trusted him and hung upon his words. There are times when one loses heart and almost concludes that the conditions of tangible success in English life are these: to be well built, giving pledges to fortune, with a moderate stoutness; to have a solemn expression of face suggesting the possession of more wisdom than has been given to any single person; to be able to hold one's tongue till some incautious talker has afforded an idea, and to have the gift of oracular commonplace. If to such valuable talents can be added an impressive clearance of the throat, there are few positions short of the highest to which their owner may not climb in Church or State. My advice therefore to younger men is to congratulate themselves that by the will of Providence they have been cleansed from this dangerous quality, or if this be not their fortunate case to hide the possession of humour behind a mask of sustained and impenetrable solemnity until they have made their fortunes, and then to give it play as the foolish freak of a rich man.

There was an element of seriousness in all this. Watson severely controlled the expression of his sense of humour. He controlled it to the utmost of his power in the pulpit and in ecclesiastical courts, and it was only in the circle of his friends that he let himself go free. Even there he restrained rigorously his dangerous power of sarcasm. He was so successful in this that many who knew him intimately did not know how formidable he could be in that way. He was the master of a deadly irony, but he was wont to say that the power of irony was one which could never be employed to any good purpose by a Christian minister. Occasionally he had great provocation, and he knew well that he had the use of a weapon which would punish his assailant, but he deliberately kept silence. Few if any knew 'the weight of his terrible hand.' Only on rare occasions, and in the security of confidence, would he sometimes show what his power was in this way.

It was the humour of the Scot in which he was most at home. English fun he delighted in, and would say that it had lent a certain flavour of geniality to private life in this country, and had saved public life from rancorous bitterness. He would declare that in his professional experience he had never known trouble in a house where the father chaffed his sons, and the sons teased their father. He frequently expressed his admiration for *Punch*, and its long tradition of purity and dignity. 'I dare to say that we ought to be thankful for the services our master caricaturist has rendered to the amenities both of public and private life.' He had a delight in the captivating, irresistible, unexpected, unreasonable way of Irish drollery. Mrs. Watson's uncle, Sir Samuel Ferguson, the eminent Irish poet and scholar, was a man in whose society he particularly delighted, and from him he learned much. Irish drollery, he would say, was more captivating, more unexpected, and more unreasonable than anything else on the face of the earth: 'If the just and honourable, but perhaps also over-sensible and somewhat phlegmatic persons who have in recent times had charge of Irish affairs, and have been trying to unravel the tangled skein, had appreciated the tricksy sprite which inhabits the Irish mind, and had made a little more allowance for people who are not moved by argument and the multiplication table, but are touched by sentiment and romance as well as vastly tickled by the absurdity of things, they might have achieved greater success, and done more good to a chivalrous, unworldly, quick-witted and warm-hearted people.'

In the matter of Scottish humour he drew a sharp contrast between the Highlander and the Lowlander. The Highlander is impulsive, imaginative, gallant to a fault, regardless of consequences, pure in life, courteous in manner, chivalrous in ideals. He is at home in the world which is dying, and makes the best of raiders and of fighting soldiers, as he is the most loyal of clansmen and the most faithful of friends. But he has been the child of beaten causes, and of dark moods, dwelling under the shadow of the mountains and by the side of sea-loch in a country of wreathing mists and weird, lonely moors. The Lowlander is self-controlled, far-seeing, persevering, industrious, with a genius for the accumulation of money. Watson would tell of a gentleman in the west-end of Edinburgh who was accustomed to ask a number of the poorer students from the University to the evening entertainment at his house that they might see what was done in the higher levels of life and be better prepared for their place in the professions. At one of these solemn and improving functions a Highlander and a Lowlander met upon the stair.

'Angus,' said the Lowlander, 'hoo are ye gettin' on? I 'm daein' fine. The girl I have appears to be greatly pleased with me, and she 's no ill-lookin'.' One may safely conclude from what one knows of the manner of a Scots country lad that he had sat upon the extreme edge of his chair all the evening, and had hardly uttered a word, and that the poor young woman had been bored to death. But there was in him the imperturbable and abounding satisfaction of the Lowland Scot which makes him impervious to rebuffs, and in the long-run carries him to the place where he would be. 'Jock,' said the Highlander, 'the young lady who wass so good as to speak to me, and whom I am desiring to serve, asked me to get her what she called "blackmange." I am willing to do her bidding, and would be ready to go anywhere and take that blackmange from any man who hass it. But I do not know what it is. I would not be saying that to the young lady, but I am feeling very sore in my heart that I cannot get her the blackmange, and, Jock, I wish to heaven I was outside this house with honour to myself.'

The humour of the Celt is an immovable and drawn-out waggery which he tastes without a smile, and of which one might suppose he was unconscious.

'Who had this place last year?' asked a Southern shooting tenant of his keeper.

'Well,' said Donald, 'I 'm not denyin' that he wass an Englishman, but he wass a good man whatever. Oh, yess, he went to kirk and he shot very well, but he was narrow, very narrow.'

'Narrow,' said the other in amazement, for he supposed he meant bigoted, and the charge was generally the other way about. 'What was he narrow in?'

'Well,' said Donald, 'I will be tellin' you, and it wass this way. The twelfth (the beginning of the grouse shooting) wass a very good day, and we had fifty-two brace. But it was warm, oh! yess, very warm, and when we came back to the Lodge, the gentleman will say to me, "It is warm," and I will not be contradicting him. Then he will be saying, "Maybe you are thirsty," and I will not be contradicting him. Afterwards he will take out his flask and be speaking about a dram. I will not be contradicting him, but will just say, "Toots, toots." Then he will be pouring it out, and when the glass was maybe half full I will say, just for politeness, "Stop." And he stopped. Oh! yess, a very narrow man.'

Another tenant was making arrangements for the coming winter before he went South, and told the keeper to get the woman who had looked after the Lodge the previous winter to take charge of it again.

'You will be meaning Janet Cameron, but I am not advising you to have Janet this year. Oh, no! it will maybe be better not to have Janet this winter.'

'Why, what was wrong with her?' And then with that painful suspicion of the Highlander which greatly hurts his feelings, 'Did she drink?'

'Janet,' replied Donald with severity, 'iss not the woman to be tasting. Oh, no! she is a good-living woman, Janet, and has the true doctrine, but I will not be saying that you should have her.'

'I see; so you and she, I suppose, quarrel?'

'It iss not this man who will be quarrelling with Janet Cameron, who is his wife's cousin four times removed, and a very good woman, though she be a Cameron.'

'Well, ask her to take the Lodge, and offer her the same wages as last year, and a little more if that will please her, and tell me what she says.'

'It is not for wages Janet Cameron will work. Oh, no! that iss not the kind of woman Janet iss, and it is no use asking her, for she will not come.'

'Well,' said the Englishman, getting nettled, 'do as you are bid, and give her the chance at any rate, and tell me what she says.'

'No, sir, it will be wasting my time going, and I will not be asking her.' Then after a pause, 'Ye would maybe not be knowin' that Janet iss dead.'

Does any one say with impatience why did he not tell that at once? If you can answer that question you lay bare the secret of the Celtic mind, so subtle that it dislikes statements of downright brutality and prefers to suggest rather than assert, as is seen in this story:—

'Why, Hamish,' said the Laird to a young fellow whom he met on the road, 'what are you doing here? Have you left the situation I got for you?'

'It is a great sorrow, sir, to this man, but I could not be staying in that place, and so I have just come back, and maybe I will be getting something else to do.'

'Look here, I don't understand this,' said the Laird. 'Was the work too heavy, or did they not pay you enough wages? Tell me what ailed you at the place.'

'I would be ashamed to complain of work, and there was nothing wrong with the wages, but it was just this way, and though I'm making no complaint, maybe you will be understanding. There was a sheep died on the hill of its own accord, and the master had it salted and ate that sheep. By and by there was a cow died suddenly, and we did not know what was wrong with her, but the master had that cow salted and we ate her. And then the master's mother took ill and we were feeling very anxious, for we will not be forgetting the sheep and the cow. And the master's mother died, and I left.'

You cannot, he would say, get a right answer from a Highlander. A distinguished Highland minister who understood his race through and through desired to know whether a certain candidate for a parish had approved himself to the people, and was likely to be appointed. He called upon one of the religious worthies of the district, being perfectly certain that if he found out what he thought he would have the answer. Duncan knew quite well why the minister had come, and the minister knew that Duncan knew, but they talked on the weather and the crop, and the last heresy case, and the spread of false doctrine in the Lowlands for half an hour. After that they came as it were by accident on the name of the candidate, and Duncan simply covered him with praise. The minister knew that that counted for nothing. A little later the minister said to Duncan, 'I would like to have your mind about that young man,'—his mind observe being very different from his speech. Then Duncan delivered himself as follows:—

'Yesterday I was sitting on the bank of the river, and I was meditating when a little boy came and began to fish. He was a pretty boy, and I am judging was very well brought up. He talked very nicely to me, and had the good manners. He had a very nice little rod in his hand, and he did not fling his line badly. It was very pleasant to watch him. But it was a great pity that he had forgot to put a hook on the end of the line, for I did not notice that he caught many fish, but he was a very nice boy, and I liked him very much. And it is a great mercy that we are getting good weather for the harvest, for we are not worthy of such goodness with all our sins and backslidings.'

Then the minister knew that the candidate would not get the parish, but Duncan was entitled to say that he had never mentioned the candidate's name, or said a single word against him.

He held that the Lowland Scottish mind was austere and restrained even in its humour. Thc helplessness of men in the hands of the almighty and inscrutable powers is always present to the Scots mind, and is a check upon gaiety. Any extravagance of speech or any permissible satisfaction with success is called a tempting of providence, the underlying thought being that if we walk humbly and quietly the unseen powers will leave us alone, poor creatures of a day, but if we lift our little heads and make a noise the inclination to strike us down is irresistible. The Scotsman has a sombre delight in funerals.

'Peter,' says one mourner to his neighbour at the tail of a walking funeral, 'div ye see Jamie Thompson walking in the front, side by side wi' the chief mourner, and him no drop o' blood to the corpse?'

'Fine I see him, a forward upsettin' ambcctious body, he would be inside the hearse if he could'—the most awful and therefore the most enviable position for a sober-minded Scot.

According to the Scots idea it is more profitable to go to a funeral than to a wedding, and anything that would detract from the chastened satisfaction of such an occasion is deeply resented, and the following conversation between a dying wife and her husband would only be possible in Scotland:—

'I 've been a very guid wife to you, John, a' thae years?'

'I 'm no denyin', Jean, ye havena been a waster; I 'll admit ye hae been economical, and verra attentive to the calves and hens.'

'Ye 'll no refuse me, then, my last request?'

'I will not, Jean, if it 's reasonable, but will hear it first.'

'Well, my mither has taken a terrible notion o' gaein' to the funeral, and I canna get her off it. Noo, John, will ye promise to hev her wi' ye in the first coach?'

'Oh, wooman, ask somethin' else, I canna do that.'

'But, John, I 'll never ask anything else o' ye; ye micht pit up wi' her juist for my sake.'

'Weel, Jean, if ye put it that way I suppose I maun agree, but I tell ye plainly ye 've spoiled the pleasure of the day for me.'

As he thought, there was no humour so dry and stringent with such a bite upon the palate as that of Scotland, and one of his grimmest examples was this. An unhappy Scot was condemned to death after a careful trial for the murder of his wife under circumstances of considerable provocation, and the verdict was no doubt a just one. There is something good, however, in every man if you walk around him long enough to find it, and his Counsel was so much interested in his client that he visited him in the condemned cell.

'There is no hope, Robertson, of a reprieve,' said the advocate frankly, 'and you know you don't deserve it. But if there's anything else I could do for you just tell me.'

'Well,' said Robertson, 'I count it very kindly to give me a cry like this, and if ye could get me one thing I would feel easier on the occasion'—which was a rather felicitous name for the coming function. 'Could ye get me Sabbath blacks, for I would like to wear them?'

'Well,' said the advocate, 'I dare say I could, but why in the world, Robertson, do you wish to wear your Sabbath clothes for the . . . occasion?'

'I thought maybe you would see that for yourself, sir, just as a mark of respect for the deceased.'

A favourite tale of his was about one of the most characteristic ministers of the Scottish Church, Dr. Norman Macleod, who was a friend of the whole nation. Working men turned to look at him as he went down the street saying one to the other, 'There goes Norman, he's looking well the day.' A minister in the next parish to that of Dr. Macleod was sent for to see a working man who was dangerously ill.

After he had visited him in his bedroom he came into the kitchen to have some conversation with the man's wife.

'Your husband is very low: I hope he may be spared. I am afraid it 's typhus fever.'

'Ay, ay,' the wife replied with mournful pride; 'it 's no ordinary trouble.'

'I didn't know your husband's face, and I didn't want to ask him questions. Do you attend my church?'

'Na, na,' with a fine flavour of contempt both for the kirk and the minister, 'we gang to Norman's.'

'Well, that 's all right, you couldn't go to a better. But why did you send for me?'

'Losh, bless ye, div ye think that we wud risk Norman wi' typhus fever?'

Another was a tale of a dull Scottish village where on a dull morning one neighbour called upon another. He was met at the door by his friend's wife, and the conversation went thus:—

'Cauld?'

'Ay.'

'Gaen to be weety (rainy), I think.'

'Ay.'

'Is John in?'

'Oh ay, he 's in.'

'Can I see him?'

'No.'

'But 'a winted to see him.

'Ay, but you canna see him. John 's deid.'

'Deid?'

'Ay.'

'Sudden?'

'Ay.'

'Very sudden?'

'Very sudden.'

'Did he say onything about a pot of green paint before he deid?'

This brought to his mind a passage from Shakespeare, which was specially dear to Walter Bagehot.

SHALLOW. Certain, 'tis certain; very sure, very sure; death, as the Psalmist saith, is certain to all; all shall die. How a good yoke of bullocks at Stamford fair?'

SILENCE. Truly, cousin, I was not there.

SHALLOW. Death is certain. Is old Double of your town living yet?

SILENCE. Dead, sir.

SHALLOW. Dead! See! See! A drew a good bow—and dead! A shot a fine shoot: John a Gaunt loved him well, and betted much money on his head.—Dead! A would have clapped i' the clout at twelvescore; and carried you a forehand shaft a fourteen and fourteen-and-a-half, that it would have done a man's heart good to see. How a score of ewes now?

SILENCE. Thereafter as they be; a score of good ewes maybe worth ten pounds.

SHALLOW. And is old Double dead?

The point in both is the strange mixing of the things of eternity with the things of half a minute.

One of his favourite stories before his last journey to America was one which illustrated the imperturbable gravity of the Lowland Scot and the humour of the tourist Englishman.

Genial Englishman (*as the collector punches his ticket*). 'Oh, I say, come now, you 've no right to damage my property. Eh, what! I paid for that ticket.'

Collector (*after a long pause*). 'Ye didna' pay for the ticket—ye paid for yer hurl, and ye 're gettin' yer hurl.'

Of Watson's continual and brilliant talk about literature, religion, and politics, I can attempt no reproduction. His literary hero was Sir Walter Scott, for whom his admiration was almost unbounded. He had his criticisms to make, and he held strongly that Scott was not fair to the religion of the mass of the Scottish people. He declared that with almost no exception Scott introduced clergymen of the Scottish Church in names suggestive of fanaticism and ridicule, Kettledrummle, Poundtext, Mucklewrath, or Blattergowl. If Scott had been writing about the Roman Catholics of a district of Scotland, and introduced them as Father Singmass or Father Hocus Pocus, this would have been called insolence and bad taste, and it was equally insolent to name Protestant ministers as he named them. When it was argued that Jeanie Deans was the flower of Scottish religion, and that the disputation in *The Abbot* between the champions of Catholicism and Protestantism gives Scott's real mind, he refused to change his view. He thought also that Scott had no understanding of the Highlander; that Scott's Highlanders were absurd, transpontine, and stagey. There was nothing of the bewitching and lovely mysticism of the Highlands in Scott. However, he would say that when Scott confined himself to strictly Scottish life he never once went wrong. His chief triumph was Bailie Nicol Jarvie; his failure was Helen Macgregor. Next to Scott in his talk came Burns, the poet of the Scottish people. On the ethical questions involved he took a moderate view. He thought that so far as the Christian Church had endeavoured to shield the purity of the family, and to bring home to man the absolute folly of supposing that moral laws could be broken without punishment, she had the poet's support, his example, his penitence on her side. Where the Church had possibly erred so far as she had touched this great man had been in her ignoring the fact that he was beyond most poets the poet of the people, for whom the Church lived, for whom the Church must suffer, and whom the Church must continuously serve. She did not sufficiently emphasise the fact that Burns had done more than any man in Scottish theology or Scottish literature to expose and kill and blast and carry for ever away everything unreal and hypocritical.

He kept himself well up in current literature, and was highly appreciative of his contemporaries. Most of all he appreciated Rudyard Kipling, whose poems he used to read and repeat with infinite zest. Mr. Kipling was dangerously ill in New York during Watson's second visit to America, and Watson wrote: 'The lamentable news that Rudyard Kipling is in danger of death comes with a shock of grief to a fellow-countryman and a reading man. Almost since the beginning of his career I have read every word he wrote, and have found in his words an inspiration beyond that of any living novelist. He deals at first-hand with the half-dozen passions which mould human nature, and always with insight and nobility. His death, which may God forbid, would in my humble judgment deprive English letters of our greatest name, and England of her real poet-laureate.' To this view he always adhered.

Of his views on theology and the Church I have already written. He was passionately convinced that in proportion as the Church made Christ central in her teaching and in her living, in that proportion she would grow and prevail. He earnestly sympathised with all forward movements for the Christianising of the people, but he was steadfastly opposed to the cheapening and degradation of Christian work, and resolutely firm in holding and preaching the Deity of Christ as defined in the Catholic faith.

When he talked about politics he almost invariably expressed his passionate desire that the Conservative party, with as many Liberals as would join them, should deal effectively and generously with the condition of the people. He thought that the Conservatives should promote measures for the creation of peasant proprietors on a great scale, and while preserving liberty and refusing to pauperise the people, they should generously acknowledge the claims of labour and provide for the necessities of aged toilers. He held that it was in this way, and only in this way, that great social dangers might be averted. But in his last years he looked with interest rather than with hope on the immediate political future of England. In spite of his bitter disappointment over the South African war he remained a firm Imperialist.

I should add that he very seldom talked about individuals. When he did he almost invariably spoke of them with great kindness. His own preferences in preaching were all for the simplest and most real expressions of experience. I have heard him single out Dr. Whyte, Dr. Parker, and Dr. Maclaren as three preachers of genius. In comparatively early years he was exceedingly impressed by certain Jesuit preachers whom he heard in Paris. On his holidays he delighted to attend little chapels, and he enjoyed the homely addresses of the lay preachers. One day a farmer was preaching in a Methodist chapel where Watson often worshipped, and at the conclusion of his sermon said, 'Why do I preach Sunday after Sunday? Because I cannot eat my bread alone.' Watson shook him warmly by the hand after the service, and said later, 'I count that one of the greatest conclusions to a sermon I have ever heard—He could not eat his bit of bread alone.'

His correspondence was immense in his later years, and he received many anonymous letters which he made a point of reading. They often added to the hilarity of his breakfast-table. He would read with great zest epistles stating his faults in a frank, straightforward spirit, and not seldom in soldierly language without any fastidious restraint of charity or delicacy. His anonymous letters of this kind gave him many an hour of simple enjoyment. There were others. He used to talk of one letter which made the sun shine on him when the sky had been grey. It was signed 'Twenty-one,' and he declared that the writer could have done few more human, cordial, and helpful things than the writing of that letter. Another anonymous letter he received was one without a signature informing him that the writer had been so touched by the sentiment of one of his stories and was generally so much impressed by his remarkable literary ability, that he had placed £1000 to his credit with a London bank as a token of gratitude. As he never heard any more of this generous gift he was reluctantly driven to the conclusion that the letter was written in a spirit of unworthy sarcasm. He paid great attention to begging letters, and hardly ever failed to answer them, though he would laugh over them.

The charm of his talk largely depended on his insight into human character, its joys, its sorrows, and its weaknesses. This peculiar insight and the power of mimicry which he inherited from his mother, together with the tones of his voice and the changing expressions of his face, put him in the front rank of talkers and after-dinner speakers. In his home his conversation was invariably cheerful. He had a perfect horror of all that was depressing, and kept away constantly from disagreeable subjects.

CHAPTER XVIII

THE UNIVERSITY OF LIVERPOOL AND LATER CORRESPONDENCE

FROM the foundation of University College, Liverpool, Dr. Watson gave the institution his whole-hearted and undeviating support. As his friend Professor MacCunn has said, he had a wide outlook on national life and a profoundly civic spirit, and, moreover, recognised the value of University institutions as vitalising and humanising forces. He had a very lofty view of the place and of the responsibilities of a University in the life of the commonwealth. Accordingly he longed and laboured for the day when the University of Liverpool should recognise itself, and be recognised as the University of the people, even as his own University of Edinburgh was recognised. Behind the University he always saw the scholar and the lover of books. As he himself loved books and felt all the fascination of a scholar's life, he was able to sympathise with every one in earnest about study.

But he was a student of life most of all. Was it not to the members of the Teachers' Guild within our walls, and then to all the world in the opening chapters of his first book, that he told the story of a Lad o' Pairts going from the parish school to the University with the eyes of the countryside upon him? Was it not on the eve of an address to the students of a Western University that the end came unexpectedly? These are not things that are likely to pass from the grateful hearts of the students of this University. The world beyond our walls is lamenting the preacher and pastor, the man of letters, the citizen, the comrade. Be it ours to keep the memory green of the believer in books, the friend of the scholar, the lover of the student.

This testimony from Professor MacCunn published in the University Magazine may be reinforced by some words from Vicc-Chancellor Dale, who frequently attended Watson's ministry. Dr. Dale writes:—

Common work brought us closely together. He became a member—and an active member—of the Executive Council of University College. He gave time and thought to its service. He used his influence in its behalf. In the movement that created the new University of Liverpool he took a foremost part. His experience and his sympathies gave him a place of his own midway between his academic and his lay colleagues. He understood the minds of both. He could interpret and he could reconcile. And when differences arose, he never rested till the differences were settled. The University owes a lasting debt to his wisdom and his strength. But some of us owe him more than this. Though not a member of his church, I often attended the services at Sefton Park, as did many of my colleagues, and many of our students. For his heart was in the work that we were doing, and with the men and women who were doing it. A new University in a great city, however staunch its friends, has an uphill fight. He helped us in many ways—notably by the place that he gave to the University in public prayer. For whatever men have learned to pray for, they will soon learn to love and to serve. His preaching, too, when he was himself, was singularly helpful. He was in touch with life. He knew what work was, and its weariness; the despondency that comes of baffled aims; the wrestling of the soul with mysteries. His sympathy was the sympathy of the strength that understands weakness, not of the weakness that would be strength. It had a touch of sternness—of austerity. But it braced one as the moorland wind braces; and at the heart of it was the peace of the sea.

Through the kindness of Dr. Dale I am able to give some letters which passed between him and Dr. Watson.

TO VICE-CHANCELLOR DALE

August 17*th,* 1903.

My dear Dale,—While on my wanderings I came across the name of the Council of the New University, and I note that almost the only ambition I have had of late years to be a member of the Governing Body of an Institution for which I have long been striving in my sphere, has been disappointed, and one of my last illusions that I might have done something to popularise the University idea among the people has been dispelled.

It would be foolish for me to complain of a choice which has secured for the Council men of greater academic ability and more pronounced popular power, and I accept the decision which finally dismisses me from University work, but I wish to offer a remonstrance on one feature of the composition of the New Council.

While there is not on it a representative of the Nonconforming clergy of the district, and yet Nonconformists have not been the worst friends of University College, the Bishop and three Church of England clergymen have been included, and altho' I would not for a moment undervalue the help given to the recent effort by any one of the Anglican clergymen, I do not know that the Church of England has been conspicuously zealous in the establishment of the University of Liverpool.

My practical reason, therefore, for writing this letter is not to question the wisdom which excluded one of the members of the old Council, which took the first step towards the New University, for it goes without saying that the most influential names ought to be chosen, but to suggest that when the opportunity occurs some representative Nonconformist clergy should be added. I will only add that when the time comes such a man can be found in Mr. Watson of Claughton, a man admirably suited both by his culture, his zeal, and his eloquence to be a member of the body on whose personality so much depends, if the University is to be made a power in the city and among the people.

I am sending a formal letter resigning my position on the University Committee if that body now exists, or I remain a member.—Yours faithfully, JOHN WATSON.

TO THE SAME

August 25th, 1903.

MY DEAR DALE,—Had I not written at once I should not have written at all, for now I care nothing about the matter. I was put into the Church by my mother, I preferred a country life or the army: My promotions were all unasked: Nicoll made me write: the Moderatorship was forced on me, and taking it was a big mistake: I have been cursed with the lack of ambition or if you like laziness. So I was rather pleased to find myself keen on the University matter, and fanned the flame: but now the flicker has died out, and I am content that L. or any other man should be in my place.

As it is, I beseech you to allow me to drop into the shadow, and indeed after writing you and after being dropped from the Council, I do not judge it expedient that I should be brought in by way of courtesy.

But to turn to the larger question, and let us not speak again of the other, I hope that you will not think me a bitter sectarian when I urge that one Nonconformist clergyman should sit on the Council, and I venture again to bring Watson before you, for he is quite the right man, and his nomination as a quite new minister would have a different complexion from offering one who had been asked to leave the Council for reasons of policy which were entirely reasonable, and then was passed over when there was an opportunity of restoring him, in favour of a man with no claims or even sympathy. You will see, I think, that it is not in such circumstances that I could accept office, but I pray you not to feel concerned for me since any sense of injustice I may have foolishly felt has faded into satisfaction that I am set free by no act of mine from what I know would have been an arduous labour to me.

With many thanks for your kindness, yours faithfully,

JOHN WATSON.

TO THE SAME

October 9th, 1903.

DEAR MR. VICE-CHANCELLOR,—I beg to acknowledge

your letter of the 7th, and I accept with much pleasure the seat on the Council of the University of Liverpool which the Council have done me the honour of inviting me to take.—Believe me, yours faithfully, JOHN WATSON.

TO THE SAME

January 5th, 1904.

DEAR DALE,—For ten days I have been in the grip of a most incapacitating cold, with much chest oppression, and altho' I go to the pulpit I can't go elsewhere, so please excuse me at University Committees.

With every good wish for the New Year for you and yours, yours wheezily, HAMISH MACWHEESSELL.

TO THE SAME

October 15th, 1904.

MY DEAR VICE-CHANCELLOR,—I regret that owing to an engagement in Brighton I shall be unable to be present at the meeting of the Council on Tuesday. By-and-by, and when the pressure of business arrangements slackens, I should like to bring before the Council some suggestions for popularising the University among the people, with a view to the creation of University ambition. Perhaps we could talk the matter over and settle times and seasons.

With every good wish for the Winter's work, yours faithfully, JOHN WATSON.

TO THE SAME

March 7th, 1905.

MY DEAR DALE,—What I want to write about is a matter I think I mentioned to you, and in which Mr. M. very cordially agreed. Whether or not we are going to have a fabric Committee, it is important that there should be some man of practical experience and ability who shall make our buildings old and new his special charge. Of course he must also be a man fit to be a member of the Council of the University. Now I have such a man to put before you, perfectly suited to undertake this duty and to join our Council. He would make the thing his special business, and I therefore am very keen to have him on the Council as soon as possible. There was something in history called the Chancellor's nod—as I have come home from the gales, snow, rain and bitter discomforts of the Sunny South, with bronchial catarrh and lumbago, my memory is not strong—but at any rate will you kindly give the nod at the earliest possible date, and I will produce my man?—Yours coldly and immoveably, JOHN WATSON.

TO THE SAME

October 6th, 1906.

MY DEAR DALE,—I am a vagrant, and as I said to you I am ready to resign whenever you think fit. Please let me know to whom I ought to write.—Yours faithfully,

JOHN WATSON.

TO THE SAME

October 11th, 1906.

DEAR MR. VICE-CHANCELLOR,—It is now my duty to resign the position of a member of the Council of the University of Liverpool, and I shall be obliged if you will place this letter before the Council.

My only reason is that I shall soon be leaving Liverpool, and that I cannot therefore give any further service.

In severing my connection with the University, I desire to acknowledge the courtesy I have ever received from my colleagues, and to express my warm goodwill for an Institution with which it was my high honour for a time to be associated.

With every assurance of respect, I am, yours faithfully,

JOHN WATSON.

(*Enclosed Note*)

TO THE SAME

DEAR DALE,—I have enclosed what is called in commercial circles the 'needful,' with inevitable regret.

Tuesday or Wednesday or Thursday evenings of next week are hungering for the sight of your face. Say when, which sounds jovial. I am not, but solemn this evening.

J. W.

FROM VICE-CHANCELLOR DALE

24th October 1906.

DEAR DR. WATSON,—The Senate are unwilling to allow your resignation of your membership of Council to pass without expressing their grateful appreciation of the services that you have rendered through many years to the University, and to the College out of which it sprang. To your advocacy and influence the success of the University movement was largely due. And your wise and sympathetic counsel has done much to strengthen the University that you had helped to found. Nor can we forget your personal kindness, unstinted and unfailing, to every member of the University staff who came in contact with you. Some of us recall faith renewed and courage rekindled by your ministry. Each of us owes you a debt of his own; you have the gratitude and the affection of us all.

I write in the name and on the instruction of the Senate, met on October 24, 1906.—Believe me, ever yours very truly,

A. W. W. DALE.

TO VICE-CHANCELLOR DALE

October 26th, 1906.

MY DEAR VICE-CHANCELLOR,—The letter which you have written on behalf of the Senate and which you have couched in such gracious terms, has touched my heart.

It has been a just ground of pride to me that I have had a modest share in the administrative work of the University and the benefit of its scholars' friendship.

Amid the daily demands of an arduous profession my leisure for the Arts, I dare not mention Science, has been very scanty, but if it has not been given one to make any addition to knowledge it is an honour to have assisted, even in a very slight measure, in building Westminster College, Cambridge, and establishing the University of Liverpool.

My association with its distinguished teachers past and present has been an inspiration, and if in any way I have helped such men in their endeavours, surely I have not altogether failed.

My thoughts will often turn to the University, and I pray that the blessing of the Eternal may ever rest on its teachers and students, on all its study and research.

Will you convey to all the brethren of the Senate my warm good wishes, and believe me, yours respectfully and gratefully, JOHN WATSON.

TO PRINCIPAL OSWALD DYKES

October 26th, 1906.

MY DEAR PRINCIPAL,—When any little honour comes my way, I count you so true a friend that I wish you to know of it, and especially when it is of an academic nature.

As you may be aware I have had a good deal to do with University College, Liverpool, and the University into which the College passed. Lately I resigned my position in the Council of the University which is the governing body, and my colleagues with whom I have been long associated passed a too generous resolution.

What however has taken me altogether by surprise is that the Senate, of which of course I was not a member, altho' I was on very intimate terms with many of the Professors, has also passed a resolution, which has both greatly touched and encouraged me, for that a body of men so varied and so distinguished should have thought so well of me, proves I have not altogether failed in my academic service in Liverpool. JOHN WATSON.

TO W. ROBERTSON NICOLL

Jan. 6th, 1904.

We shall have to fight to the death for non-sectarian education, for Temperance, and for Free Trade. I am now at heart a Liberal, but of course I remain neutral as regards parties.

TO THE SAME

17 *Croxteth Road, Liverpool, 18th February* 1904.

MY DEAR NICOLL,—This is first of all to welcome you home and to say that we hope you have enjoyed your trip to San Remo.

As I had to preach at Eastbourne last Sunday as well as address a congregational meeting, I snatched a holiday of four days with Mrs. Watson. It rained three days and blew half a gale all the four, but I had a little rest in not having to produce and it is all I am likely to get for some time, as the Bible Society are celebrating their Centenary in March, and I shall be speaking in London and half a dozen provincial towns, and have refused invitations to speak in twenty more. It is pleasant to know that when people want a spiritual and sound address on a religious subject they know where to go, and that when they want rationalistic and revolutionary orations attacking the foundations of society they do not come to me. This is not boasting, far less Pharisaism, it is simply a modest statement of facts.

I wrote to Miss Stoddart that I was half meditating a second article on the Next Revival, on which about sixty American Ministers have delivered themselves in a three months' symposium. I have changed my mind since. I don't believe in replying, and most of the criticisms were irrelevant, and none of them, that is unfavourable ones, faced the fact that the present evangelist does not reach the people outside the Churches, and secondly that the Old Testament Prophets gave a place to social righteousness which the evangelist does not. Both facts are suggestive, and it is no answer to beat me with a doctrine of the Atonement, so I shall leave the matter alone. Please say so to Miss Stoddart in the course of those consultations on the slope of Mount Olympus which the herd of common people on the plain can only imagine. JOHN WATSON.

TO THE SAME

17 *Croxteth Road, Liverpool,* 11*th March* 1904.

MY DEAR NICOLL,—I have just reached home after a toilsome week, working all Monday with the Bible Society, and speaking at their big meeting in the evening, going down on Tuesday morning to Newcastle, and reading a paper to the Free Church Council—during which the pro-Boers interrupted me, but I modestly think received no change from your afflicted friend, and never interrupted me again—speaking at a church on Wednesday evening instead of Monro Gibson, moving on to Sheffield yesterday, and haranguing a huge gathering on the Bible Society, and coming home to face the correspondence from all quarters and on all subjects.

I rather enjoyed speaking at the Mansion House and had a fairly good time; his Grace of Canterbury was very agreeable privately on Monday night, and so were all the Bishops

I have been meeting lately, especially St. Albans, who is a very agreeable and shrewd man. By the way why is it Nonconformists are not more prominent in connection with the Bible Society? I seemed to be the only man taking any share of things, and I am going up and down Lancashire trying to do my duty in connection with the Centenary. The Church of England people give me always a most cordial reception, and I am told in the Committee of Arrangements are very eager that I should be invited, which is very nice; but Nonconformists should do more to support this Society, or rather to be prominent in connection with it.

The Council was I think successful at Newcastle, and Jowett preached one of the finest sermons I ever heard. The speaking on education was fair, but a little too excited.

As regards the education decision I have my own ideas, but I did not give them. They are a little more thorough than those of the majority, and I do not believe there will be rest in the land till the State confines itself to secular instruction, and the Church teaches religion.

John Watson.

TO THE SAME

17 *Croxteth Road, Liverpool,* 19*th March* 1904.

Dear Nicoll,—By the way I am thinking of publishing my Newcastle address, although I should like you to be oversman in the question. Many people are asking for copies. It seems to have created some attention, and the pro-Boers fell upon me tooth and nail in the Liverpool papers virtually denying that I had ever said the same thing before, with the result that the *Post* published an extract from the sermon in the *British Weekly* of 1899 in almost identical words, which has rather amused Liverpool and made the pro-Boers wish they had left the matter alone. I am going out with the Bishop to Warrington on Monday and with Archdeacon Wilson, of Rochdale, to Bury on Tuesday for the Bible Society. When I spoke last Monday evening in Liverpool I do not think there was a Presbyterian on the platform except myself and very few Nonconformists of any kind. But there was a great platform, the Philharmonic Hall crowded to the door, and overflow meetings in another hall. Perhaps the comparative absence of Nonconformists from prominent places means nothing and I am doing what I can to represent that side of things.

I was struck at Newcastle by the vigour and popular power of those rising Nonconformists, Campbell, Horne, Lidgett, Dawson, Yates, and many others.

JOHN WATSON.

TO THE SAME

17 *Croxteth Road*, *Liverpool*, 21*st May* 1904.

DEAR NICOLL,—It pleased me to have even a word with you when I was dazzled by that blaze of luminaries, and I had a pleasant talk with Jacobs, and was much pleased by Chesterton's head. I have been for a week in the Forest of Fontainebleau and never felt more in my life the mystery and benediction of a great forest. I went largely for Mrs. Watson's sake who has not been well, and I think it has done her a great deal of good. For myself I am again troubled with sleeplessness, which is very trying. It is needless to say that I can always sleep at the wrong time, as when listening to any fine conversation and I nearly went to sleep at that dinner before —— had finished. He is not a bad speaker, but he has no terminal facilities.—With kind regards, yours faithfully, JOHN WATSON.

TO LADY GRAINGER STEWART

June 21*st*, 1904.

DEAR LADY GRAINGER STEWART,—Accept a line in haste

with a table of letters before me. We thank you and the children for all your kindness. I greatly enjoyed my visit and the dinner-party, and preached so well under your inspiration at North Shields that a thousand people were turned away in the evening, and the congregations stood at the open windows. I thought that I was Hugh Black, but the difference is that in a month at longest, if I were in North Shields permanently, the people would have plenty of room, but with him, they would be on the roof listening through the ventilators.—Yours affectionately,

HUGH JOHN BLACK WATSON.

TO W. ROBERTSON NICOLL

17 *Croxteth Road, Liverpool,* 8*th July* 1904.

DEAR NICOLL,—Your letter gave me much pleasure because it was written in your own hand, which I have not seen for a long time, and your writing has greatly improved. It is evident you have been attending one of those classes which teach you French in four lessons, or to write distinctly in either longhand or short in five. I like to see a man of your age steadily fighting with your faults and striving after better things. I am inviting offers for the letter from collectors because our house has been an hotel for the last week for Pans, and the family finances are running low.

The Pans[1] have almost driven me crazy partly entertaining them, partly listening to them, and partly being introduced, first to one Pan, who then introduces me to seventeen other Pans, and every one of the seventeen has a complete kitchen range behind him, till in pure absence of mind I shook hands with the venerable partner of my life and trials a few

[1] The reference, I fear, is to the Pan-Presbyterian Council.

days ago with a mechanical grin and the mystical words 'very glad to meet you Mrs. Watson, hope you are enjoying our country.' They say it was a very successful meeting. JOHN WATSON.

TO MRS. STEPHEN WILLIAMSON

October 9th, 1906.

MY DEAR FRIEND,—Just a brief sketch of our proceedings since we left your beautiful country home, before we settle down to the winter's work.

From Glenogil the 'partner of my joys and sorrows' went to an old friend of my boyhood's, Lady Grainger Stewart's in Glenisla, while her man went to preach in St George's Edinburgh, to packed congregations, hundreds being turned away; then I joined my 'helpmeet,' and we had three pleasant days with the Stewarts. We motored to Tulchan deer forest and toured home by a high mountain road. Had a view of sunset on the Grampians, never to be forgotten; another day we ran down to Rossie Priory to call on the Kinnairds, with whom we ought to have stayed this year; Lady Kinnaird spoke faithfully on my conduct, but we have made it up with promises of good behaviour in the future. From Glenisla we went to Strathgarry, and there we visited Urrard House and saw the Burghcleres, whom I had met before, who were very kind, and have asked us, if we come back, to stay with them, and Blair Castle, where Lady Tullibardine and Lady Helen Murray took immense trouble and showed us everything outside and in. Many interesting people in the district were there. Thence Mrs. Watson went home, and I to Dundee where I preached to two more crowds and lectured to a third. I stayed with the Lord Provost and his wife, nice people, and lunched at Glamis on Monday. The Strathmores are kindness itself. Lord

Strathmore got out the ancient 'Bear Drinking Cup' of which only a facsimile is shown, and having ordered up a rare wine from the cellar I drank their health in a touching scene. This I understood was a quite extraordinary honour. They all came down and gave us a great send-off.—Yours faithfully,

JOHN WATSON.

CHAPTER XIX

RESIGNATION OF SEFTON PARK CHURCH

WHILE Dr. Watson was still in the full flush of his power, he decided to resign the charge of Sefton Park Church. The news was received with universal amazement. It perplexed the public as much as Dr. Chalmers's resignation of his work in Glasgow astounded his contemporaries. It seemed as if a great post was to be abandoned and a great work relinquished long before the time. That so powerful and energetic a figure should suddenly pause in the career shaped for him at the height of a success over which not the faintest shadow seemed to have come, seemed inexplicable. But it was the determined will of Watson to make this change, and he never seemed to have any doubt as to the wisdom and necessity of the step. He determined to shake himself free of labours and cares to which he no longer found himself equal. Like Chalmers, he held that it was impossible for him to combine a due attention to his sermons with the innumerable calls of his personal and pastoral work. Even his most intimate friends wondered. But the strain of his various toils began to tell upon him. His family observed that after the year of his Moderatorship he was never the same man again. He suffered much from insomnia; he was often nervous and anxious; and though in public the old buoyancy still characterised him, at home he often showed unmistakable signs of fatigue and depression. Also he had always held that twenty-five years of such a church as that at Sefton Park were enough for any man. He had observed that many ministers who refused to resign at the natural period marred their previous work, and lived in a delusion. He was resolved that no one should say of him that he had outstayed his welcome. In his humility Watson fancied that his attractive power was decaying, and that if he continued in his sphere the congregation would decline. He could not bear to think of this. I can see in the retrospect that he never anticipated for himself a long life, in fact he ever and anon gave expression to his Celtic presentiment of early death. His life he would say was not to be a long one, and perhaps he was not unpleased to see it passing. He contemplated almost too early the softer fading aspects of our earthly years, the joy and rest and reunion of the world of hopc. He had no thought of undertaking any other office; he purposed to preach and lecture and to write books. He pleased himself with the prospect of some quiet years in a place near London where he could be happy with his family and friends. The weight of responsibility was more than he could bear, and it was evident that his spirits rose whenever he thought about the prospect of relief.

The Sefton Park congregation understood their minister. They saw that he meant what he had said. Whatever could have been done to lighten his labour they were more than willing to do. But they came to see that this was not a practicable plan with a man so anxiously conscientious as Watson was. They did all they could in kindness to change his mind, but when they saw that his purpose was fixed, they made things as easy for him as they could. Watson was profoundly touched by their delicate sympathy. He found that the wrench of parting with them was even greater than he believed it would be. In fact some of us thought that he would never leave Liverpool. He gave them a year's notice of his intention to resign in order that he might help them in choosing a successor. Perhaps the highest proof that a congregation can give of their affection for a retiring pastor is when they ask him to help them in choosing a successor. There was some difficulty in discovering a successor, though the congregation acted with marked loyalty and unanimity. It was no light task to succeed John Watson. He found it necessary to remain in Liverpool longer than he intended, and he frequently took services in the church after his resignation. But in the end all went well. Watson's work was magnificently recognised, and a successor after his own heart, the Rev. Alexander Connell, of Regent Square, London, was found and settled. The story of this period will best be told in Watson's own letters.

TO W. ROBERTSON NICOLL

Sefton Park Church, Liverpool, Sept. 8, 1904.

DEAR NICOLL,—If I cannot call you one of my oldest friends, you are certainly one of my best, and I wish therefore to acquaint you with an important decision which I have finally made during the quiet time in the country.

On Sept. 30th I propose to tell my Session that at the end of Sept. 1905, when I shall have completed my quarter of a century in Sefton Park Church, I shall resign my charge. My reason for giving this early intimation to the elders is that my Assistant has left and various arrangements have to be made which would be affected by my future, that a sudden resignation would be unfair and might suggest wrong ideas to those who do not know the happy tie between me and my people, and not least that during next winter I may give them the opportunity from time to time without prejudice on either side of hearing some suitable men for the succession.

I shall ask the elders to receive this announcement in confidence and to say nothing about the matter this year: in February of next year, when we hold our Congregational Meeting I shall review the past and tell the people.

During spring they may make up their minds about my successor, and before the holidays the necessary steps to secure him could be taken. Then he should go for a holiday in August and September, and I would fill the pulpit till the beginning of Oct. 1905, when he would enter on his ministry at the opening of the winter's work. Of course before he could be elected I should have formally to resign, but I could remain as *locum tenens*. This plan would preserve continuity and make no jolt in the Congregational history. But as regards details it must be as God wills: all I can do is to think out the matter with the set regard to the good of the congregation for which I have worked so hard and which has been so loyal to me.

You will, of course, treat this as a matter of confidence till the time comes for the public announcement. But you have my plan and ideas.

When I am free from Sefton Park I shall not cease to preach: both Sundays and week days I hope to preach for years in all kinds of pulpits: I hope also to do some literary and theological work. And I shall have leisure to read and to 'make my soul.'

For some time I have found the pastoral work and organisation hard: my yearly visitation began in April and will not be finished till November, and has taken all my spare time, and the Guilds, etc., etc., do not find me as energetic or as fertile with addresses as once I was. And I am convinced that a pastor is as necessary as a preacher for a congregation. . . .—Yours faithfully, JOHN WATSON.

FROM MR. ANDREW CARNEGIE

October 23rd, 1905.

MY DEAR FRIEND,—Congratulations upon taking the 'armour off,' having long fought the good fight well.—Now spend a wise old age, with honour, love, abundance, troops of friends surrounding and loving you.

My kindest regards, and every good wish, yours always,

ANDREW CARNEGIE.

FROM MR. HALL CAINE

October 24th, 1904.

My dear Dr. Watson,—I see the startling announcement of your intended retirement, and I send you at once an expression of my sincere sympathy. I feel that, however early in life it may seem to others, it is for you first to know what it is best to do. And I shall hope that tho' you are stepping out of the severe duties of your Pastorate, you are reserving your great powers for ever wider usefulness. The world will not let you rest altogether. You will not wish to be idle. In the best sense you must die only in harness.

With kindest greeting. Hall Caine.

TO PRINCIPAL OSWALD DYKES

October 26th, 1904.

Dear Dr. Dykes,—Accept my sincere gratitude for your kind letter: it was the weight of the pastoral and organising work I could no longer carry, and I felt Sefton Park must not be allowed to fail. It is a great sacrifice for me in every way, and I hope, therefore, that I have not been selfish in my motive, however I may have erred in anything else. I hope to preach as long as I have a voice, where I can.

When any suitable man occurs to you for Sefton Park, let us know: we have plenty of time to look round.

In haste.—With affectionate respect, John Watson.

The announcement made in 1904 evoked widespread sympathy, but few believed that Watson's career was really at an end, though all allowed that he had thoroughly earned a long rest. Liverpool and his congregation took leave of him in a royal way. They were puzzled. When they heard him talk of a 'younger, abler, and more modern minister,' they reflected that there was not likely to be found any man abler, and that no modern light or modern gift had been absent from the Sefton Park pulpit. But after pleading their hardest, they wisely and kindly accepted the inevitable. At the semi-jubilee in February 1905 Dr. Watson reviewed his ministry, and on March 13th, 1905, he gave in his resignation to the Presbytery. 'I am worn out,' he said, 'and cannot go on. If in a year or two I broke down entirely the congregation might have the burden of an invalid minister. That would have fretted me and undone what I have already done. And therefore when Sefton Park was at its best, and before my health had utterly failed, I resolved to resign that this great congregation unburdened and unfettered might pass into the hands of my successor.' It was on October 15th, 1905, that he took his farewell of the Sefton Park people. Cordial tributes were paid by the Liverpool papers, the *Post* and the *Courier*. Sir Edward Russell in a touching article bore witness to the place that Watson had held in the heart of Liverpool. 'He will be greatly missed. We can all look forward to times when everybody will be saying: "What would John Watson have said to that?" "How John Watson would have denounced this scandal!" "How John Watson would have riddled that fallacy!" "How John Watson would have exposed that piece of bigotry or fanatical zealotry!" And amid these more casual reflections will be much grave and sympathetic yearning for a renewal of those inspiring suggestions of spiritual sympathy with human needs and of spiritual responses to eternal and divine requirements which have rendered John Watson's teachings the guides, the suggestions, the warnings, the encouragement of hundreds of his fellow-citizens for these twenty-five years past.' A gift of £2600 was privately presented to him and acknowledged in a letter to Mr. T. Rowland Hughes. At a great civic function in the Town Hall, where the Lord Mayor and Lady Mayoress (Mr. and Mrs. John Lea) received several hundred guests representing all ranks and classes, speeches were made by the Lord Mayor, the Bishop of Liverpool, the Rev. Dr. Aked, Sir Edward Russell, Vice-Chancellor Dale, Mr. Samuel Smith, M.P., and others. The Bishop of Liverpool, Dr. Chavasse, said that Dr. Watson's career was not yet done. He was still very far from even the youth of old age, and it was the prayer of many that he would be spared for many a year to do some of his best work by pen and word of mouth to help in the future, as in the past, the Church of Christ, the citizen life of England and individual men and women. There was nothing to mar the occasion save the regret of parting, which told very severely at the time on Watson himself. His own speech was full of modesty and tenderness. He asserted his immovable belief that there was no city like Liverpool with so broad a spirit in society, or with such persuasive examples of municipal patriotism.

No man could know William Rathbone, that civic saint, or Charles Garrett, in whom the evangelistic spirit of John Wesley lived, or Monsignor Nugent, the type of that pity for the poor which has been one of the chief glories of the Catholic Church, or Alexander Balfour, who illustrated the *perfervidum ingenium* of the Scot, or his dear friend Samuel Rathbone, one of the ablest and most modest men of his day, without being shamed out of selfishness, and inspired to imagine and do something for the commonwealth. My Lord Mayor, you have done me many acts of kindness, and now you have added an act of honour of which I shall be proud while I live, and my sons after me. It is little I can do to show my gratitude, but if in years to come the place of my habitation be elsewhere and this city judges that I can be of any service, then I shall hasten to answer the call as a soldier rejoining his colours. And till death closes my lips I shall pray for the peace and prosperity of Liverpool.

It soon became apparent that the Church at large was not prepared to allow John Watson's retirement from labour. The Presidency of the National Free Church Council was pressed upon him. He was surprised but gratified. As he had come to understand better the Free Churches of the country, he was more and more drawn to them. He preached many sermons on their great occasions, and was universally popular. He appreciated the great place of Nonconformity in modern England, and was well disposed to meet its representatives at closer quarters. Though he declined at first, feeling that the physical strain would be too great for him, he was ultimately led to accept. In his own Church, the Presbyterian Church of England, there was a general desire that John Watson should be retained in the regular ranks. His friends all knew that after a period of rest his great energies would revive, and they wished to find for him a sphere in which they would be exerted without exhaustion. Such a sphere seemed open when the revered Principal of Westminster College, Cambridge, Dr. Oswald Dykes, intimated his intention to retire. A minister who had worked as hard as John Watson could not pretend to the higher academic acquirements, but it was well known that though he deprecated all claim to learning, he was no mean authority on certain subjects, and particularly on Church History. Westminster College seemed to need a man who would bring the institution into closer relations with the scattered congregations of the Church. Dr. Watson had shown what he could do in this direction as Convener of the College Committee. It was desired also that the students should come into close relation with one who had been a great preacher and pastor. The

Presbyterian Church of England needed him as a leader in a forward movement. He himself believed that the Church could do great things if wisely and boldly led, and of all Presbyterians he was the man who spoke to England. It was desired, therefore, by a large part of the Church that he should become Principal of the College in succession to Dr. Dykes. Only a nominal salary could be paid, and it was not contemplated that he should take full professorial work. There was opposition in important quarters of the Church, but on the whole the general feeling was strongly in favour of this step being taken, and it commended itself particularly to those who best knew Watson.

At first he was wholly averse from the proposal. He was weary and enamoured with rest. He shrank from accepting further heavy responsibilities, and he believed that the climate of Cambridge would be unsuitable to his wife's health. But gradually the idea seemed to attract him, and the reservations and the hesitations slowly disappeared. Mrs. Watson herself, who had noticed her husband's great influence over students, was willing to acquiesce in the arrangement, and it seemed as if it held the promise of new vigour and potency in the Presbyterian Church of England.

Dr. Watson was invited to deliver at Cambridge a series of lectures, and he chose as his subject a very favourite theme, 'The Scot of the Eighteenth Century.' The lectures were well received, and have been published since his death. He was stirred by what he saw. The preaching of Mr. Johnston Ross, the Presbyterian minister at Cambridge, greatly moved him, and he reckoned him with Mr. Jowett as the foremost of the younger Nonconformist preachers. But he saw difficulties which he thus expressed :—

TO W. ROBERTSON NICOLL

26th September 1905.

As regards myself and the proposal which you shadow forth I have the most serious difficulties—difficulties which seem to me insuperable. First I want to be free in order to write if I please, or study, especially in one period of Scots History, and to preach where I please when I am moved thereto, and to preach what I please, or rather what seems true to me, and to travel as I please. I do not mean to be an idle and useless man, but I do want to have some freedom after thirty-one years' regular and compulsory work.

Next I have not the scholarly equipment for any Chair, although I could do something in Pastoral Theology or Christian Ethics, and possibly in Church History, with which I have a growing acquaintance. Neither Greek nor Hebrew criticism, nor pure dogma would I venture to touch. In my busy life I have not had the opportunity of pursuing systematic study, and I am therefore out of the running for a position which should be occupied by a scholar, and by a scholar I mean an expert.

It is very good of you to offer to face the practical difficulty, but I am afraid it would be very serious. I doubt very much whether the staff would care for the introduction of a man whom they would with some justice regard as an absolute outsider, and I am sure that there would be extreme difficulty about the finance. What you propose would be the subject of committees and motions for the next five years. . . .

There is another serious question and that is health, both with regard to my wife and myself. I do not think Cambridge would suit either of us, and I am sure it would not suit her, and that is a serious matter. . . .

If you love me, come down for October 17th, when the Lord Mayor gives a public reception at the Town Hall in recognition of my twenty-five years' service to the city. This has nothing to do with the congregation, and is, I think, somewhat remarkable. He intends that it should encourage other men who besides doing their own work remember the Commonwealth, and it is, I believe, the first recognition of this kind given in our municipal history. I wish it had been given to my dear friends Monsignor Nugent and Charles Garrett, but Nugent has had a statue at any rate.

But gradually these objections were borne down. Watson decided to recruit himself after the pain of parting from Liverpool by a tour in America to which he looked forward with great eagerness. By the time he left he had accepted the Presidency of the National Free Church Council, and had also consented to be nominated for the Principalship of Westminster College, Cambridge.

Before starting Watson fulfilled many public engagements, and on October 14th, 1906, he preached in Sefton Park Church on the 'Embassy of the Gospel,' and introduced his successor, the Rev. Alexander Connell, saying: 'While you will find your minister firm in the faith of Christ, he is not the man to shut his mind against any new light God may give; and while he will be sympathetic to the ancient customs of our worship, he is not the man to forget that even good customs may corrupt the Church.'

Among the many affectionate letters of farewell received by Watson I may quote the following:—

FROM SIR EDWARD RUSSELL

January 8th, 1907.

MY DEAR WATSON,—We are looking forward with great pleasure to the happiness of being at your house, and having a good evening with you before your departure which itself is a sad event, not only to us in particular, but to all Liverpool. I received your letter with a deep feeling of the privileges of your friendship, which I have so long enjoyed. I note with delight your high appreciation of the co-operation I have sometimes been able to afford you, but it is really I who am the debtor, because having my duties, as I apprehend them, it is indeed always a satisfaction to support a man of insight and courage in public affairs, whether religious or secular.

With our united regards, yours faithfully,

EDWARD RUSSELL.

FROM PRINCIPAL OSWALD DYKES

January 25th, 1907.

MY DEAR DR. WATSON,—I saw your son the other day,

who told me you were to sail on the 30th. I wish you and Mrs. Watson from all my heart a pleasant voyage, in spite of February gales, and on the other side a good time to your hearts' content. And I also wish you a safe and certain home-coming, for I believe there is work for you yet to do in the old country, and nowhere a warmer welcome or appreciation from your friends.

Bless you for your generous, too generous words of kindness in this as in all your letters. The years before me cannot be numerous now, but if it please God they may not be unuseful or unpleasant, with health and a little strength. I shall not forget you and your wife in your absence, not for a day, for I value your friendship extremely, and what is more I value highly your gifts and the service it is in you to render, God willing, to this Church, for which I have spent the best of my days, and which dwell where I may I cannot cease to love.

God bless you, dear friend, you and yours continually.—Yours with respectful affection, J. Oswald Dykes.

FROM FATHER HENRY C. DAY

January 25th, 1907.

Dear Dr. Watson,—I am deeply obliged to you for your very kind letter, but I will not accept the farewell yet. That must be delayed as long as possible, and would that the possible were very much longer. It will indeed require a very urgent call, and one of peremptory duty to prevent my seeing you off on Wednesday next, besides I am promising myself the pleasure, if they will have me, of being at your farewell dinner on Monday. I need not tell you how much I shall feel your loss, and that of your family on merely personal grounds. I also feel very keenly the privations of the city, of your great and good influence. But enough of selfish repining. May wider fields have the advantage of your labour, and yourself an ever-increasing reward of success and of gladness.—Believe me to be, dear Dr. Watson, always yours very sincerely,

HENRY C. DAY.

CHAPTER XX

LAST VISIT TO AMERICA, AND DEATH

Dr. and Mrs. Watson sailed for New York on January 30th, 1907. Two nights before the Presbyterians of Liverpool entertained them at a banquet at the Adelphi Hotel. In reply to the toast of his health, Dr. Watson said there ought to be most absolute liberty with regard to theories, but when they came to deal with facts which lay at the heart of our religion, which were the foundation on which the Church rested, and on which the souls of men rested for time and eternity, there we must be clear, we must be sure; there we must stand with all our strength of mind and heart. He made no reference to controversies that were going on at present; he was not to be understood to criticise any teacher or thinker with imperfect information at hand. He welcomed every one who was looking at things with his own eyes, and seeking to help his fellow-men in the clearer light. But he registered his conviction that our Church should stand or fall according as she went forth to the people holding the central faith fast, and preaching that faith clearly regarding the two great facts, the Deity of the Lord Jesus Christ as the eternal Son of God and the virtue of the great sacrifice which He accomplished on Calvary for the salvation of the world. When the parting came many prominent Liverpool citizens, including Mr. Alexander Connell and Mr. John Lea, were present to say good-bye, and it is certain that not one among them dreamed that this was the last good-bye.

SS. 'Baltic,' January 30th, 1907.

My dear Mrs. ——,—I was much touched by the white heather, and by the message. The plant is now with some others in our sitting-room, for Mr. Ismay had us removed to a suite of rooms with the most delightful bathroom attached, beautifully furnished, and heated with electric stoves. This is the merchant prince way of travelling I suppose, and it is rather nice, because we have writing-tables, couches, electric lamps, arm-chairs, and so on. If only the sea is friendly we shall be very comfortable, but this is more than we can expect.

Many saw us off, and we held a kind of reception in our rooms. As Liverpool disappeared and we remembered that it was farewell to the city of our habitation, a feeling of sadness came over us, for a chapter of our life is closed. May God forgive its sins, and accept its work.

Whether we meet again or not, allow me to sign myself your friend, John Watson.

It seemed to some of his fellow-passengers that Dr. Watson was suffering from exhaustion and strain, but to others he appeared as buoyant as ever. The travellers on arriving at New York were received by their host, Mr. Frank H. Dodd, of Messrs. Dodd, Mead and Co. Mr. Dodd tells me that during the time of his stay Watson seemed to have recovered all his old spirits. He preached twice for his friend Dr. Aked in Fifth Avenue Baptist Church, and great crowds were present, and many were turned from the doors. He commenced at once the course of sermons, lectures, and addresses which he had undertaken. During his stay in Philadelphia he was the guest of Mr. Harold Peirce. Mr. Peirce has very kindly forwarded me some of his last letters and particulars about his journey. From these and from letters written home, I am able to give a fairly full account of his last journey. He had many engagements when he arrived in America, but his time was not filled up, and he accepted many additional invitations to lecture and preach, somewhat to the anxiety of his friends. So far as I can make out his course was as follows. At Philadelphia he preached, lectured, and delivered a course of addresses at Haverford College on the Religious Condition of Scotland in the Eighteenth Century. He was at Boston in the beginning of March. There he preached for Dr. Gordon in the Old South Church, lectured, and stayed a fortnight. He went to New York again on March 24th to fulfil an engagement. Then he returned to Philadelphia, from which he took a tour in the West, lecturing in Winnipeg and returning through Montana, an exceptionally long and trying journey. It was on Friday, April 12th, that he lectured in Winnipeg, and his last appearance was at Valley City, N.D., where he preached on Sunday, April 21st. He arrived at Mount Pleasant, Iowa, on April 23rd, intending to deliver a course of lectures in the Iowa Wesleyan University, but he was taken ill, and the end came on May 6th. These details will explain the letters to his sons and the kind communication from Mr. Peirce.

TO HIS SONS

PHILADELPHIA, *February 14th,* 1907.

MY DEAR F.,—It occurs to me that I might send to you a record of our tour in America, and then you could forward the letters to Freddie and to Harry. This would preserve a complete history and would save your mother and myself writing separate letters. Please get the letters back both from Cambridge and from the barracks and preserve them against our return home.

To begin at the beginning, we had after the first day very rough weather lasting for five days, and the ship's log had North-west gale and South-west gale, heavy sea, stormy sea, head sea, cross sea, entered in day by day. The last day was good weather. You know what bad sailors your mother and I are, and yet I was never ill, and your mother was only ill I think once for half an hour, which proves what a good boat the *Baltic* is. She never rolled and only pitched a little, which was quite unavoidable in the circumstances. We sat at the Captain's table, and several other people at the table we knew or they knew us, so we had pleasant companionship. We had little parties after dinner in our sitting-room, and you would have liked to drop in and see a distinguished member of the English Foreign Office, and a professor and a Scotch mill-owner and your father all smoking together and putting the universe to rights in the middle of the Atlantic with a north-west gale blowing. When we entered the river at New York, the ice was around us on every side, and it was piercingly cold. Every one had told us shocking stories about the custom house officers—how they would ask questions and open our boxes and confiscate our goods. As a matter of fact, they were most courteous. The officer who came on board before whom I signed my declaration, asked me when I gave my name as John, whether I had any other name that began with 'I.' Then we shook hands and he gave me no further trouble. I told him that all bad characters had several names because it enabled us to escape the police. When we had our luggage examined on the quay, the officer was quite delightful. He only asked us to lift the lid of the boxes and pretended to look at them, and he actually helped to fasten them up himself, a thing I am told which they very seldom do. Mr. Dodd was waiting for us, and we drove through banks of snow to his house in New York, where we received a warm welcome.

But the excitement had begun before that, for four reporters interviewed me on the steamer and took your mother's photograph and mine on the deck. We were asked questions on every subject under the sun, and especially what we thought of the Thaw trial. It is a disgraceful trial going on in New York just now on which I passed no opinion. On Saturday evening I was rung up at dinner by one of the New York papers, who asked me to represent them at the Thaw trial and to write an article on my impressions, and they offered me any sum I liked to ask. This is thought to be the most impertinent thing any New York paper has ever done, and the paper that did it is the lowest down of the New York press. I had one luncheon with literary men at the Century Club in New York and a dinner party with bankers and clergymen. On Sunday the 10th of February, I preached to very large crowds in a New York church, hundreds being turned away, and the crushing was so great that a reserve of police had to be telephoned for from the station. On Monday among other things I went to the New York Hippodrome, where we saw some excellent horsemanship and the most beautiful coloured spectacle of Neptune's Palace below the sea I have ever seen on the stage. On Monday evening I lectured in the Savoy Hotel to an appreciative audience. Every hour almost the telephone went at the house where I was living, and my likeness was taken in the house and also at a studio for the press. On Tuesday morning we came to Philadelphia and went to live in an extremely beautiful house in the country belonging to Mr. Peirce, who you may remember was at our house about two years ago. He has the most beautiful library in construction I have seen in a private house, and is a great book lover. The country where we are living is covered with snow. Yesterday I had a glorious sleigh ride with a fine trotting horse. Since coming to Philadelphia I have preached once and lectured once, and I am to lecture again to-night at a college. I have also been at one dinner and one luncheon party. My photograph has been taken again here, and I have been interviewed about six times. Over against this interviewing, however, I have met a number of distinguished Philadelphia citizens, very interesting and very able men. This brings the record up to the present date, and I will resume the history in another letter. . . . With our love to all three.—Your affectionate father, JOHN WATSON.

TO THE SAME

Philadelphia, February 26th, 1907.

MY DEAR F.,—Since I wrote you last, I have been fairly busy and also received marked kindness. To-night, I deliver the last of my course of Haverford lectures. I have also preached three times to two large congregations and one that was smaller. Of course we had a little blizzard, what is called here a 'baby blizzard.' I have also been out to some interesting social functions where I met a number of very bright people, especially judges and other lawyers. The snow was rather heavy where we are living and has been too soft for sleighing, but we have had some good drives. Owing to the changeableness of the climate, I had an attack of hoarseness which was a new thing for me. I have now got over it. I am only afraid the frequent changes in temperature may make it trying for a speaker. I am told that singers suffer a good deal in the States. We are both well apart from this and your mother is enjoying herself. On Saturday we go to Boston and then we shall go out for a short lecturing tour.

I suppose you have had my letter asking you to send an account of the sale and any news of that kind. Yesterday I saw the *British Weekly* and discovered that the opposition to my appointment at Cambridge is very strong in London and I should think it is very unlikely I shall be sent there, so you must be keeping your ears open to hear of a nice place near London where we can live. Send letters always to the Lecture Agency, 6 Beacon Street, Boston.

With our love,—Your affectionate father,

JOHN WATSON.

TO THE REV. R. C. GILLIE

March 2nd, 1907.

Dear Gillie,—We have had a most successful visit so far. I have preached to crowds, and twice to students, once men, once women. I have addressed a meeting of ministers on preaching with effect. I have delivered a course of lectures at Haverford College. I have lectured to two literary societies. I have been dined by four clubs, where I met the most interesting men of letters, and I have seen some lovely houses full of books and art. Everything has been very delightful and inspiring. As I have been asked to deliver the annual address at many colleges I hope to see more than ever of academic life which may be useful to me.

John Watson.

FAMILY

April 1st, 1907.

This is to take up a letter I wrote to Frank some time ago, which described our proceedings up to Boston. There we were for a fortnight and had a good reception, and met some nice people, we then separated, your mother went to stay with some New York friends, who took her to the country, and gave her a good time, and I worked here and there. After some wanderings I joined her on the 24th, preached to huge congregations in New York, and then went with her to stay with the leading editor at Philadelphia, who gathered some literary men together, and we had a charming evening. We then visited a lady's college and a boy's public school in one of the most beautiful places in the States. I was much interested in the school. There were four hundred boys, and they go in for athletics very much, and are also good singers. They are well fed, with as much milk as they can face, and strawberries at all meals in summer. You see they all dine together, and there are no housemasters making money out of the boys. I lectured to them, and we stayed with the headmaster. Good Friday we spent at Philadelphia, and on Saturday I had a magnificent motor run, visiting Valley Forge, where Washington encamped for a winter in the crisis of the War of Independence. If the English General had followed Washington up after the battle, he could have scattered the American troops and closed the war, but he was either too fond of the gay society of Philadelphia, or he was, as some think, a sympathiser with the Americans, so he left Washington alone and in the Spring the latter inflicted one defeat after another on the British, and turned the tide of the war.

We have now set out on a little tour in the West in which we shall visit Winnipeg, and come down through Montana where there is very fine scenery. Then at the end of this month I am due at the University of Nashville for a course of lectures. When this reaches you one-third of our absence will be over, yet it seems a very short time since we left. We are wondering where we shall go on our return. People say Cambridge, but I don't think so. . . . Whichever way it goes we shall have regrets.

With our love.—Your affectionate father,

JOHN WATSON.

FROM HAROLD PEIRCE TO W. R. NICOLL

Philadelphia grew fonder and fonder of him, for in addition to delivering the Library Lectures at Haverford College, and preaching at various church services, he had been the guest of honour at several social functions, and had frequently met many people in the most informal way. He preached five times in the Bryn Mawr Presbyterian Church, of which I am a member. He came to us the day before Ash Wednesday, and as our pastor was sick he took the service Ash Wednesday evening. From the text 'What then shall I do unto Jesus who is called Christ,' he preached a most solemn and earnest sermon which will live always in the memory of those present. Ten days after that he preached again for us, but the sermon that made the most impression on the community was the one he preached Easter morning. Early in March our pastor had died, and as a special favour to me he returned to my home the afternoon of Good Friday in order to preach on Easter and spent two or three days with us. He took charge of both services on Sunday, but that Easter morning he preached as I had never heard him preach, from the text 'In my Father's house are many mansions: if it were not so, I would have told you. I go to prepare a place for you. And if I go and prepare a place for you, I will come again, and receive you unto myself; that where I am, there ye may be also.' As we recall that service we can almost believe, as my wife has suggested, that he was preaching his own farewell sermon. He sought to impress upon us the same as he had done many years before in the chapter on 'The Continuity of Life' in *The Mind of the Master*, that the word mansions meant 'rooms, stations, stages in that long ascent of life that shall extend through ages of ages,' where we would simply tarry for a while preparatory to our going forward to still greater and more glorious work.

He closed with two stories which must be quite familiar to you. One was that of 'Blind Margery' in *The Vision of the Soul*, the last story in *His Majesty Baby*. The other was the story of the old woman who was afraid to go to Edinburgh because she had to pass through a tunnel before reaching her destination, but as she drew near the tunnel she fell asleep, and on awakening found herself in the glorious sunshine beyond. From these and other stories he drew the most beautiful lessons regarding death. He made us feel it should not be dreaded but that it was simply the mode by which Christ takes us to Himself and places us where we can do greater and more glorious work. It was his last prepared sermon, for though he had used the framework before yet he wanted to deliver what he thought under our peculiar circumstances would be the appropriate message. Saturday, March 30th, was a glorious day. It was bright and warm and almost June-like. Adjoining my place are the beautiful links of the Merion Golf Club, and so on that morning he walked several times over those links preparing this, his own farewell sermon.

To me his only address in Philadelphia comparable with this Easter sermon was the one delivered before the Presbyterian Social Union on the evening of February 25th, in which he so recounted his early experiences in the ministry that we felt we had been taken into his confidence and made his close and intimate friends. All present went away feeling that never again was it likely that we should hear such a personal recital of trials and triumphs.

This was the beginning of our acquaintance which ripened this year into close and intimate friendship. . . .

I think the two addresses Dr. Watson most enjoyed delivering were those in aid of the project for marking the final resting-place of Francis Makemie, the founder of organised Presbyterianism in America, and that delivered before the Colonial Dames in Independence Hall. Rev. Henry C. McCook, D.D., the well-known writer and a man much beloved in Philadelphia, had purchased on his own responsibility, as the only way to make sure of the property, the farm in Maryland which had belonged to the Makemie family and where Francis Makemie had been buried. Last October or November I sent Dr. Watson the circular Dr. McCook had prepared in reference to this object, and Dr. Watson wrote me that it not alone met his entire approbation, but he would be glad to aid in every way possible. He called on and dined with Dr. McCook, who was too ill to leave his house. He entered at once into the project, and by his aid at a public reading such a substantial sum was added to that fund that the project has become an assured success. HAROLD PEIRCE.

Dr. Watson seemed to pass through the travels and adventures of the North-West without injury, but when on a journey across the prairie he was very suddenly caught with what appeared to be an ordinary sore throat. However, he went on to Valley City, N.D., where he delivered his last lecture and preached his last sermon. He was not well when he arrived, but showed his usual equanimity and patience. When he arrived he found that no room had been reserved at the hotel, and that the place was full to overflowing. He found refuge in the house of Mr. William McKinney. Describing the experience to his friends he said: 'Why, the clerk just said, "You see, we don't take in tramps here. You're not in our class at all."' He lectured on Saturday, April 20th, and preached at a union service in the Armory Opera House. His sermon on Jacob made a deep impression. He never preached again.

When he arrived at Mount Pleasant, Iowa, he was very ill, and the doctor called in declared him to be suffering from an acute attack of tonsilitis. At first he seemed to improve, but the fever was very high, and the physician found that he was suffering from tonsilitis and quinsy with complications, and declared that he must do nothing for at least three weeks. He suffered very much from insomnia, but still cherished the hope of being able to deliver his Nashville lectures. On May 3rd his wife wrote: 'This loathsome catarrh is now slowly departing by way of the ears. All this leaves him very weak. He is only now sitting up in his room for a few hours.' On Sunday he again appeared to be improving, though swelling of the limbs and rheumatic pains indicated that the blood was becoming infected. On that day a telegram was received from Mr. Andrew Carnegie, and about nine o'clock in the evening Dr. Watson dictated a reply to Mr. Carnegie, 'Thanks for your inquiry.' This was his last earthly message. He then passed into a deep sleep. He spoke once or twice to Dr. Laird, who was with him until near morning. He then fell asleep again, and from sleep drifted into a coma from which he never regained consciousness. When Dr. Laird called on the Monday morning he at once saw that the crisis was at hand, and Drs. Smith and Sternberg were hastily sent for. It was too late, however, for mortal help, and at a quarter past eleven o'clock John Watson passed away. He died in the Brazelton Hotel, and he had with him day and night the presence of the cherished wife who was with him to the very end.

It does not appear that he was at all conscious

of his danger. Three days before he died he was up attending to business. It was said after his death that he had remarked to the physician on his arrival at Iowa, 'Doctor, this is my last illness.' There is no foundation for this story. He never said anything of the kind to his wife. On Sunday he read with the greatest interest the pathetic story of Edward Everett Hale, *The Man without a Country*, and was strangely touched by it. 'How dreadful,' he said, 'to be without a home.' On Monday morning, as a cup of milk was raised to his lips he murmured 'Good, good,' and never spoke again. During his illness, and especially towards the end, he became restless and anxious about Westminster College. 'Why do they not let me hear?' he said again and again, and became at times depressed. He felt that as Principal he could do great service to the Church.

The Hon. Judge Smythe, who was travelling on circuit and staying at the hotel during the week, was the only person who was permitted to see Watson, and a strong friendship was established between the two men. After the death Judge Smythe cancelled his engagements and took care of Mrs. Watson until she reached friends in New York. Mrs. Watson left by the midnight train on the next day, and a large body from the College with members of the University acting as pall-bearers, were present to wish her God-speed. During the short time preceding the arrival of the train the old College bell tolled off the fifty-seven years of Watson's life. Just before the train arrived and the party were on the platform to await its drawing into the station, there rang out sweetly and comfortingly on the still night air the strains of the hymn, 'Nearer my God to Thee.'

In anticipation of his election as Principal of Westminster College, Dr. Watson had written as follows to the Rev. R. C. Gillie:—

TO THE REV. R. C. GILLIE

April 15*th*, 1907.

DEAR GILLIE,—As the time draws near when the direction of my future life is to be decided by other hands than mine, I write to thank you for all your loyalty and kindness, which we can never forget, and to say that I should be obliged if you will cable me the result.

It occurs to me that in the event of my election, some one should have power to convey my acceptance, and I also enclose a letter to that effect. This you are authorised to read to the Synod, or give to the mover or seconder of my name, to read, as you judge most fitting. We are both well, and making our way through fine scenery to Nashville, for my lectures on 'The Bible in the Pulpit.' I have had the opportunity of preaching to huge audiences, and have received much kindness.

Many thoughts are in my mind, and I feel myself at the disposal of the Highest Power, in Whose Hands I leave myself, and with many regrets for the faults of the past, and absolute submission for the future.

With our affectionate regard, yours faithfully,

JOHN WATSON.

To be read in the event of my election—

MODERATOR AND REVD. BRETHREN,—I accept with profound respect and humility the honourable and responsible charge to which the Synod has called me, and I trust by the grace of God, so to carry myself that the confidence of the Church will be justified, and the highest interests of Westminster College be advanced.

It is with a feeling of deep solemnity that I consecrate what remains of my work in life, to the service of the College and of the Church.—I am, your obedient and grateful servant in Jesus Christ, JOHN WATSON.

It would be utterly impossible for me to give any adequate account of the universal sorrow with which the startling news of his death was received in this country, in America, in all the English-speaking lands. Volumes might be filled with the tributes paid to his beloved memory from the pulpit and the press. To his friends it seemed impossible that a personality so charged with life and energy should have passed away from them in the very fulness and ripeness of his powers. He himself fully believed that the servants of God departed in God's chosen time because their work was done. This was what he said about his own friend Henry Drummond, who died earlier. But it was very hard to think this about himself. It seemed as if the great work of his life was just about to begin. To think of what he might have done in Westminster College, as the President of the National Free Church Council, as an author, as a Christian leader, opened a future of magnificent possibilities. We lost him, as it seemed, when he was most precious to us. We saw in him a man who had the ear of England, and when we most need such a man we must look for him no more. He had gathered his stores—his strength, his experience, his seriousness, his grasp of his own thoughts—and was ready to guide us into the new era, and then he was taken from us. It was indeed a bitter loss—how bitter we shall realise through the days and years. But the thoughts of many lingered mostly on the loss of a friend. Many of us know that the loss is beyond repair. No new friendship can make up for it. Dr. Watson had a watchful solicitude for those admitted to his inner circle. He never lost sight of them. He was always ready to succour and to comfort at the hour of need ; he was for ever doing kindnesses, and he appreciated and magnified the most trivial kindness to himself as very few men ever did. And yet, as his friend Sir Oliver Lodge said in brave and heartening words :—

The departure of the cheery and invigorating personality of John Watson to the other side should not be over much lamented by his friends who remain, in spite of the gap which it leaves in the ranks of those who are working for the coming of the kingdom. Save for the pang of leaving his loved ones solitary for a while, he would welcome the transition. He looked forward to a welcome from his mother, with whom he had a sacred compact of which he occasionally spoke among intimate friends, and which he had found a bulwark against early temptation. To his mind there was no such impenetrable barrier between the two states as is sometimes supposed; and he himself was the recipient of intuitions that helped him to be a comfort to others. It should be a pleasure to us to realise that he worked up to the last minute here, with all his powers and strenuous energy unimpaired, and has now gone to continue his career of beneficent activity among other and perhaps still more efficient conditions.

Nor could we forget what he wrote himself:—

The continuity of life lifts the shadow also from another mystery—the lives that have been cut off in their prime. When one is richly endowed and carefully trained, and has come to the zenith of his power, his sudden removal seems a reflection on the economy of God's kingdom. According to Jesus he has not sunk into inaction, so much subtracted from the forces of righteousness. He has gone where the fetters of this body of humiliation and embarrassment of our adverse circumstances shall be no longer felt. We must not think of him as withdrawn from the field; we must imagine him as in the van of the battle. We must follow him, our friend, with hope and a high heart. . . . As a mother who expects her son from foreign parts would arrange his room to remind him of his boyhood, gathering into it the things he loved and the treasures he sent on before him, so will the Master reconstruct our life out of the kindly circumstances that shall fit into our character and work with this difference, that the scale shall be of heaven; and place us once more among those we love and have lost for a while with only this difference, that we shall not then see 'through a glass darkly,' but 'face to face.'

During his illness he reached after the words of a Scottish hymn, 'My Ain Countrie,' but could not quite get them. His physician was able to bring him a copy of the verses, and they seemed to give him comfort. The hymn begins with the lines:—

> 'I am far frae my hame, an' I'm weary aftenwhiles,
> For the lang'd-for hame-bringing, an' my Father's welcome smiles,
> I'll ne'er be fu' content, until my een do see
> The gowden gates of heaven an' my ain countrie.'

He died far from home, but his friends were comforted by the sympathy of the American people, and by their knowledge of John Watson's great love for America. There never was a Briton more at home in America than Watson was. It was a great consolation also that his wife was with him at the last, and to the last.

The Synod of his Church, the Presbyterian Church of England, assembled on Monday, May 6th. One of the principal items of their business was to elect a new Principal for Westminster College, and there can be little or no doubt that Watson would have been chosen by a large majority. As it was, the news came first that he was hanging between life and death, and on Tuesday it was known that he had departed. The Synod gave expression by a silent vote to their grief and reverence for the dead, and Dr. Monro Gibson offered up a prayer which expressed worthily the emotion that filled every heart. It was decided also to postpone the appointment for a year. In Liverpool, the city of his love, the most poignant sorrow was expressed everywhere.

When the bereaved wife brought home her dead husband, all hearts went out to her. Nothing but a public funeral would satisfy the community in which Dr. Watson laboured. The Lord Mayor came forward with the proposal, and it was accepted eagerly and with one consent. It was felt, as Sir Edward Russell said, that Dr. Watson's death was not merely a personal loss, but that it made a great gap in the social structure. All denominations and all parties joined in the tribute. At the funeral a great and worthy tribute of grief was paid by the city to the dead minister. The number of mourners and spectators could not have fallen short of sixty thousand. The services conducted by the Rev. A. Connell; the Rev. J. H. Scott; the Rev. Principal Oswald Dykes, who delivered an address; the Rev. Dr. Stalker and Dr. Rendel Harris, were marked by the deepest emotion. Those who were present can never forget the reality of the grief manifested everywhere. It was as if each individual were mourning a personal loss. The cortège from Sefton Park Church to the Smithdown Cemetery was headed by the Bishop and the Lord Mayor. Crowds lined the roads the whole way to the grave, and at the cemetery gates no fewer than thirty thousand were present. It was an almost unparalleled tribute of love to a Christian minister, and indicated not only the wide influence exerted by Dr. Watson, but the reality of Christian union. Long before, Dr. Watson had said to his former assistant, the Rev. J. M. Blake of Wallington: 'If I had been a General, I should like to feel that the men who had fought close by me would carry my coffin to the grave, and on it I should like my sword and any orders I had won. As it is, I should like my old colleagues to act as pall-bearers and to have upon my coffin just my M.A. hood which I really won, and a simple cross of white flowers.' Of his ten assistants eight were able to be present, and they laid him in his grave. By the grave, forming three sides of a great square, were the Liverpool Scottish Volunteers, and when the Bishop of Liverpool had pronounced the Benediction, two pipers of the Scottish played the sorrowful lament, 'Lochaber no More.' Memorial sermons were preached by Professor Stalker and the Rev. R. C. Gillie of Eastbourne, formerly his assistant and always his intimate friend.

CHAPTER XXI

CONCLUSION

THE distinguishing characteristic of John Watson was perhaps his great humanness. It was said of him at his death that nearly every man on the streets of Liverpool was more or less affected or interested in the loss. The Rev. T. Lund, Chaplain of the Blind Asylum, Liverpool, says that he was returning home late at night when an electric car pulled up, and the driver, white with emotion, leant over the rail. 'Have you heard the news?' he said. 'John Watson is dead; it is a bad day for us.' He had touched the community at many points. There was no officialism about him. He met his fellow-men simply and frankly with a steady and sure sympathy. He had not a few intimate friends among the aristocracy, and many more among the poor, and he was equally at home with both classes. He was not one of those who say war to the castle, peace to the cottage, but one of those who say peace to the cottage and peace to the castle. Wherever he travelled he talked with those whom he met, and he would frequently be so engrossed in conversation with the conductor of a tramcar that he had to be reminded of his destination. Nothing fretted him like casualness. He complained bitterly of the slackness of brother ministers in failing to answer their letters. Every correspondent received from him an immediate answer. His very foibles were intensely human. It was impossible for him to patronise any one. He was, in spite of his many labours, the most accessible of men. With this went a large generosity. His assistants, whom he invariably treated as his colleagues and more than his equals, knew most about this. One of them writes:—

> When the pressure of work was very heavy, or when his secretary was unwell, we aided in his correspondence. As might be imagined it was enormous, and letters begging for help in various forms bulked largely in it. Never to my knowledge did he leave one of these multitudinous epistles unanswered. Most of them came without any stamp for reply, but that did not make any difference, and to any appeal which he felt to be genuine he sent whatever help was in his power. It was not merely monetary help that he would send, but he would grudge no amount of private trouble by which a deserving case might be assisted.

Mr. Grant Paton, a Liverpool elder, said: 'Dr. Watson has often come to me and asked, "Do you know of any poor brother who would be the better for a £5 note? Because if you do, I have it ready." And many a £5 note have I had from John Watson to give to one of his poorer brethren.' The greater part of this charity was quite unknown. He rarely spoke contemptuously of any one's views or methods. When Evan Roberts, the Welsh revivalist, was holding his meetings at Liverpool, a fellow clergyman spoke disparagingly of his efforts to Watson, who replied: 'Well, I don't know anything about that, but remember we don't draw these audiences, so let us keep quiet.' He was present himself with Roberts on the platform a few weeks after. When Dr. Torrey and Mr. Alexander were conducting their mission in Liverpool, a wave of criticism swept over them. One afternoon Watson attended a service, and the next day a Liverpool paper had a warm yet discriminating eulogy on the missioners, signed 'A City Pastor.' The style proclaimed the author, and later on Watson owned to having written that kind letter of encouragement. He had small patience with criticisms of minor points in a man's life, and always tried to look more at the big things. For example, when Cecil Rhodes died he expressed indignation at what he called 'the tomtit opinions of commonplace pious persons to whom a man's faults were of more importance than his Imperial achievements.'

Watson's life was one of singular happiness. His delight was first in his affections, and after that in his labours, and in both he was fortunate beyond most. No one who knew his home will ever forget his chivalrous devotion to his wife, or the light and affectionate banter that passed between him and his four sons. He was also exceedingly rich in friendships, and these he assiduously cultivated. A fairly happy day with Watson was one spent in diligent work. A perfectly happy day was one in which after strenuous labour came the longed-for bright, stimulating intercourse with the well-known circle. He was not exempt from the ordinary trials of ministerial life, and the opposition and criticism of those belonging to his Church plunged him into the deepest depression. A kind word from any of his people, or any of his brother ministers, was appreciated far more than any newspaper eulogy. Regarding literature as a subordinate province of his activity, he was amused rather than annoyed by attacks, and humbly deprecated praise. It is true that he had the Celtic fear of the future. He saw in serenity something sweet and yet menacing. But he was mercifully exempted from the greater trials of life. He lost his mother when he was twenty-one, and his father when he was twenty-eight, but his wife and all his children were spared to him. It was a happy thing that one whose affections were so heavily committed was spared the trials which give life an abiding flavour of sorrow, for Watson was a man who could have died of grief.

He continued his labour to the very end, and had not to drink the thickening dregs of existence.

Watson was extraordinarily diligent, and in the latter part of his life morbidly so. The sense of duty in him was so strong that he could hardly say no. When asked to preach or to write, it seemed to him as if he must comply, and much of his work was done in extreme weariness, though to the last he seemed to retain his old vivacity and fire. It puzzled many of his friends to understand why he should take so many journeys, and do so much work that hardly seemed worth the price he paid for it. Indeed his labours in travelling, preaching, and lecturing apparently hastened his death. His activities might be described as restless and feverish. I have seen him often after an exciting day go to bed in the early morning. He would appear at breakfast as vivacious and blithe as if he had done nothing. The moment breakfast was over he would take up his task and persevere with it till it was accomplished. Then he would go out to luncheon to be the chief guest of a company which simply basked in his presence. He would pass from that to a round of visiting; he would come in tired, and at an early dinner be the life and soul of the guests. He would go out from that to a public engagement, and on his return he would carry on a conversation till three o'clock in the morning. This would go on for weeks at a time, varied only by the Sunday and by incessant railway travelling. In America he often put in three addresses in one day.

If these labours hastened his death we may be sure that his life was not thrown away wittingly. He held that a man should keep his strength and be careful of his verve, so that neither the one nor the other should become weary. But Watson could never properly distinguish between work and play. It must be remembered also that this kind of work was a great pleasure to him. His humanness made it delightful for him to meet men and women, and to make new friends. He joyfully accepted invitations from strangers, and by the time he had left them they were no longer strangers. The warm hand-grasps and expressions of kindness which he received as he travelled encouraged and strengthened him. Before leaving Liverpool for his last journey, he was examined by a doctor who pronounced his heart absolutely sound. He judged himself physically quite fit for the labour he undertook, and even those who watched him most anxiously had to acknowledge that his power of recuperation was marvellous. We have seen with what strenuous vitality he discharged his duties as student, as preacher, and as pastor.

John Watson's absorbing interest in life was the religious interest. He was first and foremost a servant of the Church of Christ, and in his judgment his work was done there. A biographer is bound to record his subject's judgment on himself, but he is not bound to agree with it. I had always difficulty in understanding Watson's insistent classification of himself as a Moderate. He was certainly a Moderate in so far as he strove to combine religious life with intellectual activity. He was a Moderate in the sense that he gave a great place to humanism, and also in the sense that he had no sympathy with many of the restrictions which the old Evangelicalism placed upon conduct. But if Moderatism means, as Mrs. Oliphant says, an easy satisfaction with the respectable fulfilment of necessary duties and an absence of strenuous religious feeling, then certainly Watson was no moderate. All the sparkle and effervescence of his nature never concealed the fact that he was a profoundly religious man. Here again I quote from one of his assistants:—

His humility was also shown in the very low estimate he had of his pulpit powers. No great preacher was ever less elated on a Sunday night than was he. After one of his most brilliant sermons he would go home covered with shame, because he felt his service had been so poor and ineffectual. This depression was almost habitual at the time of his resignation. His Celtic temperament doubtless had something to do with it; but it was equally caused by his sense of personal unworthiness. He was filled with great searchings of heart as he conscientiously reviewed his ministerial life, and they would sometimes break into speech; and by this we knew something of the secret ordeal of judgment through which he was passing, for it was very unlike him to speak much of the sacred intimacies of his inner life.

To me it seemed that of all Dr. Watson's religious convictions, one to which he most constantly returned was that of the immortal hope. Since George Macdonald there has been no such prophet of immortality. The vision always before his eyes was that of a heaven peopled with the crowding guests of God. Though he strove very hard to present the Christian ideas in the forms of his own mind and age, and to discard outworn words and phrases, though he wrote like a modern as the fathers and even the schoolmen did in their day, he was evermore convinced that in the end theology reverts to its broad immemorial features and the New Testament language. He was convinced of the emptiness of all human desires and efforts if they end in death. And if he tried to penetrate the veil of terrible mist that hangs between us and the future, it was not to re-enforce his own faith. He was perhaps not perfectly consistent in his views. It was his manner to give his convictions hospitable lodging in his mind where they had to get on together as best they could. But he had much of the mystic's certainty. Those who really knew him were aware of his wistful interest in mystical writings, and of the strength of his spiritual intuitions.

These are perhaps best expressed in his book, *The Companions of the Sorrowful Way*.

Sensitive to the difficulties of his time, he was yet an optimist. 'The day in which we are living is the best yet known, and our children will live in a better,' he said in his last sermon in Sefton Park. And when interviewed in America and asked, 'Do you think the world is getting better morally?' he answered: 'The condition of the people is getting better morally and physically. There is a great deal of unsettlement of religious thought, and I believe there will be a great change in forms of dogma, but the great fundamental truths will remain. Faith is not failing.' In his later years Dr. Watson gave much time to the study of Church history, and like Lightfoot, he drew from it a message of cheer. He came to realise the life of the Divine Society. Christ, he conceived, had promised to be with His Church in the blaze of noon, in the dark, and in the twilight between the two, wherein mainly the course of her journey lies. He saw how the Church had seemed to perish, how her defenders had seemed to be confounded, and yet how truly the Lord's promise had been kept. He perceived how these alarms, and forebodings, and prophecies of dissolution that often shake the hearts of the faithful, drop into insignificance in the course of that vast history which has *not* fulfilled them.

LIST OF WORKS

REV. JOHN WATSON, D.D.

The Order of Service for young People, . .	1895
The Mind of the Master, ...	1896
The Upper Room, ...	1896
The Cure of Souls, ...	1896
The Potter's Wheel, ...	1898
Companions of the Sorrowful Way, ...	1898
Doctrines of Grace, ...	1900
The Life of the Master, ...	1901
Homely Virtues, ...	1903
The Inspiration of our Faith, ...	1905
The Scot of the Eighteenth Century, . . .	1907
God's Message to the Human Soul, . . .	1907

IAN MACLAREN

Beside the Bonnie Brier Bush, ...	1894
The Days of Auld Lang Syne, ...	1895
A Doctor of the Old School, ...	1895
Kate Carnegie and those Ministers, . . .	1896

Afterwards and other Stories, ... 1899
Rabbi Saunderson, ... 1899
Church Folks, ... 1901
Young Barbarians, ... 1901
His Majesty Baby, and some Common People, . 1902
St. Jude's, ... 1907
Graham of Claverhouse, ... 1908

INDEX

Printed by T. and A. CONSTABLE, Printers to His Majesty
at the Edinburgh University Press

P 2. Flowers [illegible] in [illegible] garden.
3,4. Patriotism - [illegible]
7 His mother's presence with him.
21 Character [illegible] forever.
92 Keynote of his ministry
93 Conditions for a successful church.
94 f. His idea of preaching
111 Chief end of preaching.
113 [illegible] love a liturgy
120 f. Pastoral work.
124, 5. Receiving of confidences
125. His favourite motto 'Be kind, for everyone is fighting a hard battle.'
128 Visiting gives strength to preaching 128
140 Interest in social work.
142 His idea of education
276 Humanism.
305 f Humour